MW00446326

RECOVERING
MOTHER KIRK

To
Ronald Harding
Michael Rogers
John Schuurman
Craig Troxel

© 2003 by D. G. Hart

Published by Baker Academic
a division of Baker Book House Company
P.O. Box 6287, Grand Rapids, MI 49516-6287
www.bakeracademic.com

Printed in the United States of America

All rights reserved. No part of this publication may be reproduced, stored in a retrieval system, or transmitted in any form or by any means—for example, electronic, photocopy, recording—without the prior written permission of the publisher. The only exception is brief quotations in printed reviews.

Library of Congress Cataloging-in-Publication Data
Hart, D. G. (Darryl G.)
    Recovering mother kirk : the case for liturgy in the Reformed tradition / D. G. Hart.
        p. cm.
    Includes bibliographical references and index.
    ISBN 0-8010-2615-6 (pbk.)
    1. Presbyterian Church—Liturgy. 2. Public worship—Presbyterian Church. I. Title.
BX9185.H37   2003
264′.051—dc21   2002026039

Unless otherwise indicated, Scripture quotations are from the HOLY BIBLE, NEW INTERNATIONAL VERSION®. NIV®. Copyright © 1973, 1978, 1984 by International Bible Society. Used by permission of Zondervan Publishing House. All rights reserved.

Scripture quotations identified RSV are from the Revised Standard Version of the Bible, copyright 1946, 1952, 1971 by the Division of Christian Education of the National Council of the Churches of Christ in the USA. Used by permission.

Contents

Chapter 4: "Reforming Worship: Reverence, the Reformed Tradition, and the Crisis of Protestant Worship," *Touchstone* 8, no. 4 (fall 1995): 17–21. Reprinted with permission.

Chapter 5: "Evangelicals and Post-Modern Worship," *Calvin Theological Journal* 30 (1995): 451–59. Reprinted with permission.

Chapter 7: "Whatever Happened to Office? Ordination and the Crisis of Leadership in American Protestantism," *Touchstone* 6, no. 3 (summer 1993): 12–16. This essay appeared when the author was an elder in the Christian Reformed Church, before the denomination began in 1995 to ordain women as elders and ministers. Reprinted with permission.

Chapter 8: "Recovering the Keys of the Kingdom in an Age of Equipped Saints," *Modern Reformation* 6, no. 2 (March/April 1997): 16–20. Reprinted by permission of the Alliance of Confessing Evangelicals, 1716 Spruce Street, Philadelphia, PA 19103.

Chapter 9: "The Revolt of the Evangelical Elites: Gender, Equality, and Headship," *Regeneration Quarterly* 1, no. 4 (fall 1995): 30–33. Reprinted with permission.

Chapter 10: "J. Gresham Machen, Confessional Presbyterianism, and the History of Twentieth-Century Protestantism," in *Re-Forming the Center: American Protestantism, 1900 to the Present*, ed. Douglas Jacobsen and William Vance Trollinger, Jr. (Grand Rapids: Eerdmans, 1998), 129–49. Reprinted with permission.

Chapter 11: "An Old Protestant on Americanist Christianity," *Regeneration Quarterly* 1, no. 1 (winter 1995): 27–29. Reprinted with permission.

Chapter 12: "What Can Presbyterians Learn from Lutherans?" *Logia* 8, no. 4 (Reformation 1999): 3–8. Reprinted with permission.

Chapter 13: part of the program for the Tenth Colloquium on Calvin Studies, Columbia Theological Seminary, 27 January 2000.

Chapter 14: "'Reformed' or 'Revived'? Why Words Matter," *Modern Reformation* 7, no. 4 (July/August 1998): 38–41. Reprinted by permission of the Alliance of Confessing Evangelicals, 1716 Spruce Street, Philadelphia, PA 19103.

Chapter 15: "Why Evangelicals Think They Hate Liturgy," *Modern Reformation* 5, no. 1 (January/February 1996): 17–20. Reprinted by permission of the Alliance of Confessing Evangelicals, 1716 Spruce Street, Philadelphia, PA 19103.

Chapter 16: part of the program for "Hymnody in American Protestantism," a conference sponsored by the Institute for the Study of American Evangelicals, Wheaton College, 18 May 2000.

Introduction

The Westminster Shorter Catechism begins with one of its more memorable answers, stating that "man's chief end is to glorify God and enjoy him forever." Although the American Presbyterian branch of John Calvin's heirs has typically emphasized the glorification part of that answer more than the enjoyment half, practically everyone in the Reformed tradition has little reservation in affirming the Westminster divines' understanding of the theocentric nature of not only the Christian life but also human existence. But when it comes to the ways in which Reformed believers actually carry out the task of glorifying God, agreements about the necessity of honoring God usually fracture into competing understandings of what preserves God's glory best.

One of the most common tendencies among American Presbyterians and Reformed for exalting God has been to emphasize correct doctrine.[1] This Calvinistic habit has a long history in North America, going back at least to 1729, when colonial Presbyterians decided to adopt the Westminster Confession of Faith and the Larger and Shorter Catechisms as their doctrinal standards. But it achieved renewed prominence during the denominational controversies of the 1920s that pitted so-called Presbyterian fundamentalists against Presbyterian modernists. As much as that conflict involved competing views of American politics and culture, doctrine was at its core. Consequently, ever since the 1920s, to be Reformed in the United States has required, at least in the minds of many Calvinists, a strict adherence to correct and precise theological statements. In the words of J. Gresham Machen, who embodied the doctrinalist mind-set perhaps better than anyone else, "The Christian religion is based upon a body of truth, a body of doctrine, which will remain true beyond the end of

---

1. The typology that follows comes from George Marsden, "Reformed and American," in *Reformed Theology in America: A History of Its Modern Development*, ed. David Wells (Grand Rapids: Eerdmans, 1985), 1–11.

As accurate as this typology of the contemporary Reformed world in North America may be, its strangeness is also glaring to anyone at all familiar with the ministry and work of John Calvin, who did so much to define the Reformed tradition. What this description lacks is one of the chief features of church reform that Calvin spearheaded. In addition to clarifying the doctrine of justification by faith alone, the French Reformer believed that the Protestant Reformation would not amount to much without the reform of worship. In fact, Calvin placed worship ahead of justification in his list of things that, as he put it, encompassed "the whole substance of Christianity": "*first*, of the mode in which God is duly worshiped; and *second* of the source from which salvation is to be obtained."[6] If worship was so important to Calvin and the Reformed wing of the Reformation, why are contemporary expressions of the Reformed tradition not known for their interest in worship? In other words, why aren't there at least four groups of Reformed—the doctrinalists, the culturalists, the pietists, *and* the liturgicalists?

The essays collected here make the case for such a fourth sector, at least in the Reformed world and perhaps even in American Protestant circles more generally. By liturgicalism I mean an understanding of Calvinism that is firmly rooted in the ministry of the church in her gathering for worship. Liturgicalism is not simply concerned with the content or order of worship services; it involves the life of the visible church through her officers, ordinances, and public worship. Rather than making correct beliefs, sanctified endeavor, or emotional intensity the crucial piece of the Christian life, Reformed liturgicalism recognizes, as Calvin did, the importance of worship, the means of grace, and participation in the body of Christ for the gathering of new believers and the sustenance of mature saints. In fact, an implicit claim of this book is that any effort to understand Reformed doctrine, worldview, or piety in isolation from the corporate church and public worship is inherently flawed. So essential to the Christian walk are the means of grace and the ministry of the church, ordinances that transpire chiefly during public worship, that to engage in theological or cultural reflection or to pursue Christian devotion apart from the reality of belonging to the church and partaking of her ordinances is to commit a form of religious reductionism.

Several of the essays in this book offer reasons for the neglect of the church and worship in contemporary Reformed and Presbyterian self-understanding. It would be redundant, therefore, to repeat them here. What is worth commenting on by way of introduction is the startling

6. John Calvin, *The Necessity of Reforming the Church* (1544; reprint, Audobon, N.J.: Old Path Publications, 1994), 4.

indifference among twentieth-century Calvinists regarding the church and worship in pursuing the goal of glorifying and enjoying God. It is as if contemporary Calvinists have thought it possible to attend to systematic theology, cultural transformation, or Christian piety without considering the church and her ministry. They appear to assume that the work and worship of the church will simply follow from right doctrine, cultural savvy, and godly zeal. But this was clearly not the position of Calvin. Book IV of the *Institutes* contains a memorable passage on the church as mother that aptly expresses Reformed liturgicalism's point of departure:

> Let us learn even from the simple title "mother" how useful, indeed how necessary, it is that we should know her. For there is no other way to enter into life unless this mother conceive us in her womb, give us birth, nourish us at her breast, and lastly, unless she keep us under her care and guidance until, putting off mortal flesh, we become like the angels.[7]

To underscore the importance of the church's ministry, Calvin drew on this imagery and added a sentiment that many Protestants today would equate with Catholicism: "Away from her bosom one cannot hope for any forgiveness of sins or any salvation." For Calvin, at least, the church, despite all its sixteenth-century abuses, was not something to be thrown out because of such abuse. On the Protestant divide of the Reformation, the ministry of the church was still central to the Christian life and "the external means" by which "God invites us into the society of Christ and holds us therein."[8]

Attention to the church, her ordinances, those called to administer them, and the shape that corporate worship gives to Christian piety are large parts of what it means to be a liturgical or high-church Calvinist. As the essays that follow try to show, liturgical Calvinism involves more than just ecclesiology and worship; it has implications for office, piety, relations with other Christians, and the church's responsibility to society. But at the heart of the liturgical outlook is a concern for the life of the visible church as embodied in her public worship. In fact, this concern is crucial to the other ways that Reformed believers have articulated their self-identity because worship keeps doctrine, culture, and piety in proper balance. The church in worship embodies the doctrines that God's people confess. Ecclesiology and liturgy also prevent the cultural endeavors of believers from going in directions that neglect the fundamental differences between the church and the world.

7. John Calvin, *Institutes of the Christian Religion*, ed. John T. McNeill, trans. Ford Lewis Battles (Philadelphia: Westminster, 1960), IV.i.4.
8. The title of book IV of the *Institutes*.

But more important than the divide between liberals and evangelicals is the distinction between liturgical and pietist Protestantism. Here the turning point in the history of American Protestantism is the 1740s, the decade of the First Great Awakening.[12] Since that time, Protestants have tended to be divided over the propriety and character of revivals, with pietists endorsing them and liturgicalists reluctant to do so. This difference is key to understanding Reformed liturgicalism and why it has fared so poorly. Reformed liturgicalists tend to be skeptical about revivalism because they look for God to build and bless his church through Word and sacrament, not through new evangelistic techniques. Reformed pietists, in contrast, do not slight Word and sacrament but evaluate any religious activity by its evangelistic efficacy and experiential power. If the means of revivals are more effective than Word and sacrament at converting persons and generating godly zeal, then revivalism is worthy of support. This way of looking at revivals became especially prominent during the middle decades of the nineteenth century, when in reaction to the growing presence of Roman Catholics in the United States, Protestants emphasized forms of devotion that distinguished themselves from the churchly piety of the newly arrived Catholic immigrants. One important way to make this distinction was to minimize the importance of Word, but especially sacrament and clergy, and rely all the more on individualistic or non-churchly forms of Christian devotion.

Since the eighteenth century, then, the real divide, not just in American Protestantism but in American Christianity, has been between formalists and antiformalists, that is, liturgicalists and pietists. The popularity of revivalism combined with cultural factors in the United States that favor individualistic expressions of Christianity have made Protestant liturgicalism scarce.[13] But a high view of the church and the ministry of Word and sacrament was a substantial part of historic Protestantism prior to the middle of the nineteenth century. What is more, as the essays in this volume argue, high-church Calvinism may prove a welcome antidote to some of the coarseness and sentimentality that have prompted some evangelicals to look to Canterbury, Rome, or Constantinople for relief. If anything, this book's aim is to show that Geneva should be another option for Protestants seeking a corporate and liturgical expression of their faith. Just as important is the point

12. Especially helpful on the radical aspects of eighteenth-century revivalism is Harry S. Stout, *The Divine Dramatist: George Whitefield and the Rise of Modern Evangelicalism* (Grand Rapids: Eerdmans, 1991).

13. On the sociological factors that weaken the institutions and forms on which confessionalism depends, see Steve Bruce, *Conservative Protestant Politics* (Oxford: Oxford University Press, 1998), chap. 1.

that the Reformed tradition's understanding of the church, office and ordination, worship, and the sacraments is closer formally to other confessional traditions, such as Lutheran and Anglican, than it is to evangelicalism.[14] To be sure, historic Reformed practice differs from that of other Protestant traditions. One obvious difference, for example, concerns Lutheran and Reformed teaching on the nature of Christ's presence in the Lord's Supper. But both traditions hold the Supper to be essential to salvation, not as something tacked on to more authentic religious experiences outside the church. The Reformed tradition's regard for the church and ministry is so high that some of its exponents have maintained, in the words of the Westminster Confession of Faith, that outside the visible church "there is no ordinary possibility of salvation" (25.ii).

No doubt, the recurring theme throughout this book that highlights the differences between the inherently liturgical or formal character of the Reformed tradition and the essentially pietistic nature of evangelicalism, as revealed in church life and liturgical practice, will sound a divisive if not sectarian note.[15] Many Presbyterians and Reformed have thought of themselves for so long as evangelical that to point out the ecclesiastical, liturgical, and devotional oddities of the Reformed tradition is tantamount to erecting unnecessary and especially counterproductive barriers between Calvinists and other Protestants. Yet one of the convictions undergirding several chapters of this book is that the use of and reliance on evangelical and pietistic practices have weakened Reformed identity in North America. For those who desire to overcome divisions among American Protestants, a decline in Reformed self-consciousness may be a welcome development. But ironically, many Reformed and Presbyterians who desire to propagate and maintain their theological heritage see no real difference between evangelical and Reformed practices. This book challenges the notion that Reformed and evangelical pieties are fundamentally similar. It argues that Reformed identity cannot be separated from Reformed practices in church and worship.

Yet as divisive as these essays may be to evangelically minded Reformed and Presbyterians, from another perspective they are decidedly ecumenical and catholic. By demonstrating the similarities between Reformed practices and the ways that Christians have acted out the faith throughout the ages, this book is a reminder of the breadth of the

---

14. See D. G. Hart, *The Lost Soul of American Protestantism* (Lanham, Md.: Rowman & Littlefield, 2002).

15. Sectarianism is not necessarily a bad thing. For its virtues, see Stanley Hauerwas and William H. Willimon, *Resident Aliens: Life in the Christian Colony* (Nashville: Abingdon, 1989).

1

Is High-Church Presbyterianism an Oxymoron?

The words "high church" and "Presbyterian" seldom exist together, and for good reason. Anglo-American Presbyterians and their Reformed siblings on the European continent have not distinguished themselves for possessing either overly refined liturgical sensibilities or highly effective mechanisms for protecting the prerogatives of clergy. Of course, for the descendants of John Calvin, theology is a breeze. But on the Protestant ecclesiastical spectrum, running from low to high, the best Presbyterians can do is position themselves close to the Congregationalists, somewhere toward the middle, with Lutherans and Episcopalians above and Methodists and Baptists below. This may explain the old adage about Baptists being Methodists with shoes, and Presbyterians being Baptists who can read. To round out the adage, Lutherans might qualify as Presbyterians who drink to excess, and Episcopalians as Lutherans who know when to say when.

Still, as decent and orderly as it may be for Presbyterians to inhabit the moderate middle of Protestant notions about liturgy and the ministry of the church, if left to their own devices, they invariably descend to the nether regions of churchly sensibilities. For Baptists on the way up, the Presbyterian option is a happy one because it rarely demands a significant departure beyond coming to terms with infant baptism. In my own experience, my wife and I were both reared in fundamentalist Baptist congregations and now belong to the Orthodox Presbyterian Church, a communion of largely low-church proportions. What is more, five out of

Reformed liturgies in France, two to Scottish Presbyterianism, three to English developments among Puritans and the Church of England, one to the Dutch Reformed, one to the German Reformed, and finally, one to American Presbyterianism of a higher sort. All the churches ordered their services after the general pattern established by Calvin in Geneva, which ran as follows:

Invocation
Confession of Sins
Prayer for Pardon
Singing of a Psalm
Prayer for Illumination
Lessons from Scripture
Sermon
Collection of Offerings
Prayers of Intercession
Apostles' Creed (sung while elements of Lord's Supper are prepared)
Words of Institution
Instruction and Exhortation
Communion (while a psalm is sung or Scripture read)
Prayer of Thanksgiving
Benediction

Of course, with the exception of Presbyterian churches that follow the Praise and Worship liturgy by dividing the service in half, with thirty minutes of singing and another thirty of preaching, most Presbyterian congregations follow this order in some fashion. That is why the order of service is not a sufficient qualification for inclusion in the high-church wing of Protestantism. More important than a structured liturgy is the use of forms and written prayers. Again, Presbyterians might be among the most startled to learn how many prayers the Reformers wrote, not just because those who heard their sermons or lectures transcribed them but because Protestant leaders composed prayers to be used by other church members and officers. In the sense of a high-church Presbyterianism that relies on written prayers, few congregations would qualify, and those that do use forms usually mix and match liturgical elements from non-Reformed traditions, seemingly unaware of prayers used by their theological forbears. So ingrained in the Presbyterian conscience is the low-church sensibility that any hankering after a more dignified expression of worship results in scavenging through Episcopalian or Eastern Orthodox liturgies. But as books such as Baird's *Presbyterian Liturgies* indicate, the leaders of Reformed and Presbyterian churches in the sixteenth and seventeenth centuries supplied not only the order of worship but also the prayers and forms to be used. For instance, Calvin's Genevan liturgy included all the prayers for confession of sin, illumination, and intercession. The latter began in the following manner:

> Almighty God, our heavenly Father! who hast promised to grant our requests in the name of thy well-beloved Son: Thou hast taught us in his name also to assemble ourselves together, assured that he shall be present in our midst, to intercede for us with thee, and obtain for us all things that we may agree on earth to ask thee. Wherefore, having met in thy presence, dependent on thy promise, we earnestly beseech thee, O gracious God and Father! for his sake who is our only Saviour and Mediator, that of thy boundless mercy thou wilt freely pardon our offences; and so lift up our thoughts and draw forth our desires toward thyself, that we may seek thee according to thy holy and reasonable will.[2]

Calvin wrote prayers not only for pastors to use in public worship but also for parents to use at home. In fact, up until 1987, when the Christian Reformed Church introduced its new *Psalter Hymnal,* all of the denomination's hymnals included Calvin's prayers for public and private worship, along with prayers for church assemblies. The prayers for families totaled four in number and included those for the beginning and close of the day and for before and after meals. In the thanksgiving before meals, the head of the family is to pray:

> Lord God Almighty, Thou has made the world; thou dost uphold all things in it by the word of Thy power. Thou didst sustain the children of Israel in the wilderness with food from on high. Wilt Thou also bless us, Thy humble servants, and sanctify to us these gifts which we have received from Thy generous hand. May we use them temperately; help us to devote them to their proper purpose. May we thus acknowledge that Thou art our Father and Source of all good things. Grant also that we may at all times and above all things yearn for the spiritual bread of Thy Word. May our souls thus be nourished unto everlasting life, which Thou has prepared for us through the precious blood of Thy beloved Son, our Lord Jesus Christ. Amen.[3]

2. From Baird, *Presbyterian Liturgies,* 38.
3. *Psalter Hymnal* (Grand Rapids: Board of Publications of the Christian Reformed Church, 1976), 186. Calvin's prayers usually end with the Lord's Prayer, though later editions have not maintained this practice.

agogical function." For this reason it is altogether fitting for those who stand in the Calvinist tradition to speak of the real presence of Christ in the Lord's Supper. Christ's presence in the sacrament stems from the nature of signs as Calvin conceived of them. Though it is possible to distinguish the sign from the thing signified, Calvin wrote that this is a "distinction without division." In other words, it may be possible to distinguish the substance from the sign, but it was impossible to separate them. And because Christ himself is the substance of the Supper, the bread and wine are nothing less than, in the words of Gerrish, "pledges of the real presence."[6]

For this reason, Reformed believers should also be comfortable with the language of the means of grace. To be sure, the low-church outlook of today's Presbyterians makes them stutter over such a notion because of its associations with sacerdotalism. Nevertheless, the first expressions of the Reformed tradition in the sixteenth century were not hesitant to affirm that God used the means of Word and sacrament, in the words of the Westminster Shorter Catechism, to "communicate the benefits of redemption" to believers (Ans. 88). The Lord's Supper nourishes and builds up not only believers in the hope of the gospel but, as the Shorter Catechism explains, also the worthy receivers, who not corporally or carnally but by faith "partake of [Christ's] body and blood with all his benefits" (Ans. 96). Of course, to guard against sacerdotalism, the Reformed tradition has understood the efficacy of the sacraments to depend solely on the blessing of Christ, the work of the Holy Spirit, and the faith of the recipient. In other words, the Supper does not automatically confer grace, though something always happens, either in the form of blessing or curse. Still, the means of grace for the Reformed are just that—means, not merely symbols, whereby God works in the lives of his people. Such an understanding of the sacraments teaches that the Reformed tradition is not opposed to rite or ceremony. Instead, it is a question of which ordinances God has promised to use for believers' blessing and edification. The good rituals are the Word and the sacraments; the bad ones are any rite or ceremony devised by human wisdom, no matter how well intended, that have no sanction in Scripture.

Yet a high view of the Lord's Supper, according to Calvin, does not diminish a high estimation of preaching. In fact, to read some of the early Reformed creeds is to encounter a conception of preaching that makes today's Presbyterians, who stress good preaching (to the neglect of sacraments) but complain about thirty-minute sermons being too

6. Brian A. Gerrish, "John Calvin and the Reformed Doctrine of the Lord's Supper," *McCormick Quarterly* 22 (January 1969): 90–91.

short, look tame. As opposed to the contemporary image of the sermon as a teaching device that equips the laity for "every-member ministries," sixteenth- and seventeenth-century Reformed regarded preaching as a divine act. Inherent in Reformed liturgy is the dialogical principle that regards worship as a holy conversation between God and his people. God initiates through his Word, and believers respond in praise, prayer, hearing the Word preached and read, and receiving the sacraments. But God's speech does not simply extend to those elements of worship in which his Word is read, such as in the apostolic salutation, the lessons, words of institution, or benediction. It also includes the very words of the minister himself. According to the Second Helvetic Confession, "When this Word of God is now preached in the church by ministers lawfully called, . . . the very Word of God is proclaimed and received by the faithful" (1.iv).

Such a conception of preaching obviously raises the stakes for what transpires in worship when the minister goes to the pulpit. But the stakes escalate when Heinrich Bullinger adds later in the Second Helvetic Confession that preaching, even when conducted by an unregenerate man, is nevertheless the very Word of God. Here the Reformed tradition appealed to Augustine's argument against the Donatists and contended that "the voice of Christ is to be heard, though it be out of the mouths of evil ministers," in the same way that the sacraments are "effectual to the godly" even if administered by "unworthy ministers" (chap. 18). In this scheme, preaching functions almost as a ritual, obviously without a set form, but still carries the liturgical weight of other elements because the sermon itself is the time when God speaks through his under servant to his people. Preaching is not simply a common act of speech through which the minister tries to get across a particular moral or doctrinal truth. It is a holy activity that God has ordained to reveal himself in worship.

A high view of the Word (preached) and sacraments, in turn, leads to a different picture of the minister than the one that commonly prevails in contemporary Presbyterian churches. Indeed, the subject of special office and ordination is where low-church Presbyterianism comes full circle and reduces the work of the pastor to one of the many ministries that God's people conduct in all stations and walks of life. Here the doctrine of the priesthood of all believers and the Great Commission have been perverted to mean that ministers render services that are no different from what other believers do, except that pastors do it full-time, while the laity does it as an avocation. Yet if preaching really is the Word of God and if the sacraments really communicate the benefits of redemption, then the people who perform such acts are clearly different from other believers and should be set apart (ordained) to perform

they not only follow the pattern of days God established in the creation week but also look forward to the sabbath rest that awaits all God's children when Christ returns. This is especially true in worship itself when, as Reformed believe, the church gathers spiritually on the Lord's Day with the rest of the saints and angels in the presence of Christ to perform those acts of worship and service that prefigure the marriage supper of the Lamb. Looking at the Sabbath in this high-church way, as a foretaste of glory, can be a fruitful way of avoiding the kind of self-righteousness that has often surrounded the virtuous Sabbath regimen of Presbyterians.

But the question remains, Do these Reformed practices make a Presbyterian high church? The answer depends to a large degree on the convictions of each reader. Still, by looking at those observances that characterize high-church traditions and comparing them with older Reformed practices, it should at least be evident that good Presbyterians may have legitimate sympathy for the kind of piety that undergirds high-church Lutheranism or Anglicanism. What is more, Presbyterians may have the makings for an alternative version of high-church Protestantism that permits them to retain their own theological and liturgical heritage without having to look to other ecclesiastical traditions for a greater appreciation of the ministry of the visible church and its expressions in corporate worship. The question that remains is how Presbyterianism ever evolved to its current low-church status.

The Forming of a Low-Church Tradition

Whether or not the Reformed convictions outlined so far qualify as high church, they clearly differ from the current practices of most Presbyterians. Consequently, some explanation needs to be given for the disparity between older and contemporary forms of Reformed church life. Any plausible explanation will need to take into account the influence of Puritanism on American Presbyterianism, the effects of pietism on contemporary Reformed understandings of the Christian life, and the peculiar attachment that American Presbyterians have exhibited toward revivalism since the first Great Awakening.

Probably the greatest hurdle within the Presbyterian tradition to a greater recognition of the importance of liturgy in the life of Christians is the legacy of Puritanism. Puritans rightly advocated the regulative principle of worship, that is, the idea that whatever is done in public worship must find explicit warrant in Scripture. If the Bible does not require something, then it may not be done even if the thing proposed is not inherently sinful. So, for instance, the Bible may not explicitly prohibit giving testimonies during worship, but because testimonies do not find direct sanction in Scripture, they may not be included. The regulative principle finds support in both the Continental Reformed and Anglo-Presbyterian traditions and differs from Episcopalian and Lutheran practices in which the Bible is used primarily as a negative referent (i.e., What may not be done?) as opposed to a strict guideline (i.e., What does the Bible require?).

In Puritan hands, the regulative principle bred opposition to the Church of England's Book of Common Prayer. To be sure, some of this hostility stemmed from Puritan hypersensitivity to any trace of Catholicism in the liturgy. What is more, Puritans had a legitimate fear of centralized church authority that could force a minister to say prayers or use forms that ran contrary to his conscience. Indeed, a point often lost in battles over worship or disputes about the regulative principle of worship is that liberty of conscience is bound up with Calvinist understandings of worship. It's not just that the Bible has to regulate all that takes place in public worship—a fairly narrow conception. Puritans also recognized that the Bible is the only legitimate authority to bind an individual's conscience—a notion that recognizes both the legitimacy of different opinions on the circumstances of worship and that public worship, whether intended or not, forces all believers to submit to the liturgy either by participating in or refraining from the service. Corporate worship is something done by all. Because all church members should participate in all elements of worship, the best way to compel such involvement is to demonstrate that the Bible requires said practice.

But as laudable as the Puritan effort was to protect the consciences of individuals from unlawful rules, its issue has been liturgical chaos. The logic seems to be that required liturgy interferes with liberty of conscience, especially since the Bible nowhere elaborates a set order of service. This logic was especially evident in the Westminster Assembly's *Directory for Public Worship,* which only made suggestions about forms rather than actually offering prayers and forms that ministers should use. The *Directory* was a concession to Congregationalists and Independents who believed a set liturgy smacked of tyranny. So strong has been the Reformed and Presbyterian desire to protect liberty of conscience that even in churches in which there has been greater tolerance of set liturgies, such as in Scotland and the Netherlands, higher assemblies have been reluctant to require all churches to use approved forms. Instead, Reformed and Presbyterian churches have gone against Calvin's advocacy of liturgical uniformity to protect the respective powers of local pastors, sessions, and consistories.

Yet the Presbyterian commitment to liberty of conscience, while admirable, is at odds with the equally laudable Presbyterian desire for the unity of the church. Here it is interesting to see that Presbyterians have little difficulty assenting to theological and ecclesiological unity but draw the line when it comes to liturgical uniformity. For instance, rare is the Presbyterian who wonders about the value of confessing the Westminster Standards as the theological norm for ministerial fellowship. Indeed, most conservative Presbyterians take pride (the good kind) in being theologically precise. Presbyterian confessionalism is likely responsible for the large measure of theological unity that prevails in those communions that stress adherence to the Westminster Confession of Faith and the Larger and Shorter Catechisms. Likewise, Presbyterians are generally sticklers for church polity. Here the *Form of Government* and *Book of Church Discipline* supply the medicine for the Presbyterian fever for decency and order. Even though these documents, which govern church law, do not contain scriptural proof-texts, as does the Westminster Standards, few Presbyterians regard the rules governing church officers as overly onerous. In fact, without them the church would be chaotic and arbitrary.

Why is it, then, that when it comes to worship Presbyterians let indecency and disorder prevail? If Presbyterians can assent to a detailed set of confessional and catechetical documents, why not a book of common prayer? If Presbyterians can submit to the rigors of following proper procedure in session and presbytery meetings, why no set order of worship? Liturgical forms and written prayers may bind the conscience, but no more so than the Westminster Standards or the Orthodox Presbyterian Church's form for ordaining elders. Yet so wary are Presbyterians of liturgical formalism that they shun common forms for worship. The ironic exception is the OPC's *Directory for Public Worship*, which includes a form for the dedication of a new building, complete with litanies and prayers. Here the same sort of voluntary assent that informs adherence to creeds and polity needs to undergird the Presbyterian and Reformed use of liturgy. As long as church officers assent to the confession and catechisms of the church voluntarily with the idea of preserving the unity of the church, why would it be such a stretch to add liturgy to creeds and polity?

The harm, of course, is that liberty of conscience is usually a smoke screen for an experiential piety that is at odds with the formality inherent in set liturgies. Ever since the revivals of the eighteenth century, which Presbyterians for the most part embraced, the Reformed tradition in North America has been afflicted with the evangelical assumption that for Christian devotion to be sincere, it cannot be expressed in words or forms devised by someone else. Charles Hodge put that sentiment well when he wrote that written prayers "tend to formality, and cannot be an adequate substitute for the warm outgoings of the heart moved by the spirit of genuine devotion."[8] This outlook has cultivated among Presbyterians the sense that if a minister or ordinary believer uses a prayer book, he or she is simply going through the motions or, worse, exhibiting dead orthodoxy. Thereby, Presbyterianism took a wrong turn and assumed the yoke of enthusiasm, in the sense used by R. A. Knox when he wrote of "a new approach to religion" in which the Christian faith shifts from "a matter of outward forms and ordinances" to "an affair of the heart."[9] Of course, Presbyterians cannot blame their tradition's affinity for enthusiasm solely on revivalists such as George Whitefield or Jonathan Edwards. The Scottish Presbyterian practice of communion seasons, as historians have recently argued, in which churches administered the Supper only two to four times a year and did so with a week of festivities leading up to the sacrament, also worked enthusiatical leaven into the lump of Presbyterian practice. Those festivities soon evolved into camp meetings and revivals at which the excitement of receiving the Spirit overwhelmed the experience of receiving the benefits of Christ in the Supper.

The logic of Presbyterian antiformalism, however, demands closer scrutiny. The notion that genuine religion has to be expressed in a believer's own words actually leads in directions surprisingly charismatic, not Presbyterian. When Pentecostals speak in tongues, they display a kind of piety that is logically consistent with the evangelical demand for personal expression of faith. But if Presbyterians recognize that using the words of others, such as the words of Scripture or those of the confession of faith, are healthy and legitimate, then they should not balk at using the words of others in worship. In fact, the corporateness of worship requires such dependence since the demand for order means that only one person speaks or prays at a time; if everyone speaks or prays, they do so in unison. Consequently, in the case of my pastor praying the intercessory prayer, I am using his words, whether he wrote his own prayer or is using one from a book of prayer, because he is praying on behalf of the entire congregation. In the case of congregational song, everyone in the church is relying on the words of a poet to express his or her praise to God. Ironically, then, any congregation (Presbyterian included) that does not follow Quaker or Pentecostal patterns of worship, which encourage individual expression, automatically excludes

8. Charles Hodge, "Presbyterian Liturgies," in *The Church and Its Polity* (London: Nelson, 1879), 162.

9. R. A. Knox, *Enthusiasm: A Chapter in the History of Religion* (Oxford: Clarendon Press, 1950), 2.

the efforts of believers to express devotion in their own words in corporate worship.

The selectivity of Presbyterians on this point—not objecting to hymnals but opposing prayer books—has as much to do with the flip side of evangelical piety. The point is not simply that genuine devotion cannot legitimately rely on the words of others. The point is also that the hierarchy implicit in a set collection of prayers is illegitimate. After all, evangelicalism in the United States has been bound up with an anticlerical impulse that seeks to remove all barriers (i.e., authorities) that come between believers and their God. Using approved prayers not only puts words in believers' mouths but also forces them to submit to the clergy who wrote those prayers. But again, evangelical anticlericalism is unbecoming in Presbyterians because these spiritual heirs of Calvin are willing to use the words of the Westminster divines for their confession of faith, thereby assenting to the authority of those ministers and elders along with the church officers who chose the confession and the catechisms as the doctrinal standards for American Presbyterian denominations. Additionally, Presbyterians have little difficulty using the words of Scripture, thereby submitting to the authority of those God-inspired authors. Contemporary Presbyterians become edgy at the prospect of submitting to present-day church officers. Such submission appears to be a breach of the priesthood of all believers. Yet if they can acknowledge that God appoints human authorities to oversee the civil and familial realms (i.e., magistrates and parents), why do they see ecclesiastical authorities as inherently suspect? If God has ordained pastors, teachers, and evangelists to establish and nurture his people, why should church members object to using the words written and approved by ministers for use in worship? The answer, obviously, points to the strong tie between hostility to liturgy and to anticlericalism. More often than not, Presbyterians oppose liturgy because they refuse to acknowledge the legitimate authority of church officers. This connection suggests that the use of liturgies is insufficient to move Presbyterians in a high-church direction. Such a move also requires a proper recognition of the work and authority of holy office.

The abandonment of liturgical forms for heartfelt experience, so characteristic of low-church Presbyterianism, is a significant departure from the genius of the Protestant Reformation and thus puts Presbyterians in the awkward position of trying to accommodate John Calvin and John Wesley. What many contemporary Presbyterians seem to forget is that the Reformation was just that, a reformation, not a revival. The way to tell the difference between the two, according to the Belgic Confession, Article 29, is by determining whether the church uses the correct forms—namely, is the Word being faithfully preached, are the sacraments being faithfully administered, and is discipline being properly administered? The Belgic Confession, along with the rest of the Reformed creeds from the sixteenth and seventeenth centuries, has nothing to say about the typical way to spot a revival, whether by a large number of new conversions or greater earnestness on the part of existing believers. For Protestant Reformers, therefore, the issue was not whether a church was dead or alive. The evangelical concept of dead orthodoxy was virtually unknown prior to the revivals of the eighteenth century. Instead, the issue was whether a church was false or true. In the minds of Luther, Calvin, and Cramner, the way to distinguish the true church was by looking above all at the forms used in worship and the ways in which ordination took place. These matters were unambiguous. Either a prayer, sermon, or service of ordination conformed to the teaching of Scripture, or it did not (conceding that Episcopalians, Lutherans, and Reformed at times read the Bible in different ways on these points). But to tell whether a church or person was spiritually alive, revived, or dead was not so certain, and unfortunately, ever since the First Great Awakening, Presbyterians have been more attentive to the invisible work of the Spirit rather than to the visible work of the church, a form of alertness that is doomed to frustration because of the Spirit's mysterious movements.

Church as Mother or Personal Trainer?

Nevertheless, the answer to low-church Presbyterianism is not the introduction of collects, forms for the administration of the Lord's Supper, or the weekly recitation of the Apostles' Creed. As edifying and necessary as liturgical worship is, low-church Presbyterians will not recognize its virtues unless, ironically, they experience a change of heart. High-church liturgy requires a high-church piety. The same goes for high-church polity and high-church confessionalism. In other words, Presbyterians need to learn that the ministry of the church is a means of grace. According to the Westminster Shorter Catechism, "The outward and ordinary means whereby Christ communicates . . . the benefits of redemption are his ordinances, especially the word, sacraments, and prayer, all of which are made effectual to the elect for salvation" (Ans. 88). Taking care to use the right and fitting words in the ordinances or rituals used in worship or being careful about what people are ordained to the ministry are not luxuries. God has promised to use and will bless faithful prayers, songs, sermons, and sacramental forms of rightly ordained ministers.

For many American Protestants, too often the church is only an option for expression of heartfelt devotion, a choice that is the equivalent of personal forms of devotion or parachurch initiatives. To be sure, the church gathered in worship and led by ministers is the place where believers corporately express praise and adoration to their heavenly Father, and they should take great care in the way they express themselves to the sovereign Lord of the universe. But the church is also a place where, through his under shepherds, God ministers to his people. Especially in the Word read and preached and in the administration of the sacraments, God reminds his people of his forgiveness and builds them up in holiness and comfort. A high view of the church, her worship, ministry, and creed, then, requires a piety that recognizes the believer's dependence on the means that God has ordained to bless his children. If church is simply a place to display our devotion or zeal, then forms and ministers can become a burden. But if church is a place to hear the Good News from people duly ordained, then liturgy and clergy become, by the blessing of the Holy Spirit, the lifeblood of the believer's pilgrimage and devotion.

In other words, Presbyterians need to recover the notion of the church as mother. That idea is one foreign to many of Calvin's theological heirs, even though the Geneva Reformer wrote explicitly about the church's nurturing capacity. In book IV of the *Institutes,* Calvin asserts that the image of church as mother is one that expresses just how important her work is to God's children. "For there is no other way to enter into life unless this mother conceive us in her womb, give us birth, nourish us at her breast, and lastly, unless she keep us under her care and guidance until, putting off mortal flesh, we become like angels."[10] Calvin, along with a large part of the early Reformed tradition, taught that without the church a believer would wither and die, just as a baby would without her mother. The church, through her ministers, rites of preaching and sacraments, care and instruction, sustains a Christian through his or her pilgrimage, just as God provided for the Israelites during their wilderness wanderings. The means of grace that God has ordained the church to minister are like the manna and quail he fed to the Israelites until they reached the Promised Land. But to recognize the church as mother, Presbyterians also need to remember their pilgrim status. Chances are that an impoverished estimate of the church stems directly from an overly high estimate of one's self, which is only to say that Calvin's high view of the church and the care she provides was bound up with a sober view of the need believers have to be sustained and built up in the faith.

10. John Calvin, *Institutes of the Christian Religion,* ed. John T. McNeill, trans. Ford Lewis Battles (Philadelphia: Westminster, 1960), IV.i.4.

The common attitude toward the church among low-church Presbyterians is strikingly evident in their infrequent observance of the Lord's Supper. What does it say, for instance, about Presbyterian piety that most congregations celebrate the sacrament at most twelve times a year? Some might respond that such infrequency reflects a high view of the ordinance—to observe it weekly could encourage indifference and nonchalance. But just as likely, such irregularity communicates the impression that we really do not need the grace that comes with the Supper. As believers we are relatively strong, and the Word read and preached is sufficient to recharge our spiritual batteries. Again, one's estimate of the church is tied to one's assessment of the Christian life. In this case, it looks as if low-church Presbyterians have adopted the attitude of the Israelites when they complained about their diet in the wilderness. The difference is that Presbyterians are not grumbling about the monotony of the fare as much as they are following a diet that denies them the bread and cup of eternal life three out of every four weeks. Had the Israelites refused the manna with the same frequency, chances are they would have perished well before reaching the banks of the Jordan.

The only way for Presbyterians to have a high view of the church is by recovering Calvin's idea of the church as mother. To do this Presbyterians will need to abandon the notion of the church as personal trainer. For too many people in the Reformed tradition, the conception of the Christian life is one of perpetual motion. God requires good works to be performed, from midweek Bible studies to developing a Christian view of the arts, and the church's task is simply to supply pep talks and programs for personal improvement. The real work of the church, then, is what God's people do throughout the workweek, with Sunday providing a form of continuing education.

But this view of the church and the Christian life does not recognize how needy and frail God's people are and how perilous the battle is in which Christian pilgrims must fight. Less confidence about our abilities and a greater recognition of our infirmities would lead to a different view of the church. If Presbyterians continue to think of the church as a place for pep rallies, then all the formality and liturgy in the world will not make them high church. Such things will only take away the zing from their gatherings, which are supposed to add spice to the Christian life.

Perhaps Christ's instruction in John 6 is the only thing that will break through to the low-church mentality. In this passage, Christ tried to redirect his followers' earthly desires to a hunger for the bread of life. To do so he told them that the manna the Israelites received in the wilderness prefigured not the bread and fish that he had fed to the five thousand but his own body and blood. "I am the bread of life," he said. "Your fathers ate the manna in the wilderness, and they died. This is the bread which comes down from heaven, that a man may eat of it and not die. I am the living bread which came down from heaven; if any one eats of this bread, he will live for ever; and the bread which I shall give for the life of the world is my flesh" (vv. 48–51 RSV). Christ continued, "For my flesh is food indeed, and my blood is drink indeed" (v. 55 RSV). Many of the disciples responded to this teaching by remarking on what a difficult saying Christ gave: "Who can listen to it?" (v. 60).

For low-church Presbyterians, learning about the ministry of the church is similarly difficult, almost as difficult as overcoming 250 years of Presbyterian church history in the United States. But if Calvin was correct, if "our weakness does not allow us to be dismissed from [the church's] school until we have been pupils all our lives," if, in fact, "away from her bosom one cannot hope for any forgiveness of sins or any salvation,"[11] it may be time for Presbyterians to start undoing their past and relearning their tradition. The health of the doctrine and the church order they hold so dear actually depends on it.

11. Ibid.

2

Church Growth

When the apostle Peter wrote of his desire for the church to "grow in the grace and knowledge of our Lord and Savior Jesus Christ" (2 Peter 3:18), did he have in mind a bevy of megachurches, filled with American suburbanites and providing spiritual resources for every aspect of middle-class life, from Christocentric ceramics classes to marital counseling on how to recover the feeling of being naked and unashamed? Or was he thinking less in terms of quantity—i.e., attendance, giving, programs—and more in terms of quality? In other words, was he hoping for greater spiritual discernment, more evidence of sanctification, and deeper perseverance in the faith? These alternatives usually form the debating points in discussions about church growth. The evangelistically minded typically think in measurable categories, and they believe sticklers for doctrine or polity erect impediments to the spread of the gospel. Theological and procedural nitpickers, in turn, judge many church-growth schemes to be at best crass and at worst a betrayal of God's sovereignty in salvation. For them, the proper way to evaluate the growth of the church is not by counting but rather by looking at levels of commitment, fruit of the Spirit, and faithful preaching.

As spineless as it may sound, both sides have a point. The theological conservatives are likely correct to argue that Peter was more concerned with the quality of faith than with the number or size of individual congregations. Yet the evangelistically minded may also be right to think that the church must use certain techniques to facilitate growth. The question then becomes whether it is possible to have it both ways, to have well-populated and firmly faithful churches. In other words, can attention to the mechanics of numerical growth be combined with theological and ecclesiastical rigor? As much as the current scene in American evangelicalism appears to prove otherwise, it may be possible to be both big and faithful. Of course, bigness and faithfulness are debatable characteristics. But the teaching of Scripture actually suggests that evangelistic techniques are just as important as theological precision. At the same time, its instruction implies that when the church uses the right methods, doctrinal fidelity and spiritual maturity follow.

Church Growth: The State of the Art

A concern for the right techniques of church growth does not lead to an endorsement of the contemporary methods that dominate the American church scene. The most popular literature on increasing the size and influence of churches is vast, redundant, and easily ridiculed. For instance, in Rick Warren's highly popular *The Purpose Driven Church*, which many conservative Protestants use almost without a second thought, the pastor of the highly acclaimed Saddleback Church observes the hang-ups of the unchurched that he and his staff have sought to remedy. The unchurched don't like pitches for money, are suspicious of manipulation by fear, don't want to have to attend every church meeting, and don't want to have to stand up to introduce themselves. Warren and his staff also regularly send out a letter to prospective church attenders informing them that Saddleback Church is a "group of happy people who have discovered the joy of the Christian lifestyle," enjoy "upbeat music with a contemporary flavor," and listen to "positive, practical" messages that provide encouragement each week.[1] At Warren's church, then, the offense of the gospel can be easily confused as a positive-thinking, toe-tapping, grin-wearing Christianity that ignores the darker side of life.

But aside from questions about what it means to have a sober view of life, church-growth leaders don't seem to be aware of church life beyond the few "successful" megachurches in which circumstances, as much as "strategic" thinking, account for large numbers. Take the case of a recent article in *Reformed Worship* (sponsored by the Christian Reformed Church) in which Charles Arn, the president of Church Growth, Inc., a company based in Monrovia, California, recommended to Christian Reformed Church officers and members that they add another

---

1. Rick Warren, *The Purpose Driven Church: Growth without Compromising Your Message and Mission* (Grand Rapids: Zondervan, 1995), 194.

worship service to attract more people. Whether you call it a "seeker," "alternative," "contemporary," or simply a "second" service, the question is not whether to have one but when. Arn promises that the extra service will increase total attendance, giving, and conversions.[2] The piece is remarkable if only because it reads like a parody of the church-growth literature. Arn makes no reference to theology, nor does he consider the notion that God is as much the audience for worship as seekers. In fact, he looks at the church as if it were a business and at worship as if it were a consumer product.

But even worse is Arn's complete unfamiliarity with happenings in the CRC. During the same week that this issue of *RW* came out, another CRC publication, *The Banner,* the weekly denominational magazine, reported that the denomination's membership had dropped to pre-1968 figures, down from an all-time high in 1991. What Arn seemed to miss, along with his editors at *RW,* is that during precisely the same time that the CRC began experimenting with new services and expanding its worship "repertoire," the denomination lost members faster than at any other time in its 150-year history. If church-growth executives are so smart, why did the CRC decline? No doubt, the controversy over women's ordination accounted for some loss, but surely the wonders of the extra service should have more than made up for the loss of CRC conservatives. Such difficult cases, however, rarely impede the sky's-the-limit thinking of church-growth "experts."

The kingpin of church growth is Lyle Schaller, whose wisdom is legion in the pages of *Leadership* magazine. What is amazing about this man's advice to pastors and church leaders is how it fails to take into account that someone might have principled objections to such pragmatic ways of looking at the church. It is as if premodernity never happened, as if churches have always reduced the church to measurable units, as if events such as the Reformation or Vatican I are folktales, as if religious practices such as fasting, prayer, and preaching have always had no higher reference than membership statistics. For instance, in one article explaining the myths of church growth, Schaller pontificates that "the congregation averaging 150 at worship will need $16 to $18 per worshiper per weekend to pay all operational expenses, including missions."[3] Schaller states that the congregation averaging 500 at worship will need between $20 and $30 per worshiper, and when the congregation grows to 800, the figure will go up to $45. One of the rea-

2. Charles Arn, "Different Strokes: 7 Reasons Your Church Should Consider Adding Another Worship Service," *Reformed Worship* 51 (March 1999): 22.

3. Lyle Schaller, "You Can't Believe Everything You Hear about Church Growth," *Leadership* 18 (winter 1997): 49.

sons why Schaller's views are so popular is because Christians so spir-
itualize the work of the church and make it such an abstraction that
they never take into account such practical considerations as how expenses go up when attendance increases. But Schaller's general rules
cannot explain the experience of many congregations in the past whose
members sacrificed, saved, and skimped—all for the good of the church
and because of a higher sense of duty. At a certain point one begins to
wonder what kind of people are flocking to Schaller's churches? It
seems likely that people who want churches to meet their felt needs are
people who cannot feel the needs of others or bother with any notion of
higher purpose.

Equally frustrating about Schaller's laws of modern church life is his
reduction of rites and ceremonies with historic religious significance to
mere mechanics of attracting and retaining worshipers with an income
appropriate to a congregation's economy of scale. The larger and newer
the church, Schaller glibly asserts, "the more time is required for music
and intercessory prayer to transform that collection of individuals into
a worshiping community."[4] Older generations of saints were under the
impression that Sabbath preparation was supposed to accomplish
some of that transformation, but today's seekers are another matter.
Schaller further states that "the larger the crowd, and the greater the
emphasis on teaching, the longer the sermon." But in long sermons
preachers need to work in humor, "revealing personal anecdotes," and
redundancy.[5] One last liturgical tidbit from the former United Methodist minister is this: The larger the crowd, the longer the service. "Forty
to fifty minutes may be appropriate when attendance is under a hundred, but if it exceeds five hundred, that worship experience should
probably be in the sixty-five to ninety minute range."[6] It may seem like
grousing, but shouldn't Christian teaching about human nature, let
alone corporate worship, suggest that Schaller is wrong and that all
people need the same thing when they assemble to praise God and to
hear the gospel, even if their number is only two or three? Are Word and
sacrament more concentrated in a smaller setting? Such questions
never seem to trouble Schaller or his prescriptions for the church. Success apparently has no reference beyond a functional, well-staffed,
prosperous church that is dispensing what its members want to hear
and feel.

Customer satisfaction might be one way of describing Schaller's notion of a good church, which is another way of saying that he and his

4. Ibid., 50.
5. Ibid.
6. Ibid.

church-growth colleagues apply industrial and mechanical models to something that is fundamentally organic and mysterious, namely, the body of Christ. Modern ideas about church growth stem directly from business techniques and are one among many of the negative consequences resulting from the disestablishment of religion in the United States. Still, one would think it possible to resist the commodification of religion while welcoming the freedom that comes with disestablishment. Equally puzzling is that none of the promoters of these techniques appears to be aware of what their methods do to Christianity itself. So standard is the distinction between form and content that contemporary church leaders hardly bother with the effects certain practices have on the message communicated, whether implicitly or explicitly.

This is one of the many worthwhile points made by Philip D. Kenneson and James L. Street in their book, *Selling Out the Church*. They also challenge the idea that numerical growth is a reliable indicator of a church's success. They write:

> We suspect that judging success by measuring one's market share is solid business if you are Coca-Cola; we believe it is not a good idea for First Church at the corner of Main and Jefferson. Church marketers assume that numerical growth is "an indication that something exciting and meaningful is happening." It is interesting that this statement precedes [George] Barna's warning about the possible intoxicating effects of growth. He seems not to see that his assumption about growth contributes to such intoxication. . . . In other words, in a society that breeds both dissatisfaction and boredom and strips us of many traditional ways of living meaningfully, the growth of a particular church may be nothing more than an indicator that it has succeeded (for the moment) in providing two existential "products" that many people intensely desire: excitement and meaning. Of course, the excitement and meaning for which the church may be a temporary vehicle may have nothing whatsoever to do with the gospel.[7]

Even though it may feel strange to agree with mainline Protestants, Kenneson and Street are exactly right. Yet the emphasis on soul winning and evangelism in conservative Protestant circles has fostered a vacuum in ecclesiology, such that to be a conservative about the ministry of Word and sacrament is to have more in common with liberal denominations in which traditional forms remain the norm than with itinerant revivalists who refuse to let liturgy compromise effectiveness.

---

7. Philip D. Kenneson and James L. Street, *Selling Out the Church: The Dangers of Church Marketing* (Nashville: Abingdon, 1997), 125.

The Biblical Methods of Church Growth

Yet agreement with mainline critics of church growth can only go so far. Yes, faithfulness is different from and more important than effectiveness. But numbers are also important, not so much in the sense of the unsaved who need to be reached but in the sense of the baptized we let get away. Here again, the distinction between form and content is a culprit in the way Protestants conceive of the church and her growth. As much as the church needs to see how the techniques of contemporary church growth alter the content of the gospel, believers need to recognize that God has ordained certain techniques or forms for the church's growth. The one reliable God-given method is the natural and organic one of baptizing infants born to believing parents.

Once upon a time, confessional Protestants, such as Presbyterians and Lutherans, planted new churches in a remarkably calm way. Several families would move away from a community with an existing congregation to one in which none existed. Once this group of like faith and practice grew to five families, it would send word back to the office of home missions, the secretary of which would look for a pastor to shepherd the denomination's emigrants. The rest was history. The denomination would continue to support the mission work until it grew to a size that was self-sustaining. Some of the new growth came from grafting believers from other traditions on to the vine of a particular confessional tradition. Some came from the children who grew up in the new congregation and established families of their own. And, of course, some came from new converts to Christianity. This older model of church growth and planting was inherently organic and covenantal. It ran along lines of familiarity; the core group had grown up in the particular communion. It was also zealous about retaining the covenant children. The church followed those members who had been reared in her bosom, and the success of a new plant depended on another generation of believers remaining in the fold to support the new church.

In and of itself, baptism is a technique for church growth unrivaled by modern methods. It's cheap, simple, and doesn't require strategic thinking. What is more, baptism, as the Westminster Shorter Catechism teaches, signifies our "engrafting" into Christ and "partaking" of the covenant of grace (Ans. 94). It also admits persons into the visible church. In other words, it is a ready mechanism for enlarging the church. But aside from the phenomenological aspects of this sacrament (i.e., how much, how big, how many), baptism also nurtures the qualitative growth of individual believers. In the words of the Westminster Larger Catechism, the "duty of improving our baptism" is a lifelong endeavor that consists partly in "growing up to assurance of pardon of sin, and of all other blessings sealed to us in that sacrament" (Ans. 167). Pondering the significance of the sign that we wear daily because of the water of baptism, then, is actually more effective and of deeper significance than wearing a WWJD bracelet. Consequently, baptism gives exactly what church-growth experts want: numbers and spiritual depth. More important, baptism is what Christ commanded in the Great Commission, even though the legions of Protestants who look to Matthew 28:18–20 as the proof-text for all manner of evangelistic endeavors rarely remember that Christ commanded his disciples to teach *and* baptize. One way to fulfill the Great Commission, therefore, is to have more babies and see that they are baptized.

The other way is to have more babies and see that they are taught everything Christ commanded. It is not sufficient to grow churches merely by reproduction and baptism. The church also needs to see that those babies are instructed in the faith. Of course, preaching is not just for covenant children. According to the Shorter Catechism, preaching is a means of "convincing and converting sinners" (Ans. 89). One of the proof-texts for that answer is Paul's teaching in Romans 10 that people will not hear the gospel without preaching. Paul didn't ask, "How shall they hear without a clown, a dance, or a liturgical drama?" That's because he taught that preaching is the means God has ordained to convince and convert sinners and to build up believers in holiness and comfort. In other words, the Word inscripturated and the Word incarnate are specific about the right techniques for church growth: the divinely given and the divinely commanded means of Word and sacrament.

On the basis of scriptural teaching, then, one could well argue that, as opposed to the industrial and impersonal methods of church growth, the correct method of growing the church is inherently agrarian and personal. One of the better contemporary proponents of agrarian and local ways is the poet and farmer Wendell Berry, who lives and writes in Kentucky. In perhaps his most compelling book, *The Unsettling of America*, Berry contrasts industrialism and agrarianism in ways that are remarkably apt for highlighting the differences between church-growth expertise and the ministry of Word and sacrament:

I conceive a strip-miner to be a model exploiter, and as a model nurturer I take the old-fashioned idea or ideal of the farmer. The exploiter is a specialist, an expert; the nurturer is not. The standard of the exploiter is efficiency; the standard of the nurturer is care. The exploiter's goal is money, profit; the nurturer's goal is health—his land's health, his own, his family's, his community's, his country's. Whereas the exploiter asks of a piece of land only how much and how quickly it can be made to produce, the nurturer asks a question that is much more complex and difficult: What is its carrying capacity? . . . The exploiter wishes to earn as much as possible by as little work as possible; the nurturer expects, certainly, to have a decent living from his work, but his characteristic wish is to work *as well* as possible. The competence of the exploiter is in organization; that of the nurturer is in order—human order, that is, that accommodates itself both to the other order and to mystery. The exploiter typically serves an institution or organization; the nurturer serves land, household, community, place. The exploiter thinks in terms of numbers, quantities, "hard facts"; the nurturer in terms of character, condition, quality, kind.[8]

Berry not only brings into bolder relief the differences between marketing models and covenantal patterns of church growth but also underscores the fundamental discrepancy between a minister who works according to the logic of church growth and the pastors and fathers who tend God's flock in their particular pastures of congregation and family.

While traditional methods of growing the church might seem farfetched to people who live in the suburbs, shop at supermarkets, and think the Amish are quaint, others have noticed the usefulness of Berry's insights for the church. For instance, Eugene H. Peterson says, regarding *The Unsettling of America*, every time Berry "writes 'farm' I substitute 'parish' or 'congregation.' It works every time,"[9] which means that comparing church-growth experts to industrialists is no more farfetched than comparing a pastor's duties to those of a farmer. The kind of growth that church growers look for has everything to do with numbers and solvency. What does it take to maintain this particular church enterprise? What are the demographics? What products do we need to offer? How can we build brand loyalty? But a pastor, whose orientation is different from that of a Wal-Mart manager, looks on the needs of his flock no matter how large, sees those needs from the perspective of spiritual and physical health whether the flock agrees or not, and looks for growth that is qualitative and lasting. Instead of looking for ways to attract outsiders, the pastor knows that his primary responsibility is to feed his own flock and ensure their growth in grace. This explains why so many church-growth experts sound more like car salesmen than men of the cloth. It may also explain why Peterson says that he has learned "more usable pastoral theology" from Berry than from any of "his academic professors."[10]

8. Wendell Berry, *The Unsettling of America* (San Francisco: Sierra Club Books, 1977), 7–8.

9. Eugene H. Peterson, *Take and Read: Spiritual Reading: An Annotated List* (Grand Rapids: Eerdmans, 1996), 63.

10. Ibid.

Church Growth or Elect Reach?

When confessional Protestants begin to worry about the size of their churches, they should recognize that they are coming dangerously close to territory reserved for God. Only God knows how full or big our churches should be. Still, the question always lurking in the background of discussions about church growth comes back to the unsaved. Covenantal models of ministry may be wholesome and endearing, but if we rely on birth, baptism, and preaching, won't lots of people go unsaved? In other words, in an ideal world the organic ways of the church would be desirable. But we don't live in an ideal world. To reach all the lost we need to exploit every means possible, from the Internet to bumper stickers.

This is a view common in conservative Protestant circles. But it is an odd one for any Christian who claims to believe in election, for the logic implicit in most models of church growth is that the church won't grow and the lost won't be found unless we devise new schemes for growth and evangelism. If we take seriously the words of the Westminster Confession that the number of those predestinated unto eternal life is "so certain and definite, that it cannot be either increased or diminished" (3.iv), what happens to the logic of modern church-growth experts who appear to assume that the potential for growth is limitless? Instead of being depressed that our churches are small or that new converts are rare, it could be that we should be delighted with the numbers the church now has because this is exactly what God has ordained from before the creation of the world. To be sure, the doctrine of election does not excuse the church from offering the gospel freely. Instead, the point is that in addition to revealing God's eternal decree, the Bible also reveals the means God has promised to reach the elect. In the same way, then, that it might be wrong for Christians to lust after a new car, it may also be unhealthy to long for bigger churches. In both cases, God is sovereign, and it is the Christian's duty to accept the limits (better, praise God for his blessings) placed on him.

In the end, the idea of reaching the elect rather than growing the church should be a tremendous comfort to believers, especially to the officers of churches whose responsibility it is to see that the church's ministry remains faithful. Typically, the doctrine of election is a comfort to individual believers because it teaches that God is sovereign in salvation and eternal life does not depend on the fickle whims of the human heart. But the doctrine of election is also a tremendous comfort to the church corporately. Salvation does not depend on clever programs, strategic plans, or marketing savvy. It depends utterly on God and his mercy. The church, accordingly, has a tremendous responsibility to preach the Word and administer the sacraments, while parents have the equally large duty of rearing their children in the faith of their baptism. But this is all the church has to do because these are the means that God has given for the salvation of his people. The church does not need to be in a constant state of anxiety, thinking up new ways of reaching the lost. The right techniques of church growth are the means of grace that God established when our Lord commissioned the apostles to disciple the nations by Word and sacrament. These techniques are not flashy. In fact, they are rather low-key. But as the Bible reveals, God has a habit of saving his people through means that the world considers foolish. That's because, as Paul told the Corinthians, God wants everyone to see that the transcendent power of salvation belongs to him, not to us (2 Cor. 4:7).

3

The Spirituality of the Church

It has become a commonplace in the literature on Protestantism that the Reformed and Lutheran traditions differ on the relationship between the ecclesiastical realm and the civil realm. One of the classic statements of this difference comes in H. Richard Niebuhr's *Christ and Culture,* in which he distinguishes between the Lutheran view, "Christ and culture in paradox," and the Calvinist outlook, "Christ the transformer of culture." Unlike Luther, who made sharp distinctions between "the temporal and spiritual life, or between what is external and internal, between body and soul, between the reign of Christ and the world of human works or culture," and who contended that there should be "no confusion of these distinctions," Calvin, according to Niebuhr, had a more "dynamic conception of the vocations of men." The earthly callings of this life became for Calvinism activities in which believers could express their faith and love and glorify God. Niebuhr also detected this difference in Lutheran and Calvinist understandings of the state. While Luther sharply distinguished the kingdom of grace from the kingdom of the world, Calvin insisted that "the state is God's minister not only in a negative fashion as a restrainer of evil" but also in a positive fashion as a means for promoting human welfare. Thus, Calvin, like Luther, hoped for the conversion of humankind in its inward or spiritual aspects, but he went farther in arguing that the gospel of Christ would also transform this world "in all its nature and culture into a kingdom of God."[1]

1. H. Richard Niebuhr, *Christ and Culture* (New York: Harper & Bros., 1951), 171, 217, 218.

Niebuhr's understanding is one of the classic expressions of the difference between Lutheranism and Calvinism, but it has also become standard fare among mainline and evangelical American Protestants. For instance, in one of the articles on the Reformed tradition in Scribner's *Encyclopedia of the American Religious Experience*, the authors, both mainline Presbyterians, write that in contrast to Lutherans, who regarded the state as a "temporary expedient for maintaining order until Christ's second coming," Calvinists perceived the state as an "agent for bringing the Kingdom of God on earth by enforcing divine law through its civil code."[2] Evangelicals have also found the Reformed understanding of Christ and culture to be a liberating respite from older fundamentalist ideas about full-time Christian service and worldliness. The Reformed world-and-life view now frees evangelicals from having to affirm that evangelism and missions are the only Christian endeavors; artistic expression, scholarship, and politics have become legitimate vocations in which believers may serve God every bit as much as a pastor or missionary. While at many evangelical liberal arts colleges the Reformed understanding of culture has a great deal of appeal precisely because it provides a religious rationale for what used to be considered worldly endeavors, one suspects that the resurgence of political activism among evangelicals is another factor in the Reformed tradition's attraction. Indeed, the rise of the religious right and evangelical appeals to Reformed ideas about the transformation of culture appear to be more than coincidental.

While American Presbyterians naturally take a certain amount of pride in their tradition and their contribution to various political initiatives in the history of the United States,[3] the mention of the religious right in connection with a Reformed understanding of politics should prompt some misgivings, if not about the Reformed tradition per se, at least about evangelicals' appropriation of it. One evangelical historian who has expressed misgivings about what he calls "The American Christian Heritage as a 'Reformed Tradition'" is Mark Noll. Perhaps because he teaches at Wheaton College and sees the character of evangelical politics daily and also because he resides in the most Republican county in the United States, Noll recognizes the value of the Lutheran understanding of the two kingdoms. The dominant pattern of Ameri-

2. Milton J. Coalter Jr., and John M. Mulder, "Dutch and German Reformed Churches," in *Encyclopedia of the American Religious Experience*, vol. 1, ed. Charles H. Lippy and Peter W. Williams (New York: Scribner's, 1987), 511.

3. Perhaps because of the psychology of a Christian America, sectarian Presbyterians (e.g., the PCA and OPC) are now as interested in demonstrating the Christian origins of the United States as mainline Presbyterians were during the initial phase of the Cold War.

can political involvement is one of "direct, aggressive action modelled on Reformed theories of life in the world." From the seventeenth-century Puritan experiment in New England to nineteenth-century evangelical social reforms, Reformed theories, according to Noll, have "assumed the necessity of moving directly from passion for God and the Bible to passion for the renovation of society." Absent in American politics has been a Lutheran conception of public life, one that recognizes the tension between religious intentions and public consequences. Here Noll points to the Lutheran sense of irony, a sense that accepts that "precisely when Christians mount their most valiant public efforts *for* God, they run the greatest risk of substituting *their* righteousness for the righteousness of Christ." In the end, Noll is uncomfortable with embracing strictly either the Reformed or the Lutheran approach to public life, but he does believe that a little Lutheran leaven would provide a healthy alternative to dominant Reformed impulses because of Luther's recognition of the "incongruity between private and public spheres."[4]

Whatever the merits of Noll's argument, is his understanding of Reformed teaching about the relationship between religion and politics correct? To be sure, Noll differs little from Niebuhr or other interpreters of Reformed and Lutheran differences. And it would be foolish to dispute the greater number of Presbyterians as opposed to Lutherans involved in American politics (though numbers and time of migration might be as pivotal as theological differences). Still, is this distinction between Reformed and Lutheran ideas about church and state the last word on the matter? I want to suggest that it is not, that the nineteenth-century American Presbyterian doctrine of the spirituality of the church offers another perspective on what constitutes a Reformed understanding of religion and politics and that the spirituality of the church was not as novel as critics then and historians now allege. What I propose to do, then, is describe what nineteenth-century Presbyterian divines did and did not mean by this doctrine, explore their appeals to the Westminster Standards for justification of their views, and evaluate the plausibility of their appeals to the Westminster divines specifically and the Reformed tradition more generally. While I do not suppose that I will win any converts today to the spirituality of the church, I do hope, in the words of John Leith, to give the doctrine the proper "attention it deserve[s] as one way of relating church and culture."[5] Perhaps more

4. Mark A. Noll, "Ethnic, American, or Lutheran? Dilemmas for a Historic Confession in the New World," *Lutheran Theological Seminary Bulletin* 77 (winter 1991): 29–31.
5. John H. Leith, "Spirituality of the Church," in *Encyclopedia of Religion in the South*, ed. Samuel S. Hill (Macon, Ga.: Mercer University Press, 1984), 731.

important, I propose to show that Reformed believers need not look to Lutherans for a sense of incongruity between the kingdom of Christ and the kingdom of this world.

Nineteenth-Century Developments

Historians have not been overly inclined to appreciate the doctrine of the spirituality of the church. However they have described the spirituality doctrine—from a belief in a "complete divorce of religion from politics,"[6] to social justice being an illegitimate "goal" of the church,[7] to the church following "the Bible and the Bible only,"[8] to the church's abstaining from all "social comment,"[9] to the church's abandonment of secular causes[10]—students of American Presbyterianism have generally associated it with a clever or devious (depending on one's perspective) way to escape the less than noble motives of southern white Christians during the sectional crisis and debates over slavery. Ernest Trice Thompson was one of the first to criticize the teaching when he argued that it was the "distinctive" doctrine of the southern Presbyterian Church and had caused the PCUS to abandon "totally" its Calvinist heritage in the field of social ethics.[11] No less critical have been Jack P. Maddex and James Oscar Farmer, who have seen duplicity in the doctrine because of inconsistencies in the southern Presbyterian application of it. Maddex, for instance, argues that proponents of the spirituality doctrine were actually theocrats who found the teaching convenient only when the Confederacy and slavery were vanquished.[12] Farmer is more evenhanded; unlike Maddex he concedes that James Henley Thornwell was a proponent of the teaching and that Thornwell's articulation of it cannot be easily ignored. Nevertheless, Farmer concludes that "Old South Presbyterians" applied the doctrine inconsistently and wonders if Thornwell would have argued as he did had he been in a

6. Jack P. Maddex, "From Theocracy to Spirituality: The Southern Presbyterian Reversal on Church and State," *Journal of Presbyterian History* 54 (1976): 447.

7. James Oscar Farmer, *The Metaphysical Confederacy: James Henley Thornwell and the Synthesis of Southern Values* (Macon, Ga.: Mercer University Press, 1986), 257.

8. Mark A. Noll, "The Bible and Slavery" (paper presented at the conference on Religion and the Civil War, Louisville Presbyterian Theological Seminary, 14 October 1994), 34.

9. E. Brooks Holifield, *The Gentlemen Theologians: American Theology in Southern Culture, 1795–1860* (Durham, N.C.: Duke University Press, 1978), 154.

10. Leith, "Spirituality," 731.

11. Ernest Trice Thompson, *The Spirituality of the Church: A Distinctive Doctrine of the Presbyterian Church in the United States* (Richmond: John Knox Press, 1961), 25, 41.

12. Maddex, "From Theocracy," 449.

position, like Calvin in Geneva, to influence government directly.[13]
Meanwhile, Noll contends that the spirituality of the church was a
"stultifying" doctrine, preventing southern Presbyterians from recognizing differences between biblical times and the eighteenth century,
while it also, in the case of Robert Louis Dabney's argument about the
ordination of blacks, proved to be a "thoroughly unreliable guide to
exegesis."[14]

Having tried to clear the air of some criticisms, I think a brief exposition of the spirituality doctrine might be useful. Though he is rarely
cited as an exponent of the teaching—in fact, historians regularly quote
his claim that the spirituality of the church was a novelty[15]—the Yankee, Charles Hodge, in response to the Spring Resolutions of 1861, articulated a view of the church's spiritual purpose and means that,
though shorter, rivaled anything Thornwell could have written. Hodge
asserted:

> The doctrine of our church on this subject is, that the state has no author-
> ity in matters purely spiritual and that the church no authority in matters
> purely secular or civil. That their provinces in some cases overlie each
> other . . . is indeed true. . . . Nevertheless, the two institutions are dis-
> tinct, and their respective duties are different.[16]

Hodge then went on to quote from the Confession of Faith (pre-1903
revisions), chapter 31, regarding synods and councils, a point to which
I will return. Later in the article, Hodge made a statement that again
differed little from the point various southern Presbyterians tried to
make. He wrote:

> The church can only exercise her power in enforcing the word of God, in
> approving what it commands, and condemning what it forbids. A man,
> in the exercise of his liberty as to things indifferent, may be justly ame-
> nable to the laws of the land; and he may incur great guilt in the sight of
> God, but he cannot be brought under the censure of the church.[17]

Hodge's understanding of the spirituality of the church meant that
in the case of the Spring Resolutions, the 1861 General Assembly had
overstepped its proper bounds in declaring its obligation to "promote
and perpetuate" the integrity of the United States and the federal gov-

13. Farmer, *Metaphysical Confederacy*, 256, 260.

14. Noll, "Bible and Slavery," 29, 34.

15. Maddex, "From Theocracy," 441.

16. Charles Hodge, "The General Assembly," *Biblical Repertory and Princeton Review*
(hereafter *BRPR*) 33 (1861): 557.

17. Ibid., 561.

ernment.[18] The church, he believed, had no right to decide which government Presbyterians should pledge allegiance to and make that decision a condition of membership. Though Hodge clearly sided with the Union, he recognized that there was some question as to whether the federal government or the states were ultimately sovereign. The church, in its moral capacity, had every obligation to compel its members to be obedient to the government. This was clearly the teaching of Scripture. But the Bible did not settle, according to Hodge, the matter of the states versus the federal government. *"The question,"* he wrote, *"is, whether the allegiance of our citizens is primarily to the State or to the Union?"* However clear our own convictions of the correctness of this decision may be, or however deeply we may be impressed with its importance, yet it is not a question which this Assembly has a right to decide." For the church to adopt the Spring Resolutions was tantamount to singing the "Star Spangled Banner" at the Lord's Table.[19]

Lest I give the wrong impression of complete harmony between Hodge and Thornwell, I should add that in the course of declaring opposition to the Spring Resolutions, the Princeton theologian also called Thornwell's position "extreme" and, four years later, "new."[20] Hodge criticized Thornwell's opposition to a recommendation to the 1859 General Assembly to support the American Colonization Society. The South Carolinian had objected to the recommendation on the grounds that the Assembly, as a "court of the Lord Jesus Christ," not as a "body of Christian gentlemen," had no authority to support directly such an organization. Indeed, this distinction between what ministers did as citizens and what they did in their calling, a distinction crucial to apologists for the spirituality doctrine, has usually been lost on many historians.[21] No minister, Thornwell argued, could say that Christ had given him "a commission to attend to the colonization of the races." The church, he added, was not in the business of building asylums but rather dealt with "men *as men,* as fallen sinners standing in *need of salvation;* not as citizens of the Commonwealth, or philanthropists, or members of society."[22] Hodge rejected Thornwell's logic, though appar-

18. Ibid., 546.

19. Ibid., 549, 544, italics his.

20. Charles Hodge, "The Princeton Review on the State of the Country and of the Church," *BRPR* 37 (1865): 645.

21. Preston Don Graham, "The True Presbyterian: A Case Study of Border State Dissent during the American Civil War" (M.S.T. thesis, Yale University, 1995). Chapter 3 especially makes this point effectively.

22. James Henley Thornwell, "Speech on African Colonization," in *The Collected Writings of James Henley Thornwell,* vol. 4, *Ecclesiastical* (1875; reprint, Edinburgh: Banner of Truth Trust, 1974), 472–73.

ently similar to his own statement on the nature of the church, because it seemed to separate the "method of salvation" from the broad and ultimate claims of God's law. Because the church was bound to witness against all sin and error, Hodge argued, Thornwell was guilty of cowardice if not inconsistency by preventing the church from declaring God's will on colonization.[23]

Unfortunately, neither man addressed the merits of colonization, showing why he thought it a political or moral matter. Nor did Hodge or Thornwell acknowledge that their differences concerning church polity contributed to their disagreements about the spirituality of the church. In fact, their debate about church boards versus committees, which occurred during these same years, 1859 to 1861, go a long way toward explaining their differences concerning the spiritual mission of the church. Thornwell favored a circumscribed understanding of Presbyterian government, while Hodge balked at such a restricted view of ordination, special office, and ecclesiastical assemblies.[24] Indeed, Thornwell's fastidious case for conducting missions through committees of the General Assembly as opposed to boards, an argument with few advantages for the sectional crisis or debates about slavery, adds greater weight to Farmer's claim that the southern Presbyterian's view of the church cannot be dismissed lightly as a justification merely of southern politics.[25]

Nevertheless, for all their differences about church polity, Hodge agreed in the main with Thornwell about the spiritual aims and methods of the church. As Hodge wrote in his report on the 1865 General Assembly:

> The limits assigned to the power of church courts are all determined directly or indirectly by the word of God. Deriving all their authority from that source, they can rightly claim nothing but what is therein granted. As they are church courts . . . they have nothing to do with matters of commerce, agriculture, or the fine arts, nor with the affairs of the state. They can only expound and apply the word of God. . . . They may make orders for the conduct of public worship and the administration of God's house, but they have nothing to do with secular affairs.[26]

In other words, as Thornwell argued as early as 1851, the church "has a fixed and unalterable Constitution; and that Constitution is the Word

23. Hodge, "Princeton Review," 645–46.
24. See A. C. Troxel, "Charles Hodge on Church Boards: A Case Study in Ecclesiology," *Westminster Theological Journal* 58 (1996): 183–207.
25. Farmer, *Metaphysical Confederacy*, 256.
26. Hodge, "Princeton Review," 642–43.

of God. . . . The power of the Church, accordingly, is only ministerial and declarative. The Bible, and the Bible alone, is her rule of faith and practice."[27]

Defined in this way by Hodge and Thornwell, the doctrine of the spirituality of the church appears to be little more than a way of articulating the Reformed tradition's understanding of *sola scriptura*. As Thomas F. Torrance argued in the 1958 introduction to Calvin's *Tracts and Treatises,* "The formal principle which Calvin brought to [his] task was the reformation of the Church according to the Word of God as revealed in the canonical Scriptures," where Christ himself utters "His own mind" and issues "His own commands" so that the church is "begotten of incorruptible seed."[28] Though nineteenth-century American Presbyterians may have applied the formal principle of the Reformation poorly, their concern to limit the authority of the church to spiritual matters appears to be little more than what the Westminster Confession of Faith says in chapter 1: "The supreme judge by which all controversies of religion are to be determined and all decrees of councils, opinions of ancient writers, doctrines of men and private spirits, are to be examined, and in whose sentence we are to rest, can be no other but the Holy Spirit speaking in Scripture." Or as the Shorter Catechism puts it, "The Word of God, which is contained in the Scriptures of the Old and New Testaments, is the only rule to direct us how we may glorify and enjoy him" (Ans. 2). Now the rub, of course, is determining just what the Bible reveals, a difficulty that, providentially, I am not required to resolve here.

Church Power in the Westminster Standards

The mention of the Westminster Standards leads to the question of whether advocates of the spirituality doctrine made a case for it on the basis of the Westminster divines' teaching. One of the reasons why I may have taken so long to arrive at this question is that I did not find as much reference to the Westminster Confession and Catechisms as I had thought I might. Nevertheless, Hodge, Thornwell, and other nineteenth-century Presbyterians appealed to the Westminster Standards, believing that the confessional benchmark for their communion legitimated their understanding of the church, its nature, and its mission.

27. Thornwell, "Relation of the Church to Slavery," in *Collected Writings,* 383–84.
28. John Calvin, *Tracts and Treatises on the Reformation of the Church,* vol. 1 (1844; reprint, Grand Rapids: Eerdmans, 1958), viii.

Hodge provides an example of where nineteenth-century Presbyterians looked in the Westminster Standards for support of the church's spirituality. In his report on the 1861 General Assembly and the debate surrounding the Spring Resolutions, Hodge immediately appealed to chapter 31 of the Confession of Faith on Synods and Councils, which reads that the church is:

> to handle nothing but that which is ecclesiastical; and [is] not to intermeddle with civil affairs which concern the commonwealth, unless by way of humble petition in cases extraordinary; or by way of advice for the satisfaction of conscience, if [it] be thereunto required by the civil magistrate.[29]

Hodge used this paragraph from the Westminster Confession to buttress his conviction that even though the question of deciding where the power of the state ends and that of the church begins may be "difficult," still the two institutions were, in his view, "distinct" and their respective duties "different."[30] Hodge also cited paragraph 2 of the same chapter to support his contention that the political disputes at the heart of the Civil War were properly matters of private judgment and therefore beyond the church's power or authority. For that reason he dissented from the northern church's official support for the Union. The only standard for judging matters before the church was Scripture, and the Westminster Confession taught, Hodge believed, that "the decrees and determinations of councils are to be received only when 'consonant to the Word of God.'" This was only to say what chapter 31 said: that the deliverances of ecclesiastical bodies are not infallible and need to be judged by the Word of God. Thus, Hodge regarded the spirituality of the church, as he understood it, as being fully compatible with the Confession of Faith because this doctrine simply affirmed that the church could bind the consciences of men and women only on the basis of scriptural teaching.[31]

Though invoking the spirituality doctrine more frequently than Hodge, Thornwell made fewer direct appeals to the Westminster Standards. He did use the Confession of Faith, however, in his speech on African colonization, the one that Hodge regarded as an extreme expression of the church's spirituality. Like Hodge, Thornwell went straight to the chapter on synods and councils with its prohibition against the church meddling in politics. Determining whether a particular issue was ecclesiastical or political was, of course, in some cases a tough call.

29. Quoted in Hodge, "General Assembly," 557.
30. Ibid.
31. Hodge, "Princeton Review," 648.

But Thornwell did not hesitate to call African colonization a civil matter. "The relation of its classes and races, their respective rights and privileges, the position of women, the equality or inequality of citizens," Thornwell wrote, "these are questions which belong to the State." As long as the state did not violate the law of God, then the church had "nothing to do but to accept society as given, and labour to make all its parts work harmoniously."[32]

Stuart Robinson and Thomas Peck went beyond Hodge's and Thornwell's occasional references to the Westminster Standards in arguing that the spirituality of the church was the genius of Presbyterianism and therefore in complete harmony with the theology of the Westminster divines. To make this case, Robinson, who was professor of church history and polity at Danville Theological Seminary before pastoring Louisville's Second Church, wrote the book, *The Church of God: An Essential Element of the Gospel,* published in 1858. His exposition of the spirituality of the church differed little from the outlines produced by Hodge and Thornwell, though it was more elaborate. Robinson drew a series of contrasts between the ecclesiastical and the political spheres that fleshed out the doctrine: (1) The state's authority stemmed from God as creator, the church's from Jesus as mediator; (2) the state's rule for guidance was the light of nature, the church's the light "which, as the Prophet of the Church, Jesus Christ has revealed in his Word"; (3) the state's scope extended to "things seen and temporal," the church's to the "unseen and spiritual"; (4) the state's symbol was the sword, the church's the keys. For Robinson, these distinctions were not arbitrary or accidental but flowed directly from the purposes for which God ordained the state and the church. The former, as he explained, was designed to restrain the consequences of human depravity and "furnish a platform, as it were, on which to carry on another and more amazing scheme of mercy toward a part of mankind." The latter's purpose was to form "a nation of priests, a peculiar nation, not reckoned among the nations, of whom Jehovah is the God and they are his people." Such detail may explain why Jack Maddex has attributed the spirituality of the church to Robinson rather than to Thornwell.[33]

Whether Robinson deserves credit or blame is not as important for our purposes as his claim that the church's spirituality was not a "novelty" but followed directly from the "early symbols of Presbyterianism." In the appendix of his book, Robinson provided excerpts from the Scottish Kirk's first and second books of discipline; a letter from Robert

---

32. Thornwell, "Speech on African Colonization," 476; see also 474–75.
33. Stuart Robinson, *Church of God* (Philadelphia: J. M. Wilson, 1858), 85–87; Maddex, "From Theocracy," 446–48.

Baillie, one of the Scottish commissioners to Westminster Assembly; extracts from Gillespie's notes at the Assembly regarding decisions on church polity and government; and pieces from Westminster's Second Book of Discipline. While Robinson appealed to the Westminster Standards, he was particularly self-conscious about showing the dependence of American Presbyterianism on the Scottish reformation. One of the distinctive contributions of the Scots, according to Robinson, was the strict separation of church and state, a separation that lay at the heart of the church's spiritual mission and character. He believed that God's providence had uniquely positioned American Presbyterians "(for the first time, perhaps, since the apostles) to actualize fully and without hindrance her true nature and functions as a spiritual commonwealth."[34] But while Robinson believed the spirituality doctrine owed a great debt to the Scottish reformation, his exposition of church power depended heavily on the threefold office of Christ as taught in the Reformed tradition and elaborated in the Westminster Standards. As Preston Graham has recently written in a thesis on Robinson, the Kentucky Presbyterian's rationale "was that Christ no less fills the office of King as He does the offices of Prophet and Priest—The doctrines of the church, especially her goverment [sic], are derived from Christ's office as King."[35]

Thomas Peck, Robert Louis Dabney's successor at Union Seminary in Virginia, continued the tradition of the spirituality doctrine almost to the close of the nineteenth century with the publication in 1893 of his *Notes on Ecclesiology.* In the chapter on the relations of church and state, Peck gave an overview of the history of Christian teaching on the subject and credited the Reformation with discovering the genius of the church's spirituality, with Luther having "some glimpses of the grand truth" and Calvin having "a much clearer conception of the church's autonomy than Luther." Like Robinson, Peck argued that the Scottish Reformers went the farthest in developing the "autonomy of the spiritual commonwealth." In addition, Peck claimed that the spirituality doctrine found in the confessional standards of the Presbyterian Church lay at the heart of American understandings of the separation of church and state and was "universally received by all other [American] denominations, if not expressly taught in their public formularies and symbols." Like Robinson, Peck also defined the spirituality doctrine not merely negatively by contrasting the church and the state. He also positively derived this teaching from the lordship of Christ. "The church,"

34. Robinson, *Church of God,* 10, ii–xcvi, 28.
35. Graham, "True Presbyterian," 38. See Robinson's appeal to the Westminster Confession, *Church of God,* chap. 25, 73–74.

he wrote, "is called to testify for the rights of her only head and king, Jesus Christ, and for the freedom and independence which he has conferred upon herself as the purchase of his most precious blood." For this reason, Peck concluded, "The church has no legislative power, properly so-called, but only a power to declare and obey the law of Christ's kingdom."[36]

Articulated in this manner, the spirituality doctrine, no matter how successful, was an effort to describe the scope of the church's power. Stated negatively, it established a fairly clear boundary between the purpose and means of the church and of the state, though of course the claims of the moral law made some overlap necessary. Still, for the Presbyterians surveyed here, both northern and southern, the spirituality doctrine required the church to stay out of political matters, strictly defined. To justify the church's apolitical character, they appealed consistently to chapter 31 of the confession. Stated positively, the spirituality doctrine taught that the church was only to declare and minister the Word of God and that its means for doing so were the spiritual ones implied in the symbol of the keys of the kingdom. Concerning those areas that were not chiefly spiritual and about which Scripture was not clear, the church, as a corporate body, had to be silent and permit freedom for individual Christians. Thus, the spirituality of the church was closely connected to the doctrines of the lordship of Christ over individual conscience and Christian liberty. Southern Presbyterian advocates of the spirituality doctrine were more likely than their northern peers to articulate it in positive rather than in negative terms. For that reason, in addition to appealing to chapter 31 of the confession, they also cited the Westminster Standards' broader teaching about Christ as the King of the church and the Lord of conscience, the spiritual character of church ordinances, and Christian liberty. Still, in elaborating the spirituality of the church, both northern and southern Presbyterians found support in the teachings of the Westminster divines.

Spiritual Power for Spiritual Ends

The question that remains is just how successful nineteenth-century Presbyterians were in claiming support for the spirituality doctrine from the Westminster Standards. The fact that they appealed to the Standards does not settle the issue of whether they interpreted the confession and the catechisms aright. This is a question that providentially I am not

36. Thomas E. Peck, *Notes on Ecclesiology*, 2d ed. (Richmond: Presbyterian Committee of Publication, 1892), 140–41, 144, 151.

competent to settle. Here I plead ignorance as a provincial Americanist and the product of an educational system that produces authorities on the narrowest of periods, places, and subjects of human endeavor. I am not too specialized, however, to know that church-state relations were markedly different between seventeenth-century England and nineteenth-century United States and that this difference would have some bearing on determining whether the spirituality doctrine can be attributed properly to the Westminster divines. Indeed, the differences between the Old and New Worlds more generally, which forced eighteenth-century American Presbyterians to revise the Westminster Confession's teaching on the duties of the magistrate, would suggest that nineteenth-century and seventeenth-century Presbyterians differed in their understanding of the state. Thus, the fact that Parliament called for the Westminster Assembly, an instance of Erastianism if there ever was one, is at least an irony worthy of some notice to those who would appeal to the Westminster Standards to defend the apolitical character of the church.[37]

Still, the spirituality doctrine as elaborated by some of its staunchest advocates was not merely a way of arguing for the separation of church and state. Positively, the doctrine meant that the church was a spiritual institution with a spiritual task and spiritual means for executing that task. Despite my narrow range of academic competence, I am still familiar with the ever growing literature on the differences between John Calvin and the Westminster divines. Nevertheless, Calvin describes the church and the lordship and kingdom of Christ in ways that give some justification for recognizing links between the spirituality doctrine and the Reformed tradition. First, I want to cite briefly two examples from the *Institutes* that may remind us that Calvin was no stranger to the kind of dichotomies implied by the spirituality doctrine and to the view of culture contained in it. The first comes at the beginning of the section in book IV in which he writes about the state and distinguishes clearly between the civil sphere and the ecclesiastical sphere, not unlike chapter 31 of the confession. He says that the former is concerned with "merely civil or external justice," while the latter "rules over the soul or the inner man, and concerns itself with eternal life." Calvin also asserts that it is a "Judaic folly" not to recognize that "the spiritual kingdom of Christ and civil government are things far removed from one another."[38] While this section in book IV seems to be a negative statement of the spirituality doctrine, Calvin appears to articulate it positively in book II, when he describes Christ's kingship as being strictly "spir-

---

37. See Robert S. Paul, *The Assembly of the Lord: Politics and Religion in the Westminster Assembly and the "Grand Debate"* (Edinburgh: T & T Clark, 1985).

38. John Calvin, *Institutes of the Christian Religion*, ed. John T. McNeill, trans. Ford Lewis Battles (Philadelphia: Westminster, 1960), IV.xx.1.

itual in nature."[39] He adds that Christ's kingdom is "not earthly or carnal and hence subject to corruption, but spiritual" and because of that "lifts us up even to eternal life."[40]

Now, of course, critics of the spirituality doctrine can go to those sections in the *Institutes* in which Calvin describes the positive role of the magistrate in the life of the church. In addition, opponents of the spirituality of the church may argue that it seems to deny all the sociological observations, beginning with those of Max Weber, that point to the powerful influence of Calvinism's worldly spirituality in shaping the cultures of various Protestant nations. But I would suggest that sociologists have read only half of Calvin's piety and ignored that portion of the *Institutes*, repackaged as the *Golden Booklet of the Christian Life*, in which the French Reformer sounds as otherworldly as any pietist or fundamentalist.[41] In other words, nineteenth-century Presbyterians who articulated the spirituality of the church may not have been betrayers of Calvin and the Westminster divines if they saw a fairly sizeable chasm between things civil and ecclesiastical or between matters temporal and eternal.

Nevertheless, showing some precedent for the spirituality doctrine in Calvin and the Westminster Standards does not automatically make the teaching more attractive. Of course, the spirituality of the church is still associated with the southern church's defense of slavery and more generally with the fundamentalist abdication of social responsibility. Still, it must not be forgotten that the other side in nineteenth-century Presbyterianism, those who opposed the spirituality doctrine, do not in hindsight look a whole lot better in light of their politics or Christian understanding of it. Their use of Christian teaching about the magistrate to support the Union and to baptize the agenda of the Republican Party may suffer just as much from self-interest and partisan politics as did the advocates of the spirituality doctrine. So while the spirituality of the church has been a doctrine subject to abuse, so has the notion of an activist Reformed world-and-life view, which some have used to advocate in Christ's name specific politics or actions that appear to be no more than the preference of a particular interest group. Indeed, many of Abraham Lincoln's successors in the Republican Party today would like to lay claim to Christ's kingdom for their political initiatives. At times like this, the spirituality doctrine looks especially attractive.

39. Ibid., II.xv.3.
40. Ibid., II.xv.4.
41. For instance, Calvin writes in III.ix.2, "There is no middle ground between these two: either the world must become worthless to us or hold us bound by intemperate love of it." Of course, statements such as these need to be put into context. But my sense is that they are generally ignored in discussions of a Calvinist understanding of culture, or as some modern-day Calvinists put it, a Reformed world-and-life view.

One example from my own work on J. Gresham Machen, the well-known Presbyterian fundamentalist and southern sympathizer, demonstrates the usefulness of the spirituality doctrine. In 1926, he voted in his own presbytery, the Presbytery of New Brunswick, against a motion advocating the church's continuing support for Prohibition. Because his voice vote was used by his opponents to discredit him—sort of like accusing a minister today of child abuse—Machen had to explain his vote. He did so in language remarkably reminiscent of Hodge's and Thornwell's. He quoted from the Westminster Confession on Synods and Councils and argued that those, like himself, who thought Prohibition unwise "have a perfect right to their opinion, so far as the law of our Church is concerned, and should not be coerced in any way by ecclesiastical authority." Even though his failure to support the Eighteenth Amendment and the Volstead Act was a big factor in the 1926 General Assembly's failure to sustain Machen's promotion to the chair of apologetics at Princeton Seminary, in hindsight his logic appears to have some merit. Not only was Prohibition fairly ineffective as social policy, but the PCUSA now recognizes at least in informal ways how unholy its alliance with the Republican Party was. But not only were the politics of Presbyterians unwise, as Machen pointed out, but the church had also lost sight of its chief duty, namely, to bring "to bear upon human souls the sweet and gracious influences of the gospel."[42]

Thus, for the same reason that Noll finds Lutheran teaching on the two kingdoms attractive, the Reformed doctrine of the spirituality of the church may provide welcome relief from various efforts to politicize the faith. Only in this case, the spirituality doctrine shows that Presbyterians and Reformed do not have to go to Lutheran sources to justify a restrained and transcendent understanding of the nature and work of the institutional church. In other words, the spirituality of the church is the Reformed way of keeping religion and politics separate and of letting the church be the church. As Peter Berger has written, neither the left's nor the right's political agenda "belongs in the pulpit, in the liturgy, or in any statements that claim to have the authority of the Gospel. *Any* cultural or political agenda is a manifestation of 'works-righteousness' and ipso facto an act of apostasy."[43] But Reformed believers did not need a Lutheran sociologist to tell them that. In some small way, as the Presbyterian divines surveyed here show, they already knew it.

42. J. Gresham Machen, "Statement on the Eighteenth Amendment" (unpublished manuscript, Machen Archives, Westminster Seminary, Pennsylvania).
43. Peter Berger, "Different Gospels: The Social Sources of Apostasy," *This World* 17 (1987): 13.

Part 2

CONTEMPORARY
WORSHIP

4

Reverence and Reformed Worship

Within evangelical circles, clergy and laity alike are paying a great deal of attention to worship. Should congregations sing praise songs (complete with overhead projectors and guitars), or should trained choirs (complete with robes and pipe organ) sing the great works of sacred music? Should services be updated so as to be user-friendly, accessible for the unchurched, or should they continue in traditional patterns even if bewildering to visitors? Should the minister be the only leader of the service, or should the laity also lead worship, whether in prayers and/or song? In a culture that finds talking heads boring, should the thirty-five-minute sermon continue to be the central element of worship, or should congregations be open to less verbal forms of communication such as liturgical dance and drama? These are questions that bedevil not just evangelicals but also Presbyterian and Reformed congregations in North America and increasingly throughout the world.

Frustrated by what they perceive as the shallowness and emptiness of much contemporary worship, some conservatives have left evangelical and Reformed communions for the Episcopal Church as well as the Eastern Orthodox Church and the Roman Catholic Church. These people are fed up with worship that, according to one critic, is "a personalized, subjective, make-it-up-as-you-go-along affair." No one can agree what worship is. "Is it banging a tambourine, participating in evangelism, prayer, singing, speaking in tongues—what?"[1]

1. John Francis Schaeffer, "Franky Schaeffer on . . . Why I Became Orthodox," *Again* 14, no. 4 (December 1991): 14.

What is curious about the contemporary debates over worship is that the roads to Canterbury, Rome, and Constantinople never go through Geneva. Reformed worship has not been hospitable to subjectivism, individualism, or banality. Evelyn Underwood, in her book *Worship*, described John Calvin's worship as an "austere Puritanism" that "utterly concentrated on the Eternal God in His unseen majesty" and "has a splendour and spiritual value of its own." Reformed worship, Underwood continued, was "a powerful corrective of humanistic piety; driving home the abiding truth of God's unique reality and total demand, and man's poverty, dependence, and obligation."[2] This would appear to be a welcome corrective to the man-centered, therapeutic spirit that characterizes so many worship services today. Why, then, aren't more of the critics of evangelical worship dusting off copies of Calvin's *Ecclesiastical Ordinances* and the Genevan Psalter? Underwood's description of Calvin's worship provides clues to an answer.

> No organ or choir was permitted in his churches: no colour, nor ornament but a table of the Ten Commandments on the wall. No ceremonial acts or gestures were permitted. No hymns were sung but those derived from a Biblical source.[3]

People looking for elaborate liturgy, heightened experience, and high drama find little appeal in Reformed worship. The Reformed tradition stripped worship bare, critics argue, denying the human elements of worship, and left Presbyterians with no liturgy, no ritual, and hence, no room for a sacramental presence in worship.

Yet this criticism of Reformed worship (which many contemporary Calvinists would probably second) misunderstands liturgy and sacrament. After all, every church has a liturgy whether its members think of themselves as liturgical or not. Liturgy is merely the form and order of worship. Both the highest Anglo-Catholic mass and the lowest evangelical praise and worship service are liturgical in the narrowest sense of that word. Obviously, they differ dramatically in liturgy, but both embody a form and an order of worship. Even Underwood, who criticized Calvin, recognized the liturgical character of Reformed worship: "The bleak interior of the real Calvinist church is itself sacramental: a witness to the inadequacy of the human over against the Divine."[4]

From a different perspective, then, Reformed worship may be one of the highest or most churchly forms of worship, for Calvin strove to make every aspect of the service, from the design of the church's inte-

2. Evelyn Underwood, *Worship* (New York: Harper & Bros., 1936), 287.
3. Ibid.
4. Ibid.

rior to the manner of song, conform to the character and grace of the God who revealed himself in Christ and Scripture. In fact, Calvin's theology and understanding of worship seem to fit together and reinforce each other so well that one wonders how people in the Reformed tradition could possibly want or consistently try to maintain Calvinist theology without also enthusiastically embracing the elements and character of Reformed worship as formulated and practiced in the sixteenth and seventeenth centuries.

Calvin and Worship

An axiom of Calvin's theology was the importance and centrality of worship for vital and genuine Christian faith and practice. In fact, Calvin put worship ahead of salvation in his list of the two most important facets of biblical religion. The Christian religion maintains its truth, he wrote, by "a knowledge, *first*, of the mode in which God is duly worshipped; and *secondly*, of the source from which salvation is to be obtained."[5] Calvin also observed that the first table of the law—the first four commandments—all directly relate to worship, thus making worship "the first foundation of righteousness."[6]

The prominence of worship led to Calvin's articulation of the regulative principle, one of the hallmarks of the Reformed tradition. The regulative principle teaches that public worship is governed by God's revelation in his holy Word; whatever elements comprise corporate worship must be directly commanded by God in Scripture. The fact that a congregation has always worshiped in a particular way or that a certain practice stems from sincere piety are not sufficient reasons for ordering a worship service in a certain way. According to Calvin, God not only "regards as fruitless, but also plainly abominates" whatever does not conform to his revealed will. "The words of God are clear and distinct," Calvin wrote. "'Obedience is better than sacrifice. In vain do they worship me, teaching for doctrines the commandments of men' (1 Sam. 15:22; Matt. 15:9)."[7]

The desire to obey God informed Calvin's conception of the regulative principle, but just as important was the Reformer's understanding of human depravity. The principal effect of Adam's first transgression was to turn all people into idolaters. All individuals, Calvin believed,

5. John Calvin, "On the Necessity of Reforming the Church," in *Selected Works of John Calvin*, ed. Henry Beveridge (Grand Rapids: Baker, 1983), 1, 126.

6. John Calvin, *Institutes of the Christian Religion*, ed. John T. McNeill, trans. Ford Lewis Battles (Philadelphia: Westminster, 1960), II.viii.11.

7. Calvin, "On the Necessity," 128.

even after the fall possessed a seed of religion, or a sense of God in their souls. After the fall, however, this religious sense no longer led to the true God but instead forced men and women to create gods of their own making, gods that conformed to their own selfishness and vanity. The temptation of idolatry required Christians to be ever vigilant in regulating their worship by the direct commands of God in Scripture. This temptation made Calvin especially suspicious of practices in worship that were said to be pleasing or attractive to members of the congregation. He said that the more a practice "delights human nature, the more it is to be suspected by believers."[8]

Calvin's theology of worship required reforms of the Roman Catholic practices he encountered in Geneva. But the need for reform did not mean the abandonment of liturgy, nor did it require the elimination of all elements of the Catholic service. The Reformers purified the practices of their day, transforming the theological and spiritual content of Christian worship. They did not create a new order of worship out of nothing but instead altered the elements of worship to conform to the theology of the Reformation. Calvin's liturgy in Geneva, for instance, demonstrates continuity with the past while also reflecting changes derived from new insights into God's revelation. The order of worship was basically as follows:

Invocation
Confession of Sins
Prayer for Pardon
Singing of a Psalm
Prayer for Illumination
Lessons from Scripture
Sermon
Collection of Offerings
Prayers of Intercession
Apostles' Creed (sung while elements of Lord's Supper are prepared)
Words of Institution
Instruction and Exhortation
Communion (while a psalm is sung or Scripture read)
Prayer of Thanksgiving
Benediction

Even though Calvin followed a regular pattern in his worship services, he did not believe it was possible to prescribe all matters of worship.

8. Calvin, *Institutes*, IV.x.11.

He acknowledged the existence of incidental matters that Scripture did not determine. In such matters, churches had freedom under the general guidelines of the Bible to implement practices that would honor God and edify his people. While the regulative principle teaches that a specific practice must be commanded by God's Word, it also guarantees freedom regarding areas in which Scripture is not explicit.

Principles of Reformed Worship

Calvin and other Reformers hesitated to prescribe a specific liturgy for all churches, but throughout western Europe, from the sixteenth century until well into the eighteenth century, remarkable agreement existed among Presbyterian and Reformed communions about the nature and manner of worship. Indeed, the directions for worship crafted by Reformed churches from the time of Calvin through the Westminster Assembly suggested several principles that are to govern worship in the Reformed tradition.

The first is the centrality of the Word of God. God's Word not only directs the form or manner of worship but also comprises the content of worship. It is read, sung, seen (in the Lord's Supper), and preached. The centrality of God's Word is especially evident in the Reformed emphasis on preaching. In contrast to Roman Catholic worship, in which the focus is the mass and the altar is the centerpiece of church architecture, the Reformers made preaching the central part of the service and put the pulpit front and center in the sanctuary.

A second staple of Reformed theology, very much related to the first, is that worship is theocentric. Worship is God-centered, and its aim must be the glory of God. It is the highest form of fellowship between God and his people and must be done in spirit and in truth. In fact, God hates nothing more than false worship. Worship is absolutely necessary to Christian faith and practice, for God commands it and has so constituted us that worship is essential to the strengthening of our spiritual life.

This means that worship is not designed for evangelism. The fact that services on the Lord's Day have become seeker sensitive shows a perversion of the very nature of worship. Corporate worship is for God's people, for it is only his people who can worship him in spirit and in truth. Non-Christians may be welcome and should be encouraged to hear the preaching of the Word, which the Westminster Shorter Catechism describes as being an "especially" effectual means of "converting and convincing sinners" (Ans. 89). Yet the means by which God brings people to himself should not cause us to miss the nature of worship. If we incorporate evangelism into our worship, it is only a sign of laziness, not an indication that church-growth experts are correct. Evangelistic services have their place, and the church needs to take to heart Christ's command in the Great Commission. But discipleship is also part of Christ's instructions to his disciples, and worship is one of the principal means by which the benefits of Christ's redemption are applied to us.

The dialogical character of worship is the third principle governing Reformed worship. Corporate or public worship is the meeting of God with his people. Believers come at his invitation and are welcomed into his presence. God speaks through the invocation, the reading of the Word, the sermon, and the benediction. Worshipers respond in song, prayer, and confession of faith.

The dialogical character of worship raises the much debated issue of feelings or emotions in worship. To many outsiders and to many young people in Reformed churches (teenagers often show a better understanding of worship than their parents), worship appears to be remarkably boring and repressive. Many want the church to be more open, expressive, and emotional. Yet what some of these critics fail to understand is that God has told us in his Word how we should respond to him. In worship we answer God through song, prayer, and confession of faith. For some, however, this does not seem to be an appropriate vehicle for response. These people would rather respond to God in the same way they react to or participate in a rock concert, a baseball game, or even a performance by an orchestra. To note the affinity between audiences of modern forms of entertainment and congregations who participate in contemporary worship is to pinpoint one of the sources of misunderstanding in much current thinking about worship: There is a vast difference between responding to entertainment and hearing and submitting to God's Word. Yet this point is lost on many members of worship committees in numerous Presbyterian and Reformed congregations.

The topic of emotions in worship also leads to an observation about the corporate character of public worship. The *Westminster Directory for Public Worship,* crafted by the Westminster divines, is just that, a guide for public or corporate worship. In our houses of worship, we worship as a people, not as individuals. Many times people attend a service expecting that they should be able to express personal emotions as part of their response to God. What this desire fails to recognize is that worship in the church is corporate and, therefore, should be appropriate for people to do as a body or group. An analogy that may help explain this point concerns the relationship between a father and his children. A son may express himself one way to his dad when they are alone together. Such an opportunity allows the son to be intimate and expressive. But when the same son, along with his two brothers and two sisters, is in the presence of his father, he will generally not demonstrate the same level of intimacy or affection or reveal to the same degree the nature of his relationship with his father as when they are alone together. It would be downright rude, for example, for that son to expect to sit on his father's lap if that display of affection suggested favoritism or became a barrier to the other siblings' communication and fellowship with their father. Yet this is virtually what happens when some members of a congregation want their personal feelings to be incorporated into worship.

The fourth principle of Reformed worship is simplicity. The fuller revelation of God in Christ in the new covenant means that Christians are not dependent on the childish and fleshly elements of the old covenant. Because of the work of Christ, believers already sit with him in glory when they gather for worship, and this aspect of Christ's work greatly diminishes the church's need for visible or material supports in worship. Simplicity in worship, therefore, is closely related to spirituality. In the new covenant, according to Reformed theology, God is more fully present with his people than in the old covenant. But this presence is spiritual, not physical. Christ's command that his followers worship him in spirit and in truth is consonant with the new arrangement between God and his people.

Simplicity also suggests routine. Often contemporary evangelical worship services are packaged and rehearsed in an effort to manipulate the congregation into a worship experience, as if the different elements of worship were designed to arouse feelings or emotions that are somehow more intimate and more expressive than older forms of communion with God. In other words, many contemporary worship services call attention to the service and worship leaders, which may be the point of many contemporary services. Perhaps the service has been designed by people who think themselves devout and believe that if the congregation follows their example, members will also have an intimate experience with God (Why do you think they are called "worship modelers"?). In contrast, Reformed worship functions according to the premise that worship should not be novel or creative. Rather, it should be routine, ordinary, and habitual. C. S. Lewis was by no means a Reformed theologian, but he did make a point supported by the Reformed tradition when he said that a worship service "'works' best when, through long familiarity, we don't have to think about it."

> But every novelty prevents this. It fixes our attention on the service itself; and thinking about worship is a different thing from worshiping. . . . "'Tis mad idolatry that makes the service greater than the god." A still

worse thing may happen. Novelty may fix our attention not even on the service but on the celebrant. . . . There is really some excuse for the man who said, "I wish they'd remember that the charge to Peter was 'Feed my sheep'; not 'Try experiments on my rats,' or even 'Teach my performing dogs new tricks.'"[9]

The fifth and final, and perhaps the most important, principle of Reformed worship is reverence. According to Calvin, "Pure and real religion" manifests itself through "faith so joined with an earnest fear of God that this fear also embraces willing reverence."[10] Worship should be dignified and reverent, but it does not achieve these qualities through elaborate ceremonies or complex liturgies. In fact, Calvin believed that "wherever there is great ostentation in ceremonies, sincerity of heart is rare indeed."[11] This does not mean that Reformed worship has no room for joy or emotion, as some critics have charged. Joy, along with a full range of emotions—grief, anger, desire, hope, and fear—should be a part of worship. But the need for reverence and decorum dictates that any expression of emotion in worship should be tempered by moderation and self-control. To ensure that every aspect of worship is done decently and in good order, the Reformed tradition has insisted that every service be supervised by the elders, who bear responsibility for corporate worship, and that the minister, who speaks for God and for God's people, lead and direct the service.

A helpful way of understanding reverence may be to think of the ethos of a funeral service for a professing Christian (even though the Westminster divines disapproved of funeral services). At such a service when we contemplate the death of a loved one, we are obviously filled with sadness and are reminded of our own frailty. Yet when the deceased is a believer, the service is also an occasion for joy because we believe that God has called one of his children to be with him, that the believer has been "made perfect in holiness" and has "passed immediately into glory." Why should a worship service be any different, for in our services the death of our Lord is central? Of course, we do not stop with Christ's death. We go on to rejoice at his resurrection, without which, the apostle Paul says, we would not have hope. Still, the joy we experience in contemplating and worshiping our risen Savior is an emotion that is always tinged with gravity and humility. It is not the joy associated with celebrating the national championship of a college football team. It is a joy that recognizes the suffering and death of Jesus

9. C. S. Lewis, *Letters to Malcolm: Chiefly on Prayer* (New York: Harcourt, Brace, Jovanovich, 1964), 4–5.

10. Calvin, *Institutes*, I.ii.2.

11. Ibid.

Christ and also our own complicity, because of our sin, in his pain and ignominious death.

The Revisionist Impulse

Within the last twenty years, the theology and practice of Reformed worship have been stretched to the limits. Various communions have made efforts to revise directories for worship, while countless congregations have established worship committees whose sole function seems to be bringing worship up-to-date. While some proposed changes are informed by sound biblical and Reformed insights, they also expose genuine discontent within the Reformed household about worship. This discontent was probably summarized best in a recent report to one conservative Presbyterian denomination:

> There is widespread dissatisfaction or at least widespread lack of use in the church of the present Directory. There are parts of the present Directory that are so dated (e.g., "the stately rhythm of the choral") that there must be a rather thorough revision. Yet there is no consensus of where the church wants to go in worship. The current situation in the church regarding worship is diverse from near liturgical anarchy to others who feel that singing uninspired hymns is a violation of the regulative principle.[12]

How did this state of affairs come to be? Some might point to new biblical insights that show that the old habits of worship and the theology that undergirded them were bound to a specific form of cultural expression rather than to the teaching of the Word of God. Others cite the small growth of churches that do not change their worship and the inability of traditional worship to appeal to Christian youth as evidence that worship must become relevant and free from older and merely human patterns of worship. Still others see the discontent over and changes within worship as clear indications of defection from the Reformed theology of worship.

Undoubtedly, many of these changes in Reformed worship have stemmed from significant transformations within American culture. Old ways of worship no longer seem plausible; they appear to be ineffective if not alien. The effective ministry of the church, some argue, requires that it keep pace in its efforts to contextualize the gospel and

12. "Report of the Committee on Revisions to the Book of Discipline and the Directory for Public Worship," Orthodox Presbyterian Church, *Minutes of the General Assembly* (1989), 321.

make it understandable to contemporary culture. And if effectiveness means abandoning a manner of worship that dates from the 1930s, so be it. As long as the content of worship is sound, the form really doesn't matter. The changes in worship, therefore, are merely alterations of form.

It is ironic, to say the least, that believers can be so uncritical of contemporary cultural expressions—and therefore wish to use them in worship—and yet so alarmed by the evils of this culture. (It is also remarkable how Calvinists who insist that everything be done for God's glory so often judge worship on the basis of whether it is pleasing to men, women, and especially teenagers.) Most Christians would agree that the people of God face difficult times. The church is overwhelmed by the unjust policies of the government, the moral relativism of public schools, and the decadence of the media. Yet few seem to recognize the subtler dangers of American culture. One of the most insidious and subtle influences on the church comes from the media and entertainment industry. Ministers often preach about the overt dangers of Hollywood, warning about the sex, violence, and disrespect for religion in many movies, TV shows, and popular songs. A far more dangerous influence, however, is the way popular culture has altered attitudes toward worship.

Popular culture has fostered a significant shift in perceptions about corporate worship. Since people gather together now most often for some form of entertainment, Christians increasingly exhibit a willingness to regard their time together collectively in the same way they think about public forms of entertainment. Worship becomes something that the minister, choir, organist, and other musicians perform for the congregation. Addiction to popular culture has erased the conviction that the audience for worship is not the congregation but God.

Even more alarming is the way popular culture has nurtured an ethos of informality, breaking down distinctions between what is solemn and what is disrespectful. Older worship seems out-of-date—the phrase "the stately rhythm of the choral" doesn't make sense—because our culture increasingly scorns or discards what is dignified and majestic. What makes contemporary or popular forms of worship objectionable from a Reformed perspective is not that they are lowbrow, though the prayers, praise, and music of today's worship are often trivial. Believers can worship God whether or not they appreciate a sonata by Mozart or a sculpture by Michelangelo. Rather, the problem of much contemporary worship is that it does not acknowledge the insight of Calvinism, namely, that people, including Christians, are constantly tempted to fashion God in their own image. Many of the innovations in worship today convey an erroneous picture of God.

A Reformed theology of worship has always manifested the conviction that when believers gather on the Lord's Day, their practices should reflect humility and reverence. After all, Christians in worship come before the holy and transcendent one, who is the righteous judge of the universe, whom men and women offend daily, and who has wonderfully provided a way of salvation through his Son, Jesus Christ. Worship should be a reminder of the gulf between God and sinners and of what he has done to overcome that gulf, lest believers lapse into a false understanding of God.

Worship, then, is not something done lightly or without serious consideration. In worship, Christians profess and honor the character of the God whose presence they enter and who has brought them out of an estate of sin and misery. Worship always reflects a people's conception of God. True theology yields true and acceptable worship. Improper or erroneous theology yields false worship. Worship is not a matter of taste; it is a statement of theological conviction about who God is and who we are as his covenant people.

Rather than following the liberationist and irreverent impulses of American culture, Calvinists, if they are to have anything to say to the contemporary discussions about worship, need to recover in their theology and practice of worship what Psalm 2:11 talks about when it says that God's people should "rejoice with trembling." The worship recommended and practiced by Calvin, Knox, and the Westminster divines reflected a reverent combination of joy and fear, and that older manner of worship was always held in check by the sense that any display of flippancy and disrespect would offend God.

But contemporary cultural expressions rarely convey any sense of the magnitude and gravity that surround the meeting between God and his people in worship. Indeed, the forms and style of contemporary culture cannot contain the dignity and respect that should characterize the external and internal posture of Christians as they approach God's throne. Though there is therapeutic appeal in thinking of worship as entering a pub where God serves as a barroom buddy, always ready to hear what we have to say and to wipe up our spills, the God revealed in Scripture is a King who sits erect on the throne of glory, attentive to the words, thoughts, and emotions of his subjects as they assemble before him. To be sure, that King is also our Father, but in the light of what the fifth commandment and the apostle Paul say about the respect and fear children should have for parents, the image of God as our Father does not necessarily allow for nonchalance in worship.

There are no better verses to characterize Reformed worship than Hebrews 12:28–29: "Since we are receiving a kingdom that cannot be shaken, let us be thankful, and so worship God acceptably with reverence and awe, for our 'God is a consuming fire.'" This insight has characterized Reformed and Presbyterian worship since the time of the Reformation. One wonders how Reformed churches can meaningfully retain their theological heritage while abandoning the essence of Reformed worship, especially since weekly worship provides the foundation for and reinforces the very theology that Reformed believers confess. But at least the abandonment of Reformed worship may explain why those who look for a service with dignity and reverence so often turn to non-Reformed communions. If Reformed churches are going to be true to their theology and offer to weary souls some rest from the shallowness and banality of contemporary evangelical worship, they need to recover the liturgy and theology of worship of the Reformed tradition, a worship that took seriously the notion that God is indeed "a consuming fire."

5

Worship That Is Deformed

What do Billy Graham and Stanley Fish have in common? According to most participants in the ongoing culture wars, the answer would be an emphatic "not much!" With the exception of a few demographic details—both are older white men who have lived in North Carolina—little seems to unite these two figures or the movements for which they have become figureheads. Graham is, of course, the patron saint of American evangelicalism, the one who as an object of admiration or scorn determines what it means to be an evangelical. Fish, dean at the University of Illinois, Chicago, of deconstructionist, postmodernist fame, has become one of the principal cheerleaders for efforts within the academy to make the literary canon specifically, and the humanities more generally, more inclusive and less oppressive. Identified in this way, Graham and Fish, and the constituencies to which they speak, would appear to be about as far apart as John Ashcroft and Hillary Clinton.

James Davison Hunter, for instance, argues that evangelicals are a large part of the orthodox constituency that defends the traditional family, opposes political correctness and multiculturalism in the academy, and supports efforts to cut federal funding for objectionable art. This explains why evangelicals have lined up in bookstores across the land to buy and read to their children William Bennett's *Book of Virtues*. Thus, evangelicalism, at least in the common configuration of the ongoing culture wars, is the antithesis of the cultural left.

Why is it, then, that when evangelicals retreat from the public square into their houses of worship they manifest the same hostility to tradition, intellectual standards, and good taste that they find so deplorable in their opponents in the culture wars? Anyone familiar with the so-called "Praise

and Worship" phenomenon (so named, supposedly, to remind participants of what they are doing) would be hard pressed to identify these believers as the party of memory or the defenders of cultural conservatism.
P & W has become the dominant mode of expression within evangelical
churches, from conservative Presbyterian denominations to low-church
independent congregations. What characterizes this style of worship is
the praise song ("four words, three notes, and two hours") with its man-
tra-like repetition of phrases from Scripture, displayed using an overhead projector or video monitor (for those churches with bigger bud-
gets), and accompanied by the standard pieces in a rock band.

Gone are the hymnals that kept the faithful in touch with previous
generations of saints. They were abandoned, in many cases, because they
were filled with music and texts considered too boring, too doctrinal, and
too restrained. What boomers and busters need instead, according to the
liturgy of P & W, is a steady diet of religious ballads, most of which date
from the 1970s, the decade of disco, leisure suits, and long hair. Gone too
are the traditional elements of Protestant worship: the invocation, the
confession of sins, the Apostles' Creed, the Lord's Prayer, the doxology,
and the Gloria Patri. Again, these elements are not sufficiently celebra-
tive or "dynamic," the favorite word used to describe the new worship.
And while P & W has retained the talking head in the sermon, probably
the most boring element of Protestant worship, the substance of much
preaching is more therapeutic than theological.

Of course, evangelicals are not the only ones guilty of abandoning the
treasures of historic Protestant worship. Various churches in the Evangelical Lutheran Church in America and the Lutheran Church–Missouri
Synod have begun to experiment with contemporary worship. The traditionalists in Reformed circles, if the periodical *Reformed Worship* is any
indication, have also begun to incorporate P & W into their services. And
Roman Catholics, one of the genuine conservative constituencies throughout American history, have contributed to the mix with the now infamous guitar and polka mass. Yet judging on the basis of worship practices, evangelicals look the most hypocritical. Six days a week they
trumpet traditional values and the heritage of the West, but on Sunday
they are the most novel. Indeed, the patterns of worship that prevail in
most evangelical congregations suggest that these Protestants are no
more interested in tradition than their archenemies in the academy.

Postmodern Evangelicals

A variety of factors, many of which stem from developments in post-
1960s American popular culture, unite evangelicalism and the cultural

left. In both movements, we see a form of antielitism that questions any distinction between good and bad (or even not so good) or between what is appropriate and what is inappropriate. Professors of literature have long been saying that the traditional literary canon was the product, or better, the social construction, of a particular period in intellectual life that preserved the hegemony of white men but had no intrinsic merit. In other words, because aesthetic and intellectual standards are means of sustaining power, there is no legitimate criteria for including some works and excluding others.

The same sort of logic can be found across the country at weeknight worship planning committee meetings. It is virtually impossible to make the case that "Of the Father's Love Begotten" is a better text and tune than "Shine, Jesus, Shine," and, therefore, that the former is fitting for corporate worship while the latter should remain confined to Christian radio. In the case of evangelicals, the inability to make distinctions between good and bad poetry and music does not stem so much from political ideology (though it ends up abetting the cause) as from the deeply ingrained instinct that worship is simply a matter of evangelism. Thus, to reach the unchurched, the churched have to use the former's idiom and style. What is wrong with this picture?

The traditionalists are of no help here. Rather than trying to hold the line on what is appropriate and good in worship, most of those who are devoted full-time to thinking about liturgy and worship, the doorkeepers of the sanctuary as it were, have generally adopted a "united-colors-of-Benetton" approach to the challenge of contemporary worship. For instance, a recent editorial in a Reformed publication says that the old ways—the patterns that used Buxtehude rather than Bill Gaither; "Immortal, Invisible" rather than "Do Lord"; a Genevan gown instead of a polo shirt—have turned out to be too restrictive. Churches need to expand their worship "repertoire." The older predilection was "white, European, adult, classical, with a strong resonance from the traditional concert hall." But this was merely a preference and a reflection of a specific "education, socio-economic status, ethnic background, and personality." Heaven forbid that anyone should appear to be so elitist, for the traditional "worship idiom" can become "too refined, cultured, and bloodless . . . too arrogant." Instead, we need to encourage the rainbow coalition—"of old and young, men and women, red and yellow, black and white, classical and contemporary."[1] And the reason for this need of diversity? It is simply because worship is the reflection of socioeconomic status and culture. Gone is any conviction that one liturgy is bet-

---

1. Harry Boonstra, "Expanding Our Repertoire: How My Worship Credo Has Changed," *Reformed Worship* 34 (December 1994): 2–3.

ter than another because it conforms to revealed truth and the order of creation, or that one order of worship is more appropriate than another for the theology that a congregation or denomination confesses. Worship, like food or clothes, is merely a matter of taste. Thus, the logic of multiculturalism has infected even those concerned to preserve traditional liturgy.

Yet when one looks for genuine diversity in worship, multiculturalism—again, the great leveler of tradition and cultural standards—offers up a very thin band of liturgical expression. Advocates of diversity do not seem to be very interested in the way "the people" have worshiped in the past. Is there, for instance, any real effort among the various experiments in worship to recover the psalm singing of the Puritans, the simple and spontaneous meetings of Quakers, the hymnody of German pietism, the folk traditions of the Amish, the revival songs of Ira Sankey and Dwight L. Moody, or the spirituals of African-American Protestants? The answer, of course, is no, for these expressions of Protestant piety, even though originating in some groups that would hardly qualify as elite, are no better than the liturgies from the Lutheran, Anglican, and Reformed establishments. What the P & W crowd really wants is a narrow range of musical and lyrical expression, one that conforms to their admittedly limited worship "repertoire."

Indeed, contemporary worship—and church life for that matter—depends increasingly on the products of popular culture, shown in its musical mode of expression, the liturgical skits that ape TV sitcoms, and the informal style of ministers that follows the antics of late-night TV talk show hosts. Thus, just as the academic left advocates including Madonna and *Leave It to Beaver* in the canon, so the evangelical champions of contemporary worship turn to popular culture—primarily contemporary music and television programming—for the content and order of worship. This is remarkable for a Christian tradition that once found its identity in avoiding all forms of worldliness and that continues to rail against the products of Hollywood and the excesses of the popular music industry. Yet as in the case of the cultural left, the generation that grew up on TV and top-40 radio stations is now assuming positions of leadership in the church. What they want to surround themselves with in worship, as in the classroom, is what is familiar and easily accessible. Rather than growing up and adopting the broader range of experience that characterizes adulthood, evangelicals and the academic left want to recover and perpetuate the experiences of adolescence.

In fact, what stands out about P & W is the aura of teenage piety. Anyone who has spent a week at one of the evangelical summer youth camps that dot the landscape will be struck by the similarity between

P & W and the services in which adolescents participate. The parallels are so close that one is tempted to call P & W the liturgy of the youth rally. The meetings of Young Life, Campus Crusade for Christ, and Bible camps include all the elements of P & W: the evangelical choruses, the skit, and the long talk by the youthful speaker calling for dedication and commitment to Christ. While these youth ministries are effective in evoking the mountaintop or campfire-side experience, they rarely provide the sustenance on which a life of sacrifice and discipline depends. Yet P & W is attractive precisely because it appears to offer weekly the spiritual recharge that before came only once a year. Consequently, many megachurches that follow the P & W format thrive because they help many people recover or sustain the religious experience of youth.

Some may wonder what is wrong with assisting adults to perpetuate the emotions and memories that sustain religious devotion. The problem is that such experiences and the worship from which they spring are concerned primarily with affect. One searches in vain through the praise songs, the liturgical dramas, or the sermon/inspirational talk for an adequate expression of the historic truths of the faith. It is as if the content of worship or the object that elicits the religious experience does not really matter. As long as people are lifting and swaying their arms, tilting back their heads, and closing their eyes, then the Spirit must be present and the worship genuine.

What is ironic about contemporary worship is that its form is almost always the same even while claiming that older worship is too repetitive. Another standard complaint about "traditional" worship is that it is too formal. Evangelicals believe that God is never limited by outward means. Believers who rely on set liturgies or who repeat written prayers, some criticize, are merely "going through the motions." Real faith and worship cannot be prescribed. Yet for all the attempts by the practitioners of P & W to avoid routine and habit, hence boredom, contemporary worship never seems to escape its own pop culture formula. Again, the songs are basically the same in musical structure and lyrical composition, the order of the service—while much less formal—rarely changes, and the way in which people express their experience demonstrates remarkable unity (e.g., the arms, the head, the eyes). The hostility to form and the inability to think about the ways in which certain habits of expression are more or less appropriate for specific settings or purposes are what finally put evangelicalism and the academic left on the same side in the culture war. The idea that the autonomous individual must find his or her own meaning or experience of reality ends up making such individuals unwilling to follow and submit to the forms, habits, and standards that have guided a community or culture. Besides the fact that the radical individualism of modern culture has bred as much conformity as human history has ever known, evangelicals and the academic left continue to buck tradition in the hope of finding the true self capable of experiencing religion or life at its most genuine or authentic.

Bad Taste, Bad Faith

What evangelicals who prefer P & W to older liturgies share with academics who teach Louis L'Amour instead of Shakespeare is an inability to see the value of restraint, habit, and form. Evangelicals and the academic left believe that we need to be liberated from the past, formalism, and existing structures to come into a more intimate relationship with life or the divine. This is really quite astounding in the case of evangelicals whose public reputation depends on defending traditional morality. Yet the effort to remove all barriers to the expression and experience of the individual is unmistakably present in the efforts to make worship more expressive and spontaneous. This impulse in evangelical worship repudiates the wisdom of various Christian traditions that, rather than trying to liberate the self in order to experience greater intimacy with God, hold that individuals, because of a tendency to sin and commit idolatry, need to conform to revealed and ordered patterns of faith and practice. The traditions that Presbyterians follow, for instance, are not undertaken to throttle religious experience. Nor were these means arbitrarily chosen by John Calvin and John Knox. Rather, Presbyterians have conducted public and family worship in specific ways because they believe worship should conform to God's revealed truth. But just as the academic left has abandoned the great works of Western civilization because of a desire for relevance in higher education, so evangelicals have rejected the various elements and forms that have historically informed Protestant worship, again, because they are boring to today's youth.

Antiformalism also explains the stress on novelty so often found in P & W. The leader of worship planning at one of the dominant megachurches says, for instance, on a video documenting a P & W service, that she is always looking for new ways to order the midweek believers' service so that church members won't fall into a rut. She adds that people are often tired, having worked all day (an argument for worshiping on Sunday) and need something that will arrest their attention and put them in a proper frame of mind. This perspective, however, fundamentally misunderstands the relationship between form and worship. C. S. Lewis had it right when he said that a worship service "'works' best when, through long familiarity, we don't have to think about it." "The perfect church service," he added, "would be the one we were almost unaware of; our attention would have been on God. But every novelty prevents this. It fixes our attention on the service itself; and thinking about worship is a different thing from worshipping. . . . 'Tis mad idolatry that makes the service greater than the god.' A still worse thing may happen. Novelty may fix our attention not even on the service but on the celebrant."[2] This is precisely what has happened in P & W, in which the service and elements are designed to attract attention to themselves rather than functioning as vehicles for expressing adoration to God. Lewis knew that repetition and habit were better guides to the character of worship than novelty and manipulation. In fact, one does not need to be a professor of liturgics to sense that the idiom of Valley Girls is far less fitting for a believer to use to express love for God than is the language of the Book of Common Prayer. Such an instinct only confirms the wise comment of the Reformed theologian, Cornelius Van Til, who, while preferring Presbyterian liturgy, still remarked that "at least in an Episcopalian service no one says anything silly."[3]

Criticizing contemporary worship, however, to accuse it of bad taste or triviality, is almost as wicked as smoking in public. Arguments against P & W are usually taken personally, becoming an affront to the feelings of contemporary worshipers. Which is to say that the triumph of P & W, like the ascendancy of the cultural left in the academy, is firmly rooted in our therapeutic culture. The most widely used reason for contemporary worship is that it is what the people want and what makes them feel good. Again, just as there are no intellectual standards for expanding the literary canon to include romance novels, so there are no theological criteria for practicing P & W. But there are plenty of reasons that say that if we give people what they are familiar with, whether sitcoms in the classroom or soft rock in church, they will feel comfortable and come back for more. As Philip Rieff has noted, the connections between the therapeutic and the market are formidable. If we can expand our worship or academic repertoire to include the diversity of the culture, we will no doubt increase our audience.[4]

This is why P & W services are also called "seeker sensitive." They are part of a self-conscious effort to attract a larger market for the church. Yet while evangelicalism may have a large market share, its consumer satisfaction may also be low, especially if it deceives people

2. C. S. Lewis, *Letters to Malcolm: Chiefly on Prayer* (New York: Harcourt, Brace, Jovanovich, 1964), 4–5.

3. This is anecdotal evidence based on conversations with those who knew Van Til.

4. Philip Rieff, *The Feeling Intellect: Selected Writings* (Chicago: University of Chicago Press, 1990), 251–64.

into thinking they have really worshiped God when they have actually been worshiping their emotions. Thus, once again, evangelical worship turns out to be as deceptive as the academic left, which tells students that the study of Batman comics is just as valuable as the study of Henry James.

Of course, anyone familiar with the history of American evangelicalism should not be surprised by P & W. In fact, Billy Graham's recent inclusion of Christian hip-hop and rap bands in his crusades is consistent with evangelical history more generally. (It also differs little from his efforts in the 1970s, seldom remembered, to appeal to the Jesus People. With lengthy locks, an inch over the shirt collar, and long sideburns, Graham said, playing off Timothy Leary's famous psychedelic slogan, "Tune in to God, then turn on . . . drop out—of the materialistic world. The experience of Jesus Christ is the greatest trip you can take.")[5] As R. Laurence Moore argues in *Selling God,* since the arrival of Boy George, George Whitefield that is, in the American colonies, evangelicals have been unusually adept at packaging and marketing Christianity in the forms of popular culture. The intention of Protestant revivalism was "to save souls, but in a brassy way that threw religion into a free-for-all competition for people's attention." Revivalism, in fact, according to Moore, "shoved American religion into the marketplace of culture" and became "entangled in controversies over commercial entertainments which they both imitated and influenced."[6]

Seldom have evangelicals recognized that this commitment to making the gospel accessible deforms and trivializes Christianity, making it no better than any other commodity exchanged on the market. As H. L. Mencken perceptively pointed out about Billy Sunday, evangelicalism "quickly disarms the old suspicion of the holy clerk and gets the discussion going on the familiar and easy terms of the barroom." Mencken added that evangelicalism is marked "by a contemptuous disregard of the theoretical and mystifying" and reduces "all the abstrusities of Christian theology to a few and simple and (to the ingenious) self-evident propositions," making of religion "a practical, an imminent, an everyday concern."[7] Thus, the pattern of evangelical practice shows a long history of being hostile to the more profound liturgies, prayers, and hymns that God's people have expressed throughout the ages.

5. Quoted in Larry Eskridge, "'One Way': Billy Graham, The Jesus Generation, and the Idea of an Evangelical Youth Culture," *Church History* 67, no. 1 (March 1998): 86.

6. R. Laurence Moore, *Selling God: American Religion in the Marketplace of Culture* (New York: Oxford University Press, 1994), 43.

7. H. L. Mencken, "Doctor Seraphicus at Ecstaticus," *Baltimore Evening Sun,* 14 March 1916.

The reason for this hostility, of course, is that these traditional forms of expressing devotion to God are not sufficiently intelligible to outsiders. But in an effort to reach the unchurched, just as the university has abandoned its mission in order to reach the uneducated, evangelicals have reversed the relationship between the church and the world. Rather than educating outsiders or seekers so they may join God's people in worship, or rather than educating the illiterate so they may join the conversation of the West, the church and the academy employ as their languages the idioms of the unchurched and the undereducated. In effect, through P & W the church is becoming dumber at the same time that multiculturalism is dumbing down the university. In the case of P & W, the church, by embracing the elements and logic of contemporary worship, has abandoned its task of catechesis. Rather than converting and discipling the seeker, the church now uses the very language and methods of the world. Rather than educating the unbaptized in the language of the household of faith, the church now teaches communicants the language of the world.

Hughes Oliphant Old, in his fine study of worship, concludes with a reflection about mainline Presbyterian worship that applies well to what has transpired in contemporary evangelical churches. "In our evangelistic zeal," he writes, "we are looking for programs that will attract people. We think we have to put honey on the lip of the bitter cup of salvation. It is the story of the wedding of Cana all over again but with this difference. At the crucial moment when the wine failed, we took matters into our own hands and used those five stone jars to mix up a batch of Kool-Aid instead."[8] Such is the state of affairs in contemporary evangelical worship. The thin and artificial juice of popular culture has replaced the finely aged and well-crafted drink of the church through the ages. Aside from the merits of the instant drink, it is hardly what you would expect defenders of tradition and the family to choose to serve at a wedding, or at the banquet supper of our Lord. Yet just as evangelicals in the nineteenth century substituted Welches for red wine, so a century later they have exchanged the superficial and trivial for the rich forms and elements of historic Protestant worship.

8. Hughes Oliphant Old, *Worship That Is Reformed according to Scripture* (Atlanta: John Knox, 1984), 177.

6

Spirit-Filled Worship

To hear some proponents of contemporary worship, one would think that the church of Jesus Christ had not been able to worship well and properly until the advent of praise songs, Contemporary Christian Music, and greater expressiveness in church services. Bill Hybels, for instance, the pastor of Willow Creek Community Church, the flagship congregation for so many of the innovations in late-twentieth-century Christian worship, admitted in a recent interview that he did not understand worship until the mid-1980s, when he attended a conference at Jack Hayford's (the author of the now classic praise song "Majesty") Church on the Way. There Hybels witnessed a worship leader who was prepared and was able "to take us from where we were, into the presence of God." After forty-five minutes to an hour of singing, during which the leader assisted in "adoring," "confessing before," and "expressing our absolute trust and devotion" to God, Hybels went back to his hotel room and said, "This changes everything!" "Every Christian should regularly experience what I did tonight."[1]

Key to Hybels's new conception of worship was the biblical teaching that Christians are to worship their God "in spirit and truth." This meant not only that sound teaching was important for worship, as in a good sermon, but also that believers need to be "emotionally alive and engaged" in the experience of worship.[2] Indeed, what has been crucial to the success and appeal of the newer forms of worship has been a re-

1. "Hybels on Worship" (interview with Chuck Fromm), *Worship Leader* (September/October 1996): 28.
2. Ibid., 30.

discovery of the work and presence of the Third Person of the Trinity in the gathering of believers to bring praise and honor to God. One Reformed pastor, whose congregation began to incorporate some of the recent worship innovations into the services, says that when his church "discovered a new way to sing praise," the power of the Spirit "washed over us that day." Previously, this congregation had only given "lip service to the Spirit," but now they were uniquely aware of the "gentle presence of the third person of the Trinity."[3] Likewise, Hayford, writing for *Leadership* magazine, links the newer forms of worship directly with the Spirit. "Expressive worship cultivates a willingness to be taught by and to submit to the Holy Spirit."[4] This connection between spontaneity, informality, and emotional intensity in contemporary worship explains the popularity of such phrases as "Spirit-filled" or "Spirit-led" in discussions about worship. The presence of the Holy Spirit, along with the signs of his presence, means that worship is not only of God but also authentic, sincere, and right.

These appeals to the presence and work of the Holy Spirit, however much they spring from sincere devotion, reflect a profound misunderstanding of the Third Person of the Trinity. Advocates of Spirit-filled worship act as if the work of the Holy Spirit has been inextricably bound up with the use of praise songs, electric guitars, and overhead projectors. Few of these writers seem to remember exactly when and where Jesus said that his disciples were to worship "in spirit and truth." As it happened, our Lord said those words almost two thousand years ago in Samaria, and his intention in uttering that phrase was not prophetic, as if he saw a day, two millennia in the future, when his people would finally apprehend the reality of Spirit-filled worship. In fact, coming to terms with Christ's meaning in this widely appealed-to phrase clarifies what Christian worship is because it explains the work of the Holy Spirit, both in the salvation of God's people and in the period of redemptive history after the ascension of Christ.

The Age of the Spirit

The fourth chapter of John's Gospel records Christ's encounter with the Samaritan woman at the well near Sychar. After revealing himself as the water of life and demonstrating his knowledge of the woman's

3. David Beelen, "A Thirst for Expressive Worship: Restoring Balance to Our Worship," *Reformed Worship* 20 (June 1991): 8.

4. Jack Hayford, "Expressive Worship with Reluctant People," *Leadership* 15 (spring 1994): 40.

past marriages, the subject of conversation turned to worship. The woman said to Christ that the Samaritans worship at Mount Gerizim, but the Jews taught that true worship could take place only in Jerusalem. Her point concerned the proper place of worship, whether on the mountain where Samaritans worship or on the mountain where the temple was built. But Christ's response was not about place. It concerned time or, more precisely, history. Jesus said to the woman, "The hour is coming when neither on this mountain nor in Jerusalem will you worship the Father" (John 4:21 RSV). He then added, again emphasizing that time, not place, would be important for worship, "The hour is coming, and now is, when the true worshipers will worship the Father in spirit and truth, for such people the Father seeks to worship him" (v. 23 RSV). The clear implication of Christ's teaching was that time would eventually trump place. At a certain moment, the old way of worshiping God in the temple at Jerusalem would no longer be valid, and at that time God's people would worship "in spirit and truth." Worshiping in spirit and truth was not a place on earth, an attitude, or even an experience. Jesus taught instead that it was a period in the history of redemption.

The time that Jesus had in mind for the new possibilities in worship was not twenty centuries later when Protestants exchanged psalms and hymns for praise songs. Rather, the time was Jesus' own day. As he said to the Samaritan woman, "The hour is coming, and *now is*" (v. 23). The time for a new kind of worship had arrived, and Jesus was declaring that the inauguration of this new period in worship was directly connected to his own ministry. In fact, the new worship could not take place without the life and work of Jesus Christ.

The key to understanding Christ's teaching here about worship is not place but time. In the old dispensation, in the time when God revealed himself through the nation of Israel, place mattered. Whether one of God's children worshiped in Jerusalem determined whether worship was true. To be sure, God wanted his people to worship sincerely and obediently, but he also instituted the rites and ceremonies of the temple as the proper way of worshiping him. These rituals and services were appropriate because God appointed them and because they pointed to Christ, who would complete them. The Lamb of God who took away the sin of the world, that is, Jesus Christ, made the sacrifices of Old Testament worship obsolete. In the new era of redemptive history, after the coming of Christ and the fulfillment of temple worship, God's people would no longer have to worry about worshiping in a special place or on a particular mountain. Instead, they would worship "in spirit and truth." Spirit and truth were to be the characteristics of New Testament worship as much as the temple and sacrifices had been essential to Old Testament worship.

When Christ said that his followers were to worship "in spirit," he was most likely referring to the Holy Spirit. Such a conclusion is based on Christ's reference to history: "The hour is coming, and now is." Christ's advent marked the beginning of a new stage in redemptive history. This age is commonly referred to as the age of the Spirit or the last age, meaning the period between the first and the last coming of Christ (the "interadvental" period). Even the Samaritan woman knew about the epoch-making significance of the coming of the Christ, or the Messiah. She said in verse 25 of John 4, "I know that Messiah is coming. . . . When he comes, he will show us all things" (RSV). Christ answered in the next verse that he was indeed the one of whom she spoke. In effect, he was telling her that the Messiah had just taught an important lesson about worship, namely, that the time had now come when place no longer mattered because the work of Christ had ushered in the age of the Spirit.

When Old Testament believers gathered for worship, they did not have the benefit of the Holy Spirit. He was not present with them in the same gracious way that he is with the church (New Testament believers) when it meets for worship. This might sound surprising at first because we know that the Holy Spirit is always present to guide and superintend human history and the order of creation. But it is only the church, the believers who come in the period between Christ's advents, that knows and relies on the gracious power of the Holy Spirit. This is clearly the teaching of Christ later in the Gospel of John. In John 16:7, he says to his disciples that it is good that he is going away, meaning that it will be a blessing for him to ascend into heaven after his resurrection. Such an act is good because, as Jesus explains, "if I do not go away, the Counselor will not come to you; but if I go, I will send him to you" (RSV). Unless Christ ascends on high, the Holy Spirit will not descend to dwell among his people. This is the same idea that Joel prophesied when he said, "It shall come to pass afterward, that I will pour out my spirit on all flesh" (2:28 RSV). Whatever this verse may mean regarding the gifts of the Spirit, it is clearly in agreement with Christ's teaching that during a particular time in history the Holy Spirit will be more evidently present than at other times.

The evidence for the Holy Spirit's presence, about which Christ taught, was Pentecost. This event marked the transition from the old covenant to the new, from true worship being limited to Jerusalem to true worship taking place wherever two or more are gathered in Christ's name. Pentecost inaugurated the last days, the time when God's promise to Abraham that all nations would be blessed by him was fulfilled

(Gen. 12:3; Gal. 3:14). Moreover, it marked the transition from God's ways of saving his people through the means and ceremonies of Israel's laws to a time when the gospel is preached universally to all nations and the barrier between Jew and Gentile no longer matters (Gal. 3:28). This is why the presence of believers from different nations speaking in different languages was so important to the events recorded in Acts 2. On that day when the Holy Spirit began to fill the church, God fulfilled the work begun by Christ's death and resurrection, the work of inaugurating the messianic age. Only because Christ ascended did the Holy Spirit descend on God's people, and only then could the divisions between many nations be overcome by the unity provided by participating in the Spirit.

This is why Christ told his disciples that it was good for him to leave. On the surface it would seem that nothing could possibly be better than being present with Christ during his earthly ministry. But as the apostle Paul explains in the first chapter of Ephesians, Christ's absence brought with it the special work of the Holy Spirit and the benefits that believers in the age of the Spirit always enjoy. Paul writes that Christians have been sealed in the Holy Spirit, who has been given to the church as "the guarantee of our inheritance until we acquire possession of it" (Eph. 1:14 RSV). With the coming of the Holy Spirit, the church experienced the firstfruits of the final redemption. The Spirit was a deposit or guarantee of the final resurrection and glorification of the church. In effect, Christ was telling his disciples that he had to leave so that he could come again (John 14). But Christ did not leave his disciples alone to work things out according to their own wisdom and power. The Spirit would be with them, and he would be a pledge of that promised day when they would be reunited with Christ.

But Paul was not the only one to describe the benefits of Christ's ascension and the coming of the Spirit. Christ himself, as recorded in John 16, told his followers of the benefits they would enjoy once he had left and the Spirit had come. In verse 8, he said that the Spirit would convict the world "concerning sin and righteousness and judgment." The proclamation of the gospel in the power of the Spirit is one of the benefits that believers now enjoy in the age of the Spirit. Evidence of this Spirit-empowered preaching came on the day of Pentecost, when Peter witnessed to the work of Christ and the Spirit convicted the apostle's hearers of their sin. In other words, the Spirit makes the preaching of the Word an effectual means of convincing and converting sinners even as the Spirit regenerates God's chosen ones so they can believe what is preached.

Another benefit believers have through the presence of the Spirit is the inspiration of Scripture. In John 14, where Christ told his followers that the Spirit would come once he had departed, he promised that he would disclose himself to his disciples (v. 21) and that the Holy Spirit would "teach you all things, and bring to your remembrance all that I have said to you" (v. 26 RSV). In other words, Christ promised the inscripturation of God's Word in the New Testament. The witness of the apostles, through the inspiration of the Holy Spirit, would become an ongoing testimony to Christ so that the church would be led "into all truth" (John 16:13).

One further benefit that believers have because of Christ's ascension is the indwelling of the Holy Spirit. In John 14:17, Jesus promised that he would send "the Spirit of truth, whom the world cannot receive, because it neither sees him nor knows him; you know him, for he dwells with you, and will be in you" (RSV). Sinclair Ferguson writes that Jesus is teaching here that the "coming of the Spirit is the equivalent of the indwelling of Jesus."[5] It is not merely that Christ dwells with his disciples; he dwells *in* his disciples through the Spirit. In verse 20, Jesus explained how intimate his indwelling through the Spirit would be. "In that day you will know that I am in my Father, and you in me, and I in you" (RSV). In other words, the indwelling of the Holy Spirit in believers is analogous to the communion that exists within the Trinity. Paul makes the same point in Ephesians 2:11–22, where he teaches that having the Spirit is the equivalent of having the incarnate Christ dwelling in us, just as Christ is united to the Father. This is why Christ tells his disciples it is better for them if he leaves. He knew that only after his ascension would the Spirit come and would his disciples be able to enjoy benefits unavailable to God's people during the time of Moses and the prophets.

The benefits that believers receive because of the Spirit have a direct bearing on worship. Again, because we live in the age of the Spirit, we are no longer obligated to worship God in the temple in Jerusalem. Jesus indicated as much when he threw the money changers out of the temple. When the Jews asked him by what authority he cleansed the place of worship, Jesus replied, "Destroy this temple, and in three days I will raise it up" (John 2:19 RSV). As John explains, Jesus was referring to the temple of the resurrection, when his body would remain in the grave for three days and then be restored to life, not to the physical destruction and rebuilding of the place where the Jews worshiped. Still, the correspondence between the temple and the body of Christ is significant because with the resurrection the temple was in effect destroyed. Christ fulfilled all the parts of worship that had taken place in the temple because they all pointed to his sacrifice on the cross. Conse-

5. Sinclair Ferguson, *The Holy Spirit* (Downers Grove, Ill.: InterVarsity, 1996), 68. I relied on Ferguson for many points in this chapter.

quently, when Jesus said that the temple would be restored in his resurrection, he meant precisely that the place where God's people would eventually worship would be the place where Christ now is, not in the temple in Jerusalem. Thus, when believers gather on the Lord's Day, they assemble in the presence of Christ (Heb. 12:22–28). By his resurrection, Christ restored the temple.

This is why Christ could say to the Samaritan woman that the hour was coming "and now is" when God's people would worship not in Jerusalem but in Spirit and truth. Because Christ fulfilled the sacrificial system of the Old Testament, all God's people in worship are like the high priest in the temple. When they gather in Christ's name, they enter, as the writer to the Hebrews puts it, "the sanctuary by the blood of Jesus" (10:19 RSV). This is why the Protestant Reformation taught the doctrine of the priesthood of all believers. All God's children may enter into the Holy of Holies because in Christ they have become pure, spotless, and worthy to enter the place that in the Old Testament had been reserved for the high priest. Entering the Holy of Holies is precisely what happens in Christian worship. Jesus told his disciples that *wherever* "two or three are gathered in my name, there am I in the midst of them" (Matt. 18:20 RSV). The writer to the Hebrews teaches the same thing in chapter 12. When Christians gather for worship, they come "to Mount Zion and to the city of the living God, the heavenly Jerusalem, and to innumerable angels in festal gathering, and to the assembly of the first-born who are enrolled in heaven, and to a judge who is God of all, and to the spirits of just men made perfect, and to Jesus, the mediator of a new covenant, and to the sprinkled blood that speaks more graciously than the blood of Abel" (vv. 22–24 RSV). In other words, when Christians gather for worship, when they gather with Christ as their mediator, they enter the heavenly Holy of Holies. They are lifted up spiritually into heaven and assemble with all God's people and angels.

Christians do not need to go to earthly Jerusalem to enter the Holy of Holies. The temple and the services conducted there were a shadow of the heavenly worship that was to come with the ministry of Christ. Because of the incarnation, resurrection, and ascension of Christ, God's people are able to worship in the fullness of God's revelation. In the Old Testament, that revelation was only partial and looked forward to Christ. That is why Christ told the Samaritan woman that the place of worship no longer mattered. Now that the Messiah had come, all God's people from every nation and, just as important, in every nation could enter the Holy of Holies and meet with God to offer him praise and adoration.

The worship in which Christians now participate is heavenly worship because it is spiritual worship, that is, it is worship filled with and dependent on the work of the Holy Spirit, not the place of the worshiper. That is why Paul constantly contrasts true worship with worship that appears to be pious and devout. For instance, in Colossians 2, the apostle warns the church against submitting to rules and regulations that have the appearance of "wisdom" and "self-abasement" (v. 23). They are not to submit to these "decrees" because they have died with Christ and to the "elemental spirits of the universe" (v. 20). These things are a "shadow" of what is to come. But the substance "belongs to Christ" (v. 17). Likewise, in 1 Corinthians, Paul contrasts his preaching, calling it foolishness in the world's eyes, with wisdom of the world (2:14). This preaching, which is a central element of Christian worship, comes directly from the Spirit. As Paul says, he received the preaching of the gospel not from the spirit of the world but from the Spirit who is God (2:13). The simple words of preaching, again considered to be a foolish form of worship by the world, demonstrated the power of the Spirit (2:4) so that the faith of the believer would rest not "in the wisdom of men but in the power of God" (2:5). Worship in the age of the Holy Spirit is not flashy or visibly powerful but instead is so simple that it appears to be inconsequential. Yet the Spirit transforms these simple means, what Paul calls "earthen vessels" in 2 Corinthians 4:7, into powerful weapons of demonstrating God's glory and might, both through the conversion of sinners and through the praise and adoration of his people.

The Spirit-filled transformation of simple means is especially true of the sacraments of the New Testament, namely, baptism and the Lord's Supper. In these acts, the Spirit transforms ordinary elements into powerful displays of God's grace and mercy. Both sacraments point backward and forward in time. Baptism signifies in part the exodus, when God's people passed through the water of the Red Sea to their salvation as God's covenant people. It also points forward to the judgment day, when God's people will again pass through the destruction of the world while the wicked will be condemned (1 Peter 3:18–21). Likewise, the Lord's Supper points backward to the Passover meal, which commemorated God's act of passing over those households in Egypt that had the blood of a lamb on the top of their doorpost. It also points forward to the wedding banquet of the Lord, when he will be united face-to-face with his bride, the church. As significant as baptism and the Lord's Supper are, the elements of water, bread, and wine hardly compare with the grandeur of the exodus, the Passover, the judgment day, or glory. The sacraments, then, illustrate perfectly the simplicity of worship in the age of the Holy Spirit. By outward appearances they have little appeal or majesty, but through the work of the Spirit, these sacraments become signs and seals of what Christ has accomplished for his people and of the unity that exists between Christ and his church. Paul says in 1 Corinthians 12:13, for instance, that we are all baptized by one Spirit. Similarly, Paul compares the Lord's Supper to the "spiritual food" that the Israelites ate in the wilderness (1 Cor. 10:3–5, 16–18).

The point here is not to develop all the intricacies of sacramental theology but to point out that the simple and ordinary circumstances of the sacraments illustrate what Spirit-filled worship should look like. Because Christ has fulfilled the sacrifices and ceremonies of the Old Testament, Christians are no longer bound to observe those ceremonies. More to the point, because Christ has provided access into the Holy of Holies, believers may now participate in that heavenly worship to which the observances of the Old Testament pointed. To be sure, the church engages in heavenly worship in a partial way, waiting for that final advent of Christ when he will be with his people and they will bow at his feet. Still, the church participates in heavenly worship now because of the coming of the Spirit. The work of the Holy Spirit, who applies to believers the redemption purchased by Christ, allows Christians when they gather to go into the heavenly Jerusalem, which can be seen only through the eyes of faith and through the agency of the Holy Spirit.

Spirit and Truth

If this is correct, then Christians worshiped in a Spirit-filled manner long before the rise of Pentecostalism or the charismatic movement. In fact, Christians who worship between the first and second comings of Christ always worship in a Spirit-filled way because they worship in the age of the Holy Spirit. Believers in Christ do not have to go to Jerusalem to worship. Neither do they have to go to the temple and follow the rites and ceremonies in which the Israelites engaged. Of course, to say that Christians always worship in a Spirit-filled way is an overstatement. Worship in the Spirit is not automatic, and feelings or expressiveness or spontaneity are not what determine whether worship is filled with the Spirit. Rather, what determines if worship is in the Spirit is whether it is done according to the truth. This is why Christ said to the Samaritan woman that genuine worshipers would worship in spirit and truth.

The ministry of the Holy Spirit includes a number of activities that we usually take for granted. In the work of redemption, the Holy Spirit is crucial. For instance, the work of Christ during his earthly ministry cannot be separated from that of the Holy Spirit. The Spirit formed the body of Christ in the womb of the virgin Mary and provided him with all the gifts he would need for his work (Luke 1:35). Likewise, in the salvation of the individual believer, the Holy Spirit's saving work of regeneration is necessary. Only by the effectual calling of the Spirit do sinful men and women repent and believe in Christ.

The ministry of the Holy Spirit is also essential in regard to the Bible. Christians often regard Scripture as an independent form of communication from God that sits on the shelf until they pick it up and read it. But the formation of the Bible as well as the apprehension of it would not have been possible without the activity of the Spirit. The human authors of the Bible were inspired by the Holy Spirit. This is what makes their words the Word of God. For example, the prophet Micah wrote, "I am filled with power, with the Spirit of the LORD, and with justice and might, to declare to Jacob his transgression and to Israel his sin" (3:8 RSV). In a similar fashion, Paul wrote that the things he taught did not come from the wisdom of men but from God, "revealed to us through the Spirit" (1 Cor. 2:10). God does not leave his special revelation there, however, simply at the stage of inspired text. He also sends the Spirit to illuminate the minds of his children so they might know that the truths of the Bible are from God. For this reason, the Bible calls believers "spiritual," a reference that conveys their dependence on the Holy Spirit for enlightenment and guidance. This is also what Christ had in mind when he talked about the fundamental change in history that he inaugurated with his ministry. When Christ ascended, the Holy Spirit descended. And one of the reasons Christ gave for the Spirit's coming was that he might lead the church into all truth (John 16:13).

The truth-revealing work of the Holy Spirit has important implications for the way we think about worship. If the truth of the Bible rests on the inspiration of the Spirit, and if believers cannot be convinced of Scripture's truth apart from the regeneration and illumination of the Spirit, is it possible to conceive of "Spirit-filled" worship that is not also "truth-filled"? To put it another way, if we were to examine a worship service to see if the Holy Spirit were active in it, what would we be looking for? In the current rage for expressive and spontaneous worship, most people look for the Spirit's presence in the style of song, the emotions and posture of worshipers, and whether people feel blessed upon leaving the service. But this reflects a radical misunderstanding of the work of the Holy Spirit, as if the Spirit is involved with only the experiential or emotional aspects of the Christian life. In fact, the Bible teaches that the principal work of the Holy Spirit is to reveal the truth of God. This work involves the mind and the heart because the intellect and the will of a sinner both need to be changed in order for him or her to accept and believe the truths of the gospel. Still, the purpose of the revelatory work of the Spirit is to yield proper understanding, not warm feelings. This means that a Spirit-filled worship service will be one that conforms to the revelation of the Bible.

Looking at the work of the Holy Spirit this way means that so-called traditional worship, as opposed to contemporary forms, has the greatest claim to being Spirit-filled. This statement will likely startle many readers because worship in the Calvinist tradition has not been known for its zeal or intimacy. Instead, the words *cold, formal,* and *stodgy* come to mind most often when thinking about Presbyterian and Reformed worship. Yet this impression reveals how much contemporary Protestant thinking equates the work of the Spirit with emotions, not with understanding and believing the Bible. It also shows how much contemporary Protestant thought has separated the work of the Spirit from the teaching of God's Word.

Ironically, the most distinctive feature of Reformed worship is the very thing that makes it Spirit-filled, as we are using the phrase. The Reformed tradition has insisted that worship conform to the teaching of Scripture. For this reason, Protestants restored the sermon to its central place in worship as the time when God's people hear the Word of God. Reformed worship emphasizes the Bible not only by giving so much weight to preaching but also by insisting that every part of a worship service have a biblical warrant. Sometimes called the regulative principle, this doctrine teaches that the church may worship only as God has commanded his people to worship him. Because the Bible ordains prayer, preaching, the singing of praise, the reading of Scripture, and the administration of the sacraments, the Reformed believe that these elements must be part of worship. The question is not whether the Bible permits a certain practice such as dance or drama in worship. Instead, the regulative principle requires a direct charge from the Bible. Scripture, therefore, functions as the barometer for evaluating a worship service. If worship contains those things that God has commanded for his praise and honor, then it is good, and because the Holy Spirit works in accordance with the Word of God, worship that conforms to the Bible is filled with and drawn from the Spirit.

Critics of Reformed worship have argued that the regulative principle is a reflection of Calvin and the Puritan's cold, restrictive, and overly rational piety. But whatever their devotional life was like, Calvin and the Puritans had good biblical and theological reasons for insisting that everything in worship have an explicit warrant from Scripture. The first stems from God himself. Hebrews 12:28–29 says that we are to worship God in a way that is acceptable to him. The Reformed believed that the only way of knowing what pleased God was to look to what he revealed in the Bible, what practices he says in Scripture delight him. Using any other source to discover what was acceptable for worship was simply a matter of speculation or opinion.

The second reason concerned the human heart. Calvinists believe that men and women are sinful and that sin affects all parts of their being. This is no less true when men and women, including believers, think about worship. According to the Bible, the human heart, Calvin argued, was always creating idols, especially by making an idol of itself. This was the great sin of Adam and Eve in the Garden. They wanted to become as gods, and that is why they ate from the Tree of the Knowledge of Good and Evil. Because of the human propensity to manufacture idols, the Reformed tradition has insisted that the Bible, not human wisdom or preferences, serve as the arbiter of acceptable worship. Of course, simply following the Bible is no guarantee that Christians will automatically please God. People's minds wander, and people misunderstand and misapply Scripture and will sometimes try to exalt themselves in worship. But even though the Bible does not ensure pure worship, it does provide the only check on the idolatrous propensity of the human heart.

Rather than appealing to the Spirit, our appeal ought to be to the Bible to determine what makes worship Spirit-filled. Only on the basis of what God has revealed in Scripture do we know what is pleasing to him and what his will is for worship. Furthermore, God sent his Spirit to lead the church into all truth. For this reason, it is impossible to conceive of Spirit-filled worship being anything other than Bible-directed worship.

Proceeds from the Father and the Son

The Nicene Creed says that Christians believe in the Spirit, "who proceeds from the Father and the Son." The Western church (Roman Catholic) in 1054 split from the Eastern church (Orthodox) in part over that phrase. Eastern church officers believed that the words "and the Son" were not originally part of the creed. But the Western church argued that this phrase was crucial for underscoring the deity of the Third Person of the Trinity and the unity of purpose among the three Persons of the Trinity.

The argument here has been an extension of the Western church's theology in preserving the phrase "and the Son." Too often contemporary discussions of worship have isolated the work of the Holy Spirit from the activity of God the Father and God the Son. Many Protestants have been led to believe that older forms of worship paid close attention to God the

Father by stressing divine power and sovereignty. God the Son has also received a fair amount of attention historically in Protestant worship, some believe, through the emphasis on conversion and repentance in preaching. But according to current discussions, Christians have neglected the Holy Spirit in worship, forgetting the joy, spontaneity, and zeal that are allegedly so characteristic of the Third Person of the Trinity.

This process of isolating the various Persons of the Trinity and attributing different features of worship to them is unfortunate and wrong. Our Triune God is one, and his purpose in bringing his people to himself is one. For this reason, worship of God should be unified as well. Spirit-filled worship will not introduce a new element into worship, creating a style of worship that is different from worship that centers on God the Father or God the Son. The Holy Spirit enables believers to worship God the Father and God the Son. For that reason, worship in which the Spirit is active will not be different from worship in which God the Father and God the Son are praised and glorified. Worship in the Spirit was new only once, and that occurred almost two thousand years ago when Christ ascended into heaven. At that time, worship moved out of the earthly Jerusalem into all nations and among all peoples. At that point, when Christians gathered for worship through the sanctifying work of the Spirit, they entered the heavenly Jerusalem.

Christian worship, then, for the last two millennia has been Spirit-filled. It has been so when it has properly acknowledged God as the only true God who is righteous and holy and demands complete perfection for communion with him. Likewise, it has been Spirit-filled when it has recognized humankind's sinfulness and rebellion against God and its need for grace and mercy. Christian worship has also been Spirit-filled when it has been done in the name of Christ, thereby confessing that sinful men and women cannot enter God's presence without the perfect obedience and sacrifice of the only redeemer of God's people, the Lord Jesus Christ. In other words, we judge the presence and activity of the Holy Spirit in worship not by our feelings or emotions but by the truths revealed in God's infallible and authoritative Word. Christian worship is not true only when Christians are moved. Rather, Christian worship is true when it conforms to Scripture, whether worshipers experience it or not. When the church gathers for the reading of Scripture with "godly fear," the sound preaching of the Word, prayer "with thanksgiving," the singing of praise "with grace in the heart," and the administration and "worthy receiving" of the sacraments, then and only then is worship Spirit-filled (WCF, XXI.v.iii).

Part 3

OFFICE
AND ORDINANCES

7

Whatever Happened to Office?

It is difficult for some in mainline Protestant churches to understand that a few denominations like my own, the Christian Reformed Church, are still debating whether women should be allowed to serve as ruling or teaching elders (elders and pastors). For many on both sides of this debate, it is strictly a question of being faithful to Scripture. Subordinationists (those who oppose women in office) rely heavily on 1 Timothy 2 and 1 Corinthians 14, those passages that reflect the patriarchal patterns of first-century Greco-Roman culture. Ordinationists, in contrast, give much weight to the apostle Paul's egalitarian sentiments in Galatians 3. Yet both sides also reflect the assumptions rooted in their socioeconomic status. Subordinationists tend to be older or from rural society and adhere to early modern views about the role of women and the function of the home, what some have called the cult of domesticity. Ordinationists more often than not reside in the suburbs, come from two-income families, and had their consciousness raised if not shaped by the warnings of feminists.

Despite these differences, both sides have one thing in common, namely, silence about the nature and scope of the authority that the office of pastor or elder constitutes. Subordinationists, it would seem, have an easier case to make because so much of their perspective depends on a hierarchical understanding of human relationships. Whether in the church, the household, or society, subordinationists generally stand for a conception of authority that places power and responsibility in the God-ordained and male-dominated offices of magistrate, clergyman, and father. Yet one scours the writings of conservatives in vain for mention of the O-word: *ordination*. Subordinationists will gladly talk about the authority of the Bible but will rarely come clean about the hierarchical idea of office that the Bible and its culture seem to assume. Nor are they willing to argue—as Protestants used to before the French and American Revolutions—that the authority of particular offices and vocations is essential to social order and the restraint of evil. Rather, most contemporary Protestants are small-d democrats who believe that individuals should be free to pursue their own economic well-being, order their own lives, and discover their own happiness. Thus, with some irony, subordinationists have accepted virtually all the premises of modernity, premises that undermine the very notions of office and ordination they wish to defend in barring women from holding special office. But in this one area—as well as in the area of the role of women in the home—they cling to a premodern conception of ordination and office.

Such contradictions are no less evident on the ordinationist side. While progressive Protestants have come to terms with the egalitarian and functional views of authority and power that modern society encourages—even to the point of finding these very same ideas in the Bible, a remarkably premodern if not ancient text—they have not explained why the church should hold on to such antiquated notions as ministerial office and ordination. The egalitarian ethic teaches that all individuals are equal, and one hears much about the diversity of gifts and ministries that all God's people possess. Yet if all are equal, why should we set some apart or give authority to a particularly small segment of the believing community? Wouldn't it make more sense to abolish the office of minister or elder entirely, or at least ordain everyone for the special gifts they possess and ministries they perform? The way many ordinationists finesse this question is to talk about service. Clergy are not ordained to be rulers. Rather, there is a better understanding of ministerial office—the ideal of service. (Actually, the idea of leader as servant is at least as old as the Rotarians, Lions, and Kiwannis.) The minister or elder does not wield power in an authoritarian way but rather abases herself to serve—much like Christ did—for the larger good of the Christian community. The model for this service is Christ's phrase "the least shall be first." The suffering servant is certainly an appealing ideal but one that rarely characterizes denominational assemblies in which Robert's Rules provide the modicum of order and in which bureaucrats moan about the slightest drop in budgetary allocations.

Though it may be behind the times by about three decades, the debate in the CRC over the ordination of women reflects a profound crisis within historically white American Protestant denominations about the nature and function of ordination. The Christian Reformed are certainly timid about connecting the office of minister to an older conception of ordination, but mainline and evangelical Protestants also avoid defining the precise nature and function of the ministerial office. The following quotation depicting the decline in ministerial authority within the CRC has been true of Protestant clergy for some time.

> These older ministers, whose spiritual authority was enormous and sometimes tyrannical, had fixed minds. Their influence is sometimes hard to understand now when every Tom, Dick, and Sadie with a strong D average in high school has the right to expressed opinion. Then, when preachers said, "Thus saith the Lord," they were inclined to believe it.[1]

Few Protestants would deny that the sense of a minister speaking for God—and the accompanying sense that attending church was a duty with grave consequences—has been lost. Some would undoubtedly welcome the change to egalitarian forms of leadership that are accessible and hospitable to the needs and demands of the laity. Yet two developments within the Protestant household, one among mainliners, the other among evangelicals, tell us that all is not well. These developments reflect efforts to rehabilitate the role of the clergy but, as is so typical of modern times, without mentioning adequately or wrestling with what it is that happens in the service of ordination.

Within the mainline Protestant churches, there is much talk about decline, both in real numbers and in less tangible forms of cultural clout. Some of these estimates may either be a bit too dour or not sufficiently attentive to long-term historic trends.[2] Yet most would agree that mainline Protestant stock in recent decades has lost considerable value. Various medicines have been prescribed for the church's return to health. Plans for church growth, more theology, less social activism, and greater diversity all come to mind. The Hartford Seminary Executive Seminar for church leaders is a further effort to rehabilitate the American church. This program, which was funded by the Lilly Endowment and concluded at the end of 1993, was designed to bring together younger church and interdenominational leaders to examine the crises

1. John M. Timmerman, "Whatever Happened to Sunday?" *Reformed Journal* 31 (February 1981): 14.

2. William R. Hutchison, Catherine L. Albanese, Max L. Stackhouse, and William McKinney, "Forum: The Decline of Mainline Religion in American Culture," *Religion and American Culture* 1 (1991): 131–54; and Benton Johnson, Dean R. Hoge, and Donald A. Luidens, "Mainline Churches: The Real Reason for Decline," *First Things* (March 1993): 13–18.

and prospects confronting religious bodies in America. Participants in the project read a variety of manuals in business management and current affairs and developed proposals to make themselves more effective as leaders of religious organizations. The implicit rationale behind this seminar was the notion that a future generation of leaders would be better equipped to guide the churches back into a period of prosperity, relevance, and influence.

A variety of authors has also explored the crisis of leadership within American churches. One such author is Jackson W. Carroll, who wrote *As One with Authority*. Carroll argues for a model of ministerial authority rooted in "reflective-leadership," a dialogical approach to living out one's Christian identity that is based on a high degree of trust and interaction between clergy and laity.[3] While Carroll pays some attention to the sacramental character of the ministry—i.e., the minister as God's representative—the focus of the book is on how ministers can function better as reflective leaders. The clergy, according to this view, are still experts or professionals, but their expertise is less scientific, less bound by ironclad laws of cause and effect. They are ultimately more human because they are more cognizant of the contingencies of daily existence. The impression given by Carroll's book, and works similar to it, is that clergy will become better leaders if they become more effective professionals.

The model of minister as professional is rooted in developments more than a century old within American Protestantism. As Craig Dykstra and James Hudnut-Beumler have demonstrated in an astute article on the structure of American denominations, from the late eighteenth to the twentieth century, denominational governance witnessed an organizational revolution. National church bodies went from constitutional confederacies (1780–1870), to corporations (1870–1960), to regulatory agencies (1960 to the present). In the early period, the character of denominational life was local. Denominational structures served chiefly the needs and ministry of the local congregation. Since 1870, the nature and purpose of denominations have changed dramatically. The focus shifted from the local congregation to the national body, which has its own functions and duties that are different from the work of the local church and in some cases more important. This change created a large bureaucratic structure filled by church executives whose function was to manage the programs of the church. As these programs and agencies grew, they took on a life and culture of their own, different from the life and culture of the local church but similar to the corporate culture that was developing simultaneously

3. Jackson W. Carroll, *As One with Authority* (Louisville: Westminster, 1991).

in American business. The church became more a corporation than a household of faith.[4]

It is no wonder that strategies for enhancing the authority of the modern denomination use the language of professionalism and expertise, even applying these models of leadership to the work of the local minister. It also comes as little surprise that the managers of Protestant corporations turn increasingly to the literature of scientific management produced by America's corporate executives for help with everything from improving morale at the national office to making the local sales representative, the pastor, a more productive and effective agent. Yet there is a danger to corporate models for the church contained in the literature on management. As a recent book on the bureaucratic therapies of management gurus such as Peter Drucker shows, recommendations for greater participation and harmony within the corporation often obscure the strategies of powerful executives intent on preserving their own authority and status.[5]

Despite numerical growth and greater visibility, American evangelicalism has not been immune from the crisis of leadership affecting the mainline churches. The functional equivalent of mainline denominational leadership within evangelical circles is the seminary. Evangelical seminaries fill a void created by a variety of independent nondenominational congregations and evangelical churches within denominations suspicious of denominational structures. Both kinds of congregations need an agency to recruit, train, and certify church leaders. Despite the size and affluence of many of these seminaries, all is not well within the evangelical fold. Increasingly, one hears concerns about the irrelevance of traditional theological studies and the need for ministers to be better equipped to grapple with the demands of contemporary believers and modern society. Especially threatening to the evangelical seminary is the proliferation of megachurches that teach that the heart (piety) matters more than the head (theology) and yet demand that ministers be schooled in the latest social scientific and business strategies of church growth. Critics also fault the traditional seminary curriculum for being too quietistic. Some evangelicals want ministers who are more eager to promote various strategies for social justice and peace.

4. Craig Dykstra and James Hudnut-Beumler, "The National Organizational Structures of Protestant Denominations: An Invitation to a Conversation," in *The Organizational Revolution*, ed. Milton J. Coalter, John M. Mulder, and Louis B. Weeks (Louisville: Westminster/John Knox, 1992), chap. 12.

5. Stephen P. Waring, *Taylorism Transformed: Scientific Management Theory since 1945* (Chapel Hill: University of North Carolina Press, 1991).

In both cases, evangelical theological educators are having to confront tensions that have bedeviled the evangelical movement since its origins. Evangelicalism emerged during the revivals of the eighteenth century, dominated by the English evangelist George Whitefield. These revivals were important because they forged a new style of religious leadership, one that was direct, personal, popular, and depended much more on the speaker's appeal to the audience—his charisma—than on his standing in the social hierarchy. Theology and formal learning were not important to the revivalists' appeal. Instead, personality, style, and emotion were better indicators of ability. Religious disestablishment after the war for independence was like throwing gas on the fire of evangelicalism. While previously church life had been highly regulated, the separation of church and state in the American republic gave the upper hand to revivalistic ministers informed by pragmatic know-how and unfettered by the restraints of learning and certification. Little wonder then that Methodists and Baptists, the two groups that promoted revivals best, grew the fastest, while older established churches such as Congregationalist and Episcopalian declined. Even more important was what the tradition of revivalism did to evangelical patterns of leadership and governance. The most successful evangelical leaders were and continue to be individuals with enormous popular appeal who are ready and willing to use whatever techniques are available to communicate the gospel. Theology, liturgics, and office do not matter. Folksy stories, schmaltzy music, mailing lists, and satellite dishes do.

So while mainline churches pattern themselves after the model of professionalism and expertise, evangelical churches emulate the practices of popular culture. Both kinds of leadership, as Max Weber argued, exhibit the types of authority produced by modern society. The development of mainline Protestant denominations reflects the "rational-legal" variety of leadership that relies on professional training and bureaucratic certification. The revivalist practices of evangelicals are typical of the "charismatic" basis of authority that stems from an individual's exceptional personal qualities of morality and heroism. Ironically, the allegedly antimodern evangelicals have capitulated almost as thoroughly to modernity in matters of leadership as the so-called modernist mainline churches. Yet both evangelical and mainline practices are a far cry from what Christians have historically thought about ordination and the kind of leadership that proceeds from it.[6]

6. See, for instance, Max Weber, "Politics as Vocation," in *From Max Weber: Essays in Sociology*, ed. H. H. Gerth and C. Wright Mills (New York: Oxford University Press, 1946), chap. 4.

Ordination is the holy act of setting individuals apart to perform certain tasks within the church. It carries with it the conferring of authority and prescribes the tasks of office holders. The apostle Paul's injunction in 1 Corinthians 4:1 is a helpful summary of ordination's significance. He writes, "This is how one should regard us, as servants of Christ and stewards of the mysteries of God." The Geneva Confession of 1537 explained that this conception of the ministry requires church members to "receive the true ministers of the Word of God as messengers and ambassadors of God," to "hearken" to these ministers as to Christ himself, and to consider "their ministry as a commission from God necessary in the church." And just to make sure that unruly Genevans knew who was in charge regarding church matters, John Calvin wrote that true pastors were called by God, that the government of the church, in short, was not "a contrivance of men but an appointment made by the Son of God." Calvin went on to warn that those who rejected or despised the Christian ministry were in effect rebelling against and insulting Christ himself.[7]

This kind of pious language, to be sure, can be heavy-handed and sanctimonious. It can also be very repressive. Nevertheless, the idea that ordination sets one apart for ministry instituted by the very Creator and Redeemer of the universe does bring to the table an altogether different understanding of church leadership than the models bandied about within evangelical and mainline churches, one that has authority and, hence, leadership built into it. The minister does not hold authority because of special gifts (expertise), though gifts are important. Nor does the minister speak with power because he is telegenic and winsome. Rather, authority resides in the ministry because of the office of the pastor itself. The office, no matter who holds it, is authoritative. The Second Helvetic Confession expresses such a view of office when it states, "We know that the voice of Christ is to be heard, though it be out of the mouths of evil ministers. . . . We know that the sacraments are sanctified by the institution and the word of Christ, and that they are effectual to the godly, although they be administered by unworthy ministers" (chap. 18).

The authority of the ministry does not originate strictly from its ontological status but also follows from the functions ministers perform. According to older Protestant conceptions of ordination, ministers were set apart not just to rule but also to administer the Word and sacrament; they were stewards of the mysteries of God. Churches in the

---

7. Geneva Confession and Calvin translated by and quoted in J. L. Ainslie, *The Doctrines of Ministerial Order in the Reformed Churches of the Sixteenth and Seventeenth Centuries* (Edinburgh: T & T Clark, 1940), 8–9.

Reformed tradition have talked about the authority of the ministry by using the phrase "the power of the keys." According to the Heidelberg Catechism, "The preaching of the holy gospel and Christian discipline" are the means by which the kingdom of heaven is opened and shut (Ans. 83). The doctrine of the keys, in the logic of the Second Helvetic Confession, means that while Christ reserves ultimate power and authority for himself, the minister has the powers of the steward in the lord's house; the Lord gives keys to his servants in order to restrict access to the household of faith. Granted, few American Protestants today are willing to invest their minister with this kind of authority. In fact, many are quite suspicious of any structure of governance that smacks of patriarchy, much less hierarchy. But such suspicions will hardly be assuaged by remedies that make the ministry little more than a source of empowerment or therapy. Modern rationales for ministry still protect the prerogatives of ministers—there is still a distinction between the clergy and the laity under the guise of equality and service. At least, the older conception of ordination was candid about the nature and, therefore, the limits of the minster's office and power.

The older idea of ordination also reflected a clearer understanding of why the ministry was important and why it should have such power and authority. Ultimately, the power of the minister flowed from the church's confession of faith and the Christian hope for eternal life. The functions ministers performed, the administration of Word and sacrament, were means of grace, ways for the faithful to be reminded of and confirmed in their salvation from misery and death through the death and resurrection of Jesus Christ. These mysteries of God put the rest of life into a different perspective. No matter what the condition of temporal existence, whether in feast or famine, wealth or poverty, freedom or oppression, there was still hope for the life to come and assurance of that life through the work of Christ. As stewards of those mysteries, the ministry could not have performed a more valuable or vital service.

In contrast, the authority of ministers today is negligible because such a cosmic perspective on their services is largely absent. Churches no longer have a clear sense of what they do. The language of salvation and redemption is still used, but these doctrines are increasingly vague. Those who see social justice and mercy as essential to the church's redemptive mission have failed to present a vision of equality and empowerment that transcends political partisanship or that can in any meaningful sense be recognized as sacred. And if progressive believers do try to argue that a particular policy is sanctioned by divine teaching, they come perilously close to sharing with the religious right a Constantinian understanding of the political order in which God's law is the basis for the law of the land. As long as Christians disagree about what constitutes the good society, social justice and mercy will not provide ministers with much in the way of authority.

Even evangelicals, the so-called conservatives, have mucked up older ideas about the church as, what Calvin called, "the mother of salvation." Evangelicals regard redemption as a way to have a therapeutic ("personal") relationship with the sovereign and transcendent God of the universe. They want God to be their buddy. To the extent that evangelicals think at all about the clergy, they regard ministers as models of the kind of intimate relationship with God they desire. But if, as evangelicals believe, the most important aspect of Christianity is a personal friendship with God through private Bible reading and prayer, then who needs the ministry or the visible church for that matter?

The old understanding of ordination is implausible, however, not just because theological consensus no longer exists. Another difficulty, perhaps even more basic, is the social order on which churches depend. Modern society regards ritual, symbol, hierarchy, and form as unreal at best and fake at worst. Gone is any conception that the forms and shapes of temporal existence represent transcendent realities. Instead, what matters most is standard of living and gross national product. How can ministers provide any leadership, let alone exert any authority, when what ministers do as stewards of the mysteries of God is so marginal if not antithetical to the way most people spend their time? Can Protestant church leaders, with straight faces, as the president of the CRC's seminary recently suggested, encourage young people with particular gifts and abilities to go into the ministry rather than becoming doctors, lawyers, or academics? Can Protestants do this especially when their churches have blessed the current pursuit of material goods and therapeutic services as being fundamentally good? To be sure, some may object that these goods and services are not as equitably distributed as they should be, but almost no one, with the exception of a few agrarians, is willing to say that corporate-industrial society—a society that puts a premium on productivity, efficiency, and function—undermines the very idea that there is a higher transcendent reality and, therefore, that this kind of social arrangement is harmful, not just for the church as an institution but for humankind more generally.

Richard M. Weaver, the Marxist turned agrarian, was on to something when he pointed out the connections between modern economic realities and the demise of the importance of metaphysics and religious ideas. In his book *Ideas Have Consequences*, he wrote:

> The spoiling of man seems always to begin when urban living predominates over rural. After man has left the country to shut himself up in vast piles of stone, . . . after he has come to depend on a complicated system

of human exchange for his survival, he becomes forgetful of the overriding mystery of creation. Such is the normal condition of the *deracine*. An artificial environment causes him to lose sight of the great system not subject to man's control. Undoubtedly this circumstance is a chief component of bourgeois mentality, as even the etymology of "bourgeois" may remind us. It is the city-dweller, solaced by man-made comforts, who resents the very thought that there exist mighty forces beyond his understanding; it is he who wishes insulation and who berates and persecutes the philosophers, the prophets and mystics, the wild men out of the desert, who keep before him the theme of human frailty.[8]

Weaver offers no solution to the problem of clerical authority. But he does raise by implication the question of whether the church can grow, let alone subsist, in a society that is structured in such a way as to deny the very reason for its existence—to make men and women aware of their frailty and offer a divine and mysterious way for overcoming it. Until churches reconsider the function of the ministry in the light of ultimate reality—that the clergy is set apart for a special, gracious, and authoritative task—efforts to pump more vitality and efficiency into Protestant leadership will be futile.

8. Richard M. Weaver, *Ideas Have Consequences* (Chicago: University of Chicago Press, 1948), 115.

8

The Keys of the Kingdom

How would you rate the work of your church? A ministry scorecard might include the following: If your church has a children's ministry, give it 2 points; a welcome team ministry, 1 point; a tape ministry, 1 point (but if a tape and book ministry, 2 points). A couples' ministry should be worth 2 points as should an international student ministry, a mothers' ministry, and a newlywed ministry; but subtract a point if it is a newlywed mothers' ministry. A women's ministry should also receive 2 points, and in the spirit of equity, a men's ministry should receive the same. But if your men's group is an adjunct of Promise Keepers, don't give it any points—you have to start it on your own. An AIDS ministry, a ministry to the homeless, and a low-income housing ministry all receive 3 points, a score befitting a big church with many resources and talented members. Throw in 1 point each for a weekly Bible study, foreign missions, and the sacraments (2 points for the latter if your church allows the laity to set up the Lord's Supper). Finally, add 1 point for a Sunday morning service, 2 points if you have both a contemporary and a traditional service.

Now tally up your score. How did your church do? Be careful though. Before you delight in a double-digit number, you should know that this game is like golf—the higher the score, the worse the performance. The reason, of course, for this inverse method of scoring comes from our Lord himself. When he sent his disciples into the world, he prescribed the means they should use to disciple the nations. In the Great Commission, Christ told the apostles to teach and baptize. In other words, he defined the ministry of the church as encompassing two tasks only: Word and sacrament.

Of course, Reformed Protestants expanded the marks of the church not because they foresaw the importance of an ice hockey ministry (yes, I heard about this on the local Christian radio station) but because discipline was crucial to the faithful proclamation of the Word and the administration of the sacraments. It is not difficult to see how discipline fits under the umbrella of Word and sacrament whenever preachers are made accountable to church courts and wherever congregations bar the unrepentant from the Lord's Table. Even so, the Reformed marks of the church hardly allow for the bevy of so-called ministries that church-growth leaders pitch to would-be megachurches. According to the Westminster Shorter Catechism, the means by which Christ promised to bring his people to himself and to sustain them are things that today make a church supposedly in-grown and unsuccessful, not to mention backward. Those means are Christ's "holy ordinances, especially the Word, sacraments and prayer, all of which are made effectual to the elect for salvation" (Ans. 88).

Such a narrow view of the ministry means that par for the church is 4: 1 point for preaching, 2 points for the sacraments, and 1 for prayer. Any activity beyond these results in a church, to use golfing vernacular, above par or a bogey church.

How Did Churches Become Ministry Samplers?

The contemporary proliferation of ministries has many sources, but three factors are especially important: The first is the demise of the doctrine of providence; the second concerns the apparent feebleness of traditional means; and the third relates to the highly touted Reformed world-and-life view.

Providence

If one doctrine defines contemporary evangelicalism more than any other, it is a belief in miracles or the idea that God can and still does intervene directly and immediately in human affairs, thus manifesting supernatural power. Among Pentecostals and some charismatics, speaking in tongues, healing, and direct revelations from God constitute evidence of God's miraculous activities. But for evangelicals who like their God a little more subdued, the new birth or conversion experience suffices. Being born again is for many the best indication that God is still alive, active, and saving his people. This may explain why evangelicalism has been identified with the new birth and why the media refer to evangelicals as "born-again" Christians. It is a name that reinforces the miraculous and therefore proves that God still exists.

Modern-day evangelicals inherited this heightened supernaturalism from their fundamentalist grandparents. That older generation of conservative Protestants who battled liberal theology in the 1920s and 1930s did so in part because modernists abandoned supernaturalism. In liberal Protestant hands, the virgin birth of Christ became a mythological account of the advent of someone the early church revered as God, and the resurrection became simply an expression of the first Christians' wishful thinking and a way to inspire hope. Liberal Protestantism made these theological moves in part to defend Christianity from the findings of modern science that denied the possibility of miracles and limited truth to explanations derived entirely from evidence that could be verified by the human senses. But while conceding large chunks of Christian teaching to science, modernists were unwilling to abandon Christian convictions altogether. So they clung to belief in God but reduced the divine, even redemptive activities, to natural processes. God was immanent, modernists argued, and was at work in the forces of natural development and human progress. Thus, while Darwinism proved to skeptics that God did not exist, to liberal Protestants it described God's ways in fashioning higher forms of life and nobler civilizations.

Fundamentalists knew well that modernism was not the genuine article and therefore opposed liberalism as a betrayal of the gospel. Conservatives were especially keen to assert the transcendence of God, as opposed to his immanence, and to defend the miraculous character of salvation. Hence the fundamentalist habit of including the virgin birth, the resurrection, the deity of Christ, and the divine character of Scripture on various lists of essential doctrines. Creation was especially important to fundamentalists partly because it was so central to modernist theology. Fundamentalists described the creation of humans in supernatural terms, conceiving of it as a direct, immediate work of God, and they denied the liberal notions of mediation and development. Thus, what was true for conversion also became true for the creation of humans; just as God miraculously regenerated the hearts of believers, so God also supernaturally created their physical form.

The result of this otherwise commendable defense of God's transcendence and sovereignty in salvation was a neglect of the doctrine of providence. According to the Westminster Shorter Catechism, for instance, providence is "God's most holy, wise and powerful preserving and governing [of] all his creatures and all their actions" (Ans. 11). What lies behind this understanding is the belief that God works his purposes through secondary means, not simply through his direct and miraculous deeds. Even if an individual or something in nature appears to be the cause of a certain natural effect, as believers we also know that God is using that secondary cause for the effect he desires. So if we say that the sun burned off the morning fog, we are not necessarily denying God's hand in nature but are merely describing the means he used to clear the sky. Likewise, in studies of the Reformation, we point to the way that Prince Frederick III was crucial to the success of Martin Luther because Frederick served as a buffer between Luther and the higher powers of the papacy and the emperor (something that the martyrs John Wycliffe and John Huss lacked).

The same point can be made about conversion or salvation. Ordinarily, God does not treat people like the apostle Paul—that is, God does not appear in person and blind them. Instead, he uses a variety of means in a person's life to carry out his saving purpose. One example is the influence of family and friends. Statistics overwhelmingly reveal that those who make a profession of faith do so in part because of the influence of a believing family member or friend. Another example is preaching. God does not hammer believers over the head but uses the proclamation of the Word as a means of bringing them to faith and repentance. The same is true of sanctification. Paul tells us to work out our faith in fear and trembling. This means that we are, in the words of the Westminster Shorter Catechism, to make "diligent use" of the means of grace, that is, prayer, the Word, and the sacraments (Q&A 85). But we also know, as Paul adds, that it is God who is at work in us (Phil. 2:12–13).

The secondary means we see and use do not guarantee God's saving grace. His Spirit has to be at work for any of these means to be effective, thus the need for supernatural and miraculous activity as fundamentalists insisted. But Scripture clearly teaches that God uses secondary means to carry out his purposes both in restraining evil and in redeeming his people. In other words, God saves both through providence and miracles. In addition, secondary causes are as much the work of God as are miracles. If we fail to see this, we run the risk of espousing a deistic view of salvation, one in which God winds up the clock of the soul in the act of conversion and then lets it run its own course by its own powers. Contrary to deism, the Bible teaches that God is always involved and ever active in sustaining his creation. The same is no less true of redemption. Whether something occurs providentially or supernaturally, it does not happen without God's purpose.

Foolish Means

Of course, recovering a full view of God's redemptive acts, one in which we take greater notice of secondary means, does not settle the issue of ministry. Couldn't it be that God has ordained ice hockey ministries to bring some of his people to himself? Or what about evangelistic crusades? Isn't the proof in the pudding? As long as some are coming to Christ, can't we say these unusual ministries are ordained by God?

To answer these questions, we need to keep in mind the means that God has promised to bless. The apostle Paul, both in Romans 10 and Ephesians 4, places great stress on the ordained ministry and the public proclamation of the Word, even asking in the former how the elect will come to Christ without preaching. This underlines the point about the importance of means. Ordinarily, God uses means, and so these means are not something we may disregard. We may even say that they are necessary.

We should also observe that these means are ordinary, to use the language of the Shorter Catechism, not simply in the sense that they are the normal ways in which God works but also in the sense that from the world's perspective they aren't very noble or glamorous. This is why Paul describes preaching as foolishness. The cross itself is foolish to the unregenerate mind (1 Cor. 1:23), but the great and mighty redemptive power of God is also packaged or conveyed in a flimsy and unconvincing form. As Paul writes to the Corinthians, the preaching of Christ and him crucified is a stumbling block to the Jews and folly to the Gentiles (1 Cor. 1:23). This means that the church as defined by the ministry of Word and sacrament is in the business of being ordinary.

For a variety of reasons, Christians do not want to admit that the church is ordinary. On the one hand, they want to show off the greatness of God and devise different strategies (i.e., ministries) that will demonstrate just how great, mighty, and merciful God is. On the other hand, the "outward and ordinary means whereby Christ communicates to us the benefits of redemption" (WSC, Q&A 88) aren't very attractive or fun to so-called seekers. Preaching and the sacraments will hardly allow a small church to compete with the megachurch that produces a weekly dramatic video for its youth group (at a rate of $5,000 per video). Nor will Word and sacrament be very effective in luring unchurched Harry and his wife, Harriet.

But isn't this precisely the point of Paul's teaching in the first chapter of 1 Corinthians as well as of the Bible more generally? If we look at all the great redemptive acts in the history of redemption, we cannot help but be struck by how ordinary these miracles are. The exodus is probably the most spectacular event, but it relied simply upon a wind, a strong one to be sure, but not a tornado. Or take the example of Joshua and the Israelites walking and blowing trumpets to bring down the walls of Jericho. David's encounter with Goliath also speaks volumes about God's understated ways of protecting his people and slaying his foes. Of course, the greatest example is our Lord himself, who came to earth as the Messiah and Lord of glory to vanquish the ultimate enemies of sin and death but who arrived in the contemptible surroundings of a barnyard. These examples underline the apostle Paul's instruction in 2 Corinthians 4:7 that God uses "jars of clay" to show that "this all-surpassing power" is from him, not from human hands or wisdom. The same is no less true for the way God now works in his church. He uses the simple means of Word and sacrament to keep us humble and ensure that he receives all the honor and glory.

The point here is not simply that God ordinarily works through foolish means and therefore the church must do likewise. This is true. But we also need to see that the church has been commissioned to disciple the nations and that God has promised to bless her work. The only means God has promised to bless are Word and sacrament. Other ministries that appear to be more attractive and effective not only detract from God's ordained means but also imply that we are wiser than God and that we do not trust his gracious provision. If the church is to be faithful, she must also be content with the means God has given to his church. And unless he sends a word of knowledge promising to bless the youth group, we need to continue with the ordinary means of Word and sacrament.

You may ask, aren't some of these other ministries effective? Don't people come to know Christ through various ministries? But how do we know if ministries other than Word and sacrament are effective? Do we know this simply because a certain parachurch ministry announces in its newsletter that so many came to Christ? Or do we look at statistics from weekly men's group meetings? Ultimately, any so-called ministry depends on the Word and sacrament to determine its effectiveness or, in other words, to tell whether the profession of those who came to Christ is credible. If a twelve-year-old boy comes home from summer camp professing to be a Christian or if a soccer mom goes to a midweek women's Bible study, are we going to say that these professions are credible if these individuals do not gather with other believers each Sunday to hear the Word and receive the sacrament and continue to do so for the rest of their lives? If professing Christians do not participate in the means of grace and fail to assemble with God's people, just how credible is their profession? Of course, some might still defend the credibility of professions that do not draw upon the riches of Word and sacrament. If so, they will have a hard time doing this from Scripture. The

Bible does not say that either weekend retreats or church-sponsored low-income housing (even though they may be beneficial) are the means God uses to save and build his church.

Kingdom Work

Still, evangelicals are not solely to blame for the proliferation of ministries these days. The Reformed also need to shoulder some of the responsibility. Here the widespread idea of kingdom work, or a Reformed world-and-life view, requires closer scrutiny.

The notion of kingdom work stems from good intentions. Abraham Kuyper was probably its best exponent when he said, "There is not an inch in the entire area of our human life which Christ, who is sovereign of all, does not call 'Mine!'"[1] The Reformed worldview aims to do justice to the cultural mandate of Scripture, which calls us to worship God not just on the Lord's Day but also during the week in our vocations. Kuyper, in fact, refined the notion of sphere sovereignty to include not just the idea that Christ is Lord of the church, family, and state (the traditional Reformed spheres). His lordship extends to the whole range of human endeavors, from the natural sciences to the arts. This idea has greatly appealed to evangelicals and former fundamentalists who desire religious rationale for not being a missionary or an evangelist, what is sometimes called "full-time Christian service." Among believers who associate secular occupations with worldliness, the Reformed world-and-life view provides relief by recognizing the religious dimension of all legitimate vocations.

The downside of the Reformed worldview, however, comes when it leads to the idea of cultural transformation, as it usually does. Kingdom work takes on the progressive notion of Christians going into every field of human endeavor, serving God in all occupations, and eventually redeeming the culture to Christ. According to this logic, any legal form of employment is as worthwhile as the ministry of Word and sacrament. After all, Christians in various callings, so the argument runs, are transforming the culture just as much as pastors; sometimes, if the occupation is on a large enough scale, such as in the media or entertainment industry, it can be even more effective than the work of the church. It is as if writing the script of a successful sitcom is more important than the proclamation of the Word.

As it turns out, this understanding of Christian cultural engagement never really escapes the otherworldliness of fundamentalism. In order

1. Abraham Kuyper, "Sphere Sovereignty," in *Abraham Kuyper: A Centennial Reader*, ed. James D. Bratt (Grand Rapids: Eerdmans, 1998), 488.

to legitimize all nonreligious vocations, this view of cultural transformation gives them a religious purpose by saying that they are redemptive or extend Christ's lordship. Older Protestant understandings of vocation, however, recognized secular occupations as good, not because they were evangelistic or redemptive but because God had ordained them. Worldly occupations, according to this view, were still worldly, but worldliness in this sense was good because God had created a good world. This Protestant understanding of vocation still recognized the sacred and unique function of the ministry. While baking and preaching were both legitimate callings—a person was not a better Christian because ordained—the Reformers understood that preaching (even if conducted by the unregenerate), not baking, was the means God used to extend his kingdom. Thus, the popular idea of kingdom work misunderstands the nature of both secular and sacred occupations. It carries with it a fundamental misunderstanding of the kingdom of Christ and how it is realized.

The Keys of the Kingdom

Despite obvious problems with the kingdom-work model of cultural transformation, it does highlight the idea of kingdom in a helpful way. Here it might be useful to consider the nature of Christ's kingdom and what the means are by which he establishes it. Christ is indeed Lord of all things, but his rule will certainly look different in diverse spheres. For instance, Christ is Lord of the United States whether the Constitution recognizes it or not, because God has ordained the powers that be. In the same way, Christ is Lord of both Christian and non-Christian families, because he has ordained this institution as a way to restrain evil and maintain social order. But this is a different kind of rule than what we see in the church. There Christ's kingdom requires bowed knees and tongues confessing Jesus Christ as Lord.

The Westminster Shorter Catechism renders Christ's kingdom as a place where he subdues us to himself, rules and defends us, and restrains his and our enemies (Q&A 26). The point is that Christ's kingdom is a spiritual rather than a physical place, and if spiritual, then it is one where his role as Savior, not as Creator, is primary. This means that the kingdom of God exists only where the benefits of Christ's redemption have been applied, namely, among the elect, not within something as abstract as culture, society, or even television. John Calvin, for instance, limits the idea of the kingdom in just this way when he writes of Christ's kingly office. We can perceive the force and usefulness of Christ's kingship only when we recognize it to be spiritual. This is clear enough from the fact that, while we must fight throughout life under the cross, our condition is harsh and wretched. What then, would it profit us to be gathered under the reign of the Heavenly King, unless beyond this earthly life we were certain of enjoying its benefits? For this reason we ought to know that the happiness promised us in Christ does not consist in outward advantages—such as leading a joyous and peaceful life, having rich possessions, being safe from all harm, and abounding with delights such as the flesh commonly longs after. No, our happiness belongs in the heavenly life![2]

Calvin goes on to infer from Luke 17:21 and Romans 14:17, where God's kingdom is described as being among his people and as "righteousness, peace and joy in the Holy Spirit," that Christ's kingdom "is not earthly or carnal and hence subject to corruption, but spiritual" and thus "lifts us up even to eternal life."[3]

The idea of kingdom work is also helpful for pinpointing the means whereby Christ establishes his kingdom. The very words of our Lord in Matthew 16:19–20; 18:18; and John 20:22–23 are revealing. In these passages, Christ tells his disciples that he has given them the keys to his kingdom. Zacharias Ursinus, coauthor of the Heidelberg Catechism, wrote that the keys of the kingdom consist in preaching and discipline, "by which the kingdom of heaven is opened to believers, and shut against unbelievers."[4] In these spiritual means, the church declares the grace of God to those who live in true faith and repentance and simultaneously declares the wrath of God to the wicked and their exclusion from the kingdom. He goes on to explain that the metaphor of keys borrows from the image of the stewards of a house. "The church is the house of the living God," he writes, and "the ministers of the church are the stewards of God."[5] In declaring the will of God for salvation, ministers have the keys to open God's house to the elect and to shut it to the reprobate.

Aside from the high view of the church and its ministry conveyed by Ursinus, his remarks bring us back full circle to where we began. Calvin and Ursinus would have had no trouble rating an "effective" church. For them, preaching, the sacraments, and discipline were the means Christ had ordained for extending his kingdom. Anything else was sheer gimmickry, efforts that might spring from good intentions but ul-

2. John Calvin, *Institutes of the Christian Religion*, ed. John T. McNeill, trans. Ford Lewis Battles (Philadelphia: Westminster, 1960), II.xv.4.

3. Ibid.

4. Zacharias Ursinus, *The Commentary of Dr. Zacharias Ursinus on the Heidelberg Catechism* (1852; reprint, Phillipsburg, N.J.: Presbyterian & Reformed, 1985), 441.

5. Ibid.

timately detract from the means of grace and breed distrust of God's promises to bless the means of grace. The kingdom of God is not a moral American society, wholesome television programming, or more Christians in the arts. As Jesus himself said, "My kingdom is not of this world" (John 18:36). In other words, his kingdom is located in the hearts, souls, strength, and minds of those people who love and serve him. At the same time, the means by which Christ establishes his kingdom are not banners in the sanctuary, drama and dance in worship, or even a full slate of Sunday school classes. No, the keys of the kingdom, the instruments that lock and unlock it, are the tasks our Lord gives to ministers. When churches reduce the clutter of their programs and when God's people recognize the ministry of Word and sacrament for what they are, namely, the means whereby Christ communicates the benefits of redemption, then and only then will we have churches that score well.

9

Office, Gender, and Egalitarianism

The Christian Reformed Church, a Dutch Calvinist denomination headquartered in Grand Rapids, Michigan, with a little more than a quarter of a million members, bit the bullet at its 1995 Synod and decided to open the offices of minister and elder to women. This way of describing the ruling is probably too strong because the CRC's decision was more cowardly than heroic. Rather than actually changing church order, a judgment that would have required ratification by the lower courts of the church, Synod merely altered the Supplement to Church Order, a change that avoided the church at large. Nevertheless, this decision appeared to be the culmination of a long debate within the CRC about biblical teaching on male headship, the subordination of women, and the nature of ordination.

Unless you are a conservative Calvinist who cares about the health of Reformed theology and practice, you probably have no good reason to lament what happened to the CRC. By most measures, Dutch Calvinists are of no discernible importance. The CRC is a relatively small ethnic communion that, despite its post–World War II assimilation into American culture, often through evangelical guises, has been on the sidelines of American Protestant developments. Yet these Dutch Calvinists have produced (and have sometimes hired) a number of important academics who not only have emerged as leaders in their respective disciplines but also have become models for Christian (especially evangelical) scholarship. Here the names of Alvin Plantinga, Nicholas Wolterstorff, George Marsden, Mary Stewart Van Leeuwen, and Richard Mouw come to mind. Equally important has been the CRC's intellectual leadership on the issue of the ordination of women. Traditionally, evangelicals have not been able to think their way theologically out of a box. (If readers think this judgment too harsh, they should read Mark Noll's *Scandal of the Evangelical Mind.*) But the debates in the CRC have occasioned the reflections of its academics on the questions surrounding women in office, and in turn these considerations have provided cover and ammunition for evangelicals on this delicate issue.

Not that evangelicals needed much help. Historically, evangelicals, those Protestants in the forefront of promoting revivals, calling for conversion (a "born-again" experience), and making Christianity relevant to everyday concerns, have also been on the cutting edge of blurring the distinction between the ordained and the laity, or of demanding equal access to ecclesiastical office for all Christians. Nowhere is this point more strikingly illustrated than in Nathan Hatch's prize-winning book, *The Democratization of American Christianity,* in which he tells how evangelicalism, the New World faith, made the individual (sometimes read "the people") sovereign in all religious matters, relegating the clergy, church, and tradition, the corruptions of the Old World, to the ash heap of history.

The Dutch Calvinist contribution to the debates about the equality of women appears to have been in the area of eschatology. Here traditional Reformed theology about the relationship between the old and new covenants has provided a handy way for rationalizing a progressive view of history. Just as the rights of God's children expanded in the movement from Israel in the Old Testament to the church in the New Testament, so the development of greater rights and freedoms for individuals in human history demonstrates a better understanding of biblical teaching about the value of individuals and their gifts. For instance, on the eve of the 1990 Synod at which the issue of women in office was supposed to be settled, Cornelius Plantinga Jr., professor at Calvin Seminary, argued that the case for opening up offices to women rested on a hermeneutic that saw "the big movement of the history of redemption," or the "big new patterns and trajectory of the New Testament over smaller, older, and (I think) temporal and local commands."[1] So, too, Mary Stewart Van Leeuwen at the same time argued that the "unfolding drama in which God's salvation is made available to more and more groups previously considered marginal" meant that salvation included "equal access to its privileges and responsibilities."[2] More re-

1. Cornelius Plantinga Jr., "You're Right Dear—or How to Handle Headship," *Reformed Journal* 40 (May/June 1990): 20.

2. Mary Stewart Van Leeuwen, "The Contradictions of Headship," *Reformed Journal* 40 (May/June 1990): 21.

cently, in 1995, George Marsden did Plantinga and Stewart Van Leeuwen one better when he made the case for the equality of women in the church based on the older liberal Protestant distinction between the letter and spirit in Scripture. Marsden looked less at the exclusion/inclusion and hierarchy/equality dialectics than he did at the specificity of Old Testament teaching about office and ordination compared to the relative silence of the New Testament about such matters. The movement in the Bible from a detailed code for Israel to almost no regulations for the church means for Marsden that the "weight" of the argument shifts "decisively to biblical principles such as equality in Christ and the calling of all Christians to their God-given gifts."[3]

Still, the redemptive-historical flourish on standard arguments for the equality of individuals calls to mind many of the millennial expectations that evangelicals in the early nineteenth century used to break with hierarchy and tradition, whether in society or the church. The similarities are especially evident when contemporary proponents of women's ordination try to paint their opponents into a corner by comparing the exclusion of women from church office to slavery. Because no one in his or her right mind would countenance a defense of slavery, the argument seems to go, how could anyone plausibly deny the equal worth of women for holding ecclesiastical office? This logic, and the hermeneutic that spiritualized the apostle Paul's teaching about the subordination of women and about slavery, was similar to that which led evangelical reformers on the eve of the Civil War to equate the abolition of slavery and liberation of women with the central impulses of the gospel.

The appeal to slavery demonstrates that the terms of the debate over women have not changed in one and a half centuries. True freedom and equality only emerge, Christian feminists argue, when all distinctions and forms of hierarchy are removed. Put in these terms, the argument for women's ordination appears to be more the logical conclusion of American political assumptions than the application of biblical teaching, a resemblance that suggests that Dutch Calvinists are merely following in the well-worn paths of evangelicalism, that is, of trying to adapt Christian verities to the pieties of the American experiment. Thus, the CRC's recent decision may well demonstrate the denomination's capitulation to the premises on which the modern political economy has organized public and private life, the very premises on which nineteenth-century evangelicals first advocated the liberty and equality of all individuals.

3. George Marsden, "Women's Ordination for Conservative Biblicists," *Perspectives* 10 (May 1995): 5.

The fact that the argument over women's ordination is more ideological than biblical should come as no surprise. What is surprising, however, is that advocates of women's liberation do not see how their arguments facilitate the very political and social arrangements that intellectuals generally decry and that "conservative" evangelicals defend—namely, market capitalism and the rights of the rational, autonomous self to do as he or she pleases. Christian feminists love to show how their opponents are captive to bourgeois, if not 1950s, American values and sensibilities that kept women at home in the women's sphere. But they rarely seem to fathom that the egalitarianism and individualism inherent in the feminist position—whether Christian or not—is also responsible for the political economy that produced Ronald Reagan's "Morning in America."

Perhaps part of a lecture from History of Society 101 would be instructive. The modern argument to liberate women, and men for that matter, from the shackles of tradition, authority, social hierarchy—what have you—is of a piece with changes in society occurring during the eighteenth and nineteenth centuries associated with the expansion of market economies, technological development, and the consolidation of nation-states. These changes took and are still taking a tremendous toll on the family and the church, two institutions that are pivotal to God's redemptive purposes. The modern political economy weakens the family by giving to large impersonal institutions such as schools, hospitals, businesses, and governments the tasks formerly performed by the family. It is no wonder that women feel left out and unfulfilled in modern society given that the current social arrangements have taken over many of the services women used to provide. The modern political economy also disorients church life, a feature of modernity that has ensured the success of evangelicals who thrive in the parachurch. Clergy function less as heads over their congregations than as administrators and policy makers in a voluntary organization. Their teaching is received more as therapeutic than as authoritative. What is more, the task of churches has been made to conform to the principles of a social service institution rather than of a source of eternal life.

Things, of course, were not always this way, especially at the time of the writing of the Old and New Testaments. The social structure then and the one that generally prevailed until the eighteenth century was one in which the dominant approach to human life was relational rather than functional. Premodern societies were less concerned with performing tasks or producing goods than with strengthening human relationships. Families were obviously important to this kind of society because they constituted the basis for human relationships and provided most of the social services. The church was closely tied and responsive to the Christian families and communities in which it existed. The heads of the church functioned in a way similar to fathers in a family. They governed their people, taught them and watched over them, and when they were in need responded to that need. The church, in other words, was more like a people or a family than an impersonal institution.

In this setting, headship and submission, whether in the home or the church, were not foreign concepts. They were the very stuff of theology and daily life. Headship in Christian theology means that Adam is the head of the human race and that Christ is the head of the church. Christians confess, accordingly, that all humans sinned in Adam, because he acted as the representative of humankind, and that believers are saved in Christ, the second Adam, because he died on behalf of the redeemed. Headship, therefore, implies both service and authority. Christ serves by suffering and dying in our stead. He also rules as Lord.

At the same time, premodern society supported the idea that God deals with his people primarily in groups or communities, not as individuals. The church, accordingly, constitutes a people or a community, not a collection of autonomous selves. Likewise, communities have well-honed structures of governance, authority, and accountability. Subordination and submission are part and parcel of communities. Not only do wives submit to husbands, but in the ideal Christian community, all members submit to rulers, all believers submit to church officers, and all children submit to parents. These communities, with their structures of governance, have historically been the principal means for defining the identities of individual members. Individuals in community do not choose who they are; rather, their identities arise from being born into and being members of the community.

If this is the form of community in which the Bible was written, and even more, which the biblical authors assumed, how can any ideology or form of social arrangement that moves believers farther from this pattern be desirable for the church and its members? Yet this is precisely what Christian feminists are doing, whether they acknowledge it or not. The issue is not so much about whether the Bible forbids women from holding special office as it is about the unwholesome assumptions that make the Bible conform to the egalitarian and individualistic ideology on which so much of feminism depends. Thus, the irony of Christian feminism: While advocates of women's causes deride the political economy that forced domesticity on women, they champion the very idea of the self that underwrites market capitalism. The market relies on autonomous and free individuals, people who are capable of making rational choices, to produce and consume its goods. These autonomous individuals cannot be subordinate to or held in check by the demands of family or community, for if individuals are restrained by ties of blood, land, or confession, whether in the choice of job or commodity and especially in the choice of when to work and how to work, the market will not be as productive, profitable, or efficient. This is also a problem for conservative evangelicals who oppose feminism but propagate the virtues of laissez-faire capitalism. But it is hollow for Christian feminists to decry the evils of the market when their own conception of the self sustains corporate capitalism in all its fullness.

Aside from the problem of baptizing political economy, evangelical feminists make the more grievous mistake of misconstruing the gospel. Throughout arguments for women in office specifically, or for women's rights more generally, lurks the assumption that freedom or equality in Christ means virtually the same thing as political freedom or equality. Christian feminists are correct to argue that in Christ we have freedom from the law and from the curse of sin, in other words, that in Christ everyone is equal. As Galatians 3:28 reads, "There is neither Jew nor Greek, slave nor free, male nor female." In Christ, the circumstances of birth do not determine one's access to God. God is sovereign and saves whom he will, though he saves ordinarily through specific means of grace. The Westminster Confession of Faith summarizes well when it says, "The liberty which Christ has purchased for believers under the gospel consists in their freedom from the guilt of sin, the condemning wrath of God, the curse of the moral law; . . . their free access to God" (20.i).

This is why James Henley Thornwell could write:

> True freedom is the liberty wherein Christ has made us free. It consists essentially in the dominion of rectitude, in the emancipation of the will from the power of sin, the release of the affections from the attractions of the earth, the exemption of the understanding from the deceits and prejudices of error. It is a freedom enjoyed by the martyr at the stake, a slave in his chains, a prisoner in his dungeon, as well as the king upon his throne. It is precisely this freedom which the apostle enjoins upon slaves when he exhorts them to obey their masters and to do their work as in the eye of God."[4]

Yes, this was the kind of argument used to justify slavery. But that does not mean that the picture of Christian liberty it paints is untrue. The slave, according to the Bible, is just as free in Christ as the king. In other words, we miss the significance of the spiritual freedom we ob-

4. James Henley Thornwell, "Relation of the Church to Slavery," in *The Collected Writings of James Henley Thornwell,* 4 vols. (Edinburgh: Banner of Truth Trust, 1974), 4:382–83.

tain in Christ and that is taught in Scripture if we reduce it to the temporary arrangements of this world's political order.

The problem, however, is that we do not live merely in Christ. We also live in this world, in the created order, even if that order is fallen. Here a little eschatology is helpful. We are already in Christ, but at the same time we are not yet in Christ. We will be fully in Christ only in the new heavens and the new earth. Then—though this is only speculation—there may no longer be distinctions and hierarchies, though if Christ is our pattern, we will still be male and female and he will be our King, thus ruling out the chances for participatory democracy in glory. But for now we are still part of this age in God's redemptive plan, the interadvental period. And in this stage of redemption, as Paul writes, distinctions between men and women, husbands and wives, parents and children, masters and slaves, and governors and the governed are still important because they are part of the way God keeps order, restrains evil, and advances his *spiritual* kingdom. This is why the Westminster Confession goes on in the chapter on Christian liberty to say that the political powers God has ordained and the freedom purchased by Christ do not destroy but "mutually . . . uphold and preserve one another" (20.iv). Thus, it is possible—though feminists always deny it—to affirm both Christian liberty and submission to the legitimate authorities of the created order.

This is also why the authors of the Westminster Confession condemned anyone who opposed "lawful power" "upon pretence of Christian liberty" (20.iv). In the mainstream of the Reformed tradition, this distinction between liberty or equality in Christ and liberty or equality in the civil realm were, as Calvin wrote in a passage often overlooked, "things far removed from one another." As Calvin went on to state in that passage, "It is a Judaic folly to look for the kingdom of Christ among the things that make up this world, and to shut it up among them; our opinion, which is supported by the plainest teaching of Scripture, is that on the contrary, the fruit we reap from grace is spiritual fruit."[5] In other words, the standards of freedom or restraint in the political realm, the realm charged with maintaining order and restraining evil in the created order (which applies just as much to church polity because saints have a habit of needing restraint), are not the standard for the liberty we enjoy in Christ. Thus, the-proof-is-in-the-pudding appeals to women's rights and women's ordination by many Christian feminists are off base. The liberty or equality that women do or do not enjoy in the political and ecclesiastical realms does not define the liberty pur-

5. John Calvin, *Institutes of the Christian Religion*, ed. John T. McNeill, trans. Ford Lewis Battles (Philadelphia: Westminster, 1960), IV.xx.1.

chased by Christ. Liberty in Christ is of an altogether different nature, order, and finally, eschaton.

The accommodation of the gospel to the political and economic norms of our age is the reason why the arguments of Christian feminists are so alarming. To be sure, the church has negotiated different readings of difficult biblical texts for years. Paedo-baptists can genuinely recognize credo-baptists as brothers and sisters in Christ even while disagreeing on important portions of Scripture. In the same way, it is possible for those who oppose women's ordination to admit that the issue is not as central to the Christian faith as the deity of Christ or the Trinity (though equivocation on such clear passages is disconcerting). No, the problem with so many of the arguments for women's ordination is that they reduce the freedoms purchased by Christ's body and blood to the civil liberties we enjoy through the U.S. Constitution. This kind of equation should give serious Christians real pause. Ultimately, it trivializes the gospel, for it ends up positing that women are not truly liberated unless they have equal access to ecclesiastical office, a notion that flies in the face of the real comfort believers, whether male or female, slave or free, Jew or Greek, enjoy in Christ and that was so wonderfully expressed by the apostle Paul: "Neither death nor life, neither angels nor demons, neither the present nor the future, nor any powers, neither height nor depth, nor anything else in all creation, will be able to separate us from the love of God that is in Christ Jesus our Lord" (Rom. 8:38–39).

Part 4

PRESBYTERIAN PAROCHIALISM

10

Confessional Presbyterianism and the Limits of Protestant Ecumenism

At its General Assembly of 1945, the microscopic Orthodox Presbyterian Church demonstrated (depending on your perspective) either remarkable chutzpa or momentous folly when it refused to join the National Association of Evangelicals. The NAE, of course, the chief manifestation of progressive fundamentalism, was the wave of the future. It brought together in a loose way the individuals (Harold Ockenga, Carl Henry, Billy Graham) and institutions (Fuller Seminary, National Religious Broadcasters, Christianity Today) that would be pivotal for the post–World War II evangelical renaissance. The OPC, a denomination founded in 1936 in the aftermath of the foreign missions controversy in the northern Presbyterian Church, however, was clearly living off the capital of its accomplished and articulate founder, J. Gresham Machen (1881–1937). When Machen died suddenly on January 1, 1937, only six months after the start of the OPC, the luster of the new denomination quickly faded. In that same year, the church experienced a split, losing the Bible Presbyterians led by the feisty Carl McIntire. By the time of the NAE's founding, the OPC's growth had been meager at best. It surely seemed that if orthodox Presbyterians had wanted to exercise leadership within and benefit numerically from the emerging evangelical coalition, they should have accepted the NAE's invitation. Nevertheless, the OPC followed the advice of its ecumenical relations committee and refused to join the NAE.[1]

The OPC's decision would seem to be a prime example of fundamentalist separatism. One of the reasons the OPC remained separate was the NAE's openness to ministers from mainline denominations. From the perspective of the OPC, it seemed inconsistent for the NAE to offer itself as an alternative to the modernist Federal Council of Churches and yet allow ministers from mainline churches to be members. As historians of the new evangelicalism have argued, progressive fundamentalists such as those who formed the NAE were willing to work with evangelicals in mainline denominations to exert a wider sphere of influence, while separatist fundamentalists such as Carl McIntire and the orthodox Presbyterians refused to cooperate with any organization that harbored theological liberalism.

This interpretation of Protestant developments in the 1940s, while it offers more nuance than the two-party paradigm that splits American Protestantism into right (read: evangelical) and left (read: mainline) camps, nevertheless perpetuates and extends the dualism that bedevils American religious history.[2] Despite the apparent differences between neo-evangelicals and fundamentalists, religious historians still generally divide the Protestant world in two. The aim here is to make a case for the existence and importance of another type of conservatism, namely, confessional Protestantism, which is often overlooked in the standard accounts of twentieth-century religious history. Although Machen and the denomination he founded appear to be fundamentalist because of their militant opposition to liberalism, Orthodox Presbyterians also stood for beliefs and practices at odds with fundamentalism and neo-evangelicalism. For this reason, an examination of only what conservatives opposed misses important dimensions of their identity. And the reasons behind Machen and the OPC's opposition to liberalism reveal a set of concerns distinct from fundamentalism that may be called Presbyterian confessionalism. Accordingly, the OPC's reason for not joining the NAE stemmed from its confessional identity rather than

1. On the founding of the NAE and neo-evangelicalism, see Joel Carpenter, *Revive Us Again: The Reawakening of American Fundamentalism* (New York: Oxford University Press, 1997), chap. 8. On the nature of OPC's relationship with neo-evangelicalism, see D. G. Hart, "The Legacy of J. Gresham Machen and the Identity of the Orthodox Presbyterian Church," *Westminster Theological Journal* 53 (1991): 209–25. The OPC's total membership as of March 31, 1946, was 7,555, according to the *Minutes of the Thirteenth General Assembly* (1946), 126.

2. See Douglas Jacobsen and William Vance Trollinger Jr., "Historiography of American Protestantism: The Two-Party Paradigm and Beyond," *Fides et Historia* 25 (1993): 4–15.

fundamentalist separatism. In fact, at the same time that it declined membership in the NAE, the denomination also refused to join Carl McIntire's American Council of Christian Churches, an organization more representative of separatist fundamentalism. From the OPC's perspective, neither the NAE nor the ACCC was sufficiently Calvinistic, and neither organization exhibited a proper (i.e., Presbyterian) understanding of the church.

The OPC's porcupine-like conservatism, therefore, raises two significant points. The first concerns J. Gresham Machen, a figure commonly cited as the embodiment of fundamentalism par excellence. His association with the Calvinist and inerrantist theology of Princeton Seminary has been especially useful for historians who argue that the issues of the 1920s drove Princeton's Calvinists into the arms of dispensationalist fundamentalists. Closer scrutiny of Machen, however, reveals that the alliance between the Princeton theology and dispensationalism stems more from the two-party perspective of religious historians than any real similarities between Princetonians and fundamentalists. Historians have properly attributed opposition to liberalism to the Princeton theology and dispensationalism. Yet they have not recognized the tension and antagonism between Calvinists and dispensationalists. In light of an examination of the different rationales of those who opposed modernism—that is, identifying what they stood for positively instead of merely what they attacked—the reasons for the OPC's isolation not only make more sense but also reveal the distinctive thought and aims of Presbyterian confessionalists like Machen.[3]

The second and larger purpose for looking at Machen and the OPC is to give some attention to confessional Protestantism more generally. Orthodox Presbyterians were not the only group to remain separate from the NAE. Others such as the Christian Reformed Church as well as Wisconsin and Missouri Synod Lutherans were also critical of the theology and ecclesiology implicit in the NAE. The OPC, therefore, represented a wider, though not necessarily large, phenomenon. Confessional Protestants, whether Lutheran, Reformed, Anglican, or Anabaptist, did not readily fit into the dominant liberal and conservative parties that the Federal Council of Churches and the NAE represented and that historians have used to categorize Protestant history. Consequently, while this chapter focuses on the tradition of confessional Presbyterianism exemplified by Machen, its more general purpose is to add greater nuance

3. On the alleged alliance of Princetonians and dispensationalists, see Ernest R. Sandeen, *The Roots of Fundamentalism* (Chicago: University of Chicago Press, 1970); and George M. Marsden, *Fundamentalism and American Culture: The Shaping of Twentieth-Century Evangelicalism, 1870–1925* (New York: Oxford University Press, 1980).

and precision to our understanding of twentieth-century Protestantism by calling attention to Protestant confessionalism.

Machen and Fundamentalism

To argue that Machen was not a fundamentalist may strike some as a good example of special pleading. He was, after all, outspokenly hostile to Protestant liberalism and displayed the militancy that typified fundamentalism. In his most popular book, *Christianity and Liberalism,* Machen charged that liberalism was not only "un-Christian"—fighting words in and of themselves—but also "the greatest menace" the church had faced, a "type of faith and practice . . . anti-Christian to the core." To add insult to injury, he explained that while the church of Rome was a perversion of Christianity, "naturalistic liberalism" was an entirely different religion.[4]

Yet militant opposition to liberalism only goes so far in defining various constituencies within American Christianity. Roman Catholics, after all, opposed modernism long before Protestants did, and yet few scholars have called conservative Catholics fundamentalists.[5] For this reason, it is imperative to notice that Machen would not affirm the two most popular fundamentalist beliefs, creationism and dispensationalism, which together expressed uncanny certainty about the beginning and the end of human history. Machen, like most confessional Presbyterians, remained agnostic about the timing of Christ's return and grew increasingly hostile to dispensational premillennialism. In *Christianity and Liberalism,* Machen called dispensationalism a "false method of interpreting the Bible" and repeatedly rebuffed the requests of William Bell Riley to join the World Christian Fundamentals Association because of that organization's dispensationalist doctrinal plank. By the end of his career, Machen feared that the Scofield Reference Bible, with its misunderstanding of the nature of sin, was "leading precious souls astray."[6]

Machen also showed little interest in the controversy over evolution, though it was not for a lack of initiative on William Jennings Bryan's part. In preparation for the Scopes Trial, Bryan invited Machen to tes-

---

4. J. Gresham Machen, *Christianity and Liberalism* (New York: Macmillan, 1923), 160, 52.

5. See Jay P. Dolan, *The American Catholic Experience: A History from Colonial Times to the Present* (Garden City, N.Y.: Doubleday, 1985), 304–20.

6. Machen, *Christianity and Liberalism*, 49; Machen to William Bell Riley, 30 April 1929 and 1 May 1929; and Machen to J. Oliver Buswell, 19 October 1936, Machen Archives.

tify on behalf of the prosecution. Machen courteously declined, explaining that he was not a student of the Old Testament. But Machen's appeal to the rules of expertise actually concealed a perspective on creation derived from his theological mentor, Benjamin Warfield. Known for his rigorous Calvinism and doctrine of inerrancy, Warfield also believed that Christians could embrace evolutionary theories, even to the point of accepting the idea that the human form evolved from existing creatures, as long as such views allowed for a supernatural act of God in the creation of the human soul.[7]

The sociopolitical baggage that accompanied Protestant concerns about the creation and destiny of human life was another difference that separated Machen from mainstream fundamentalism. Creationism and dispensationalism became lightning rods in the aftermath of World War I for working-class and southern Protestants who were alarmed by the apparent secular drift of American society. Because the terms and categories of evolution and postmillennialism had so often been used to support progress, fundamentalist fear about America's decadence bred suspicions about evolution. Furthermore, anti-German sentiments, fueled by the war, helped to unite evolution, liberal Protestant ideas about the kingdom of God, and German barbarism in the minds of most fundamentalists. Germany became the prime example of the moral and social decline that followed logically from liberalism's naturalistic account of the universe and human affairs.[8]

Machen, however, viewed the war differently, and his perspective was indicative of a political philosophy that was at odds with the ideology of popular fundamentalism. Even though he served at the front in France as a YMCA secretary, Machen was ambivalent at best about the United States' involvement in the war and criticized the Wilson administration's military conscription policy as a breach of civil liberties. Because of his studies at Marburg and Göttingen Universities and his friendships with German students and faculty, Machen was reluctant to endorse the Allied cause. On the domestic front, his politics were equally unusual for one thought to be a fundamentalist. For instance, Machen maintained party allegiance and voted in 1928 for the first Roman Catholic presidential candidate, the Democrat Al Smith, because of Smith's intention to repeal Prohibition. As a member of the Sentinels of the Republic, a political organization founded by Massa-

7. See Machen's correspondence with Bryan: Bryan to Machen, 23 June 1925, and Machen to Bryan, 2 July 1925. For Machen's recommendation of Warfield, see Machen to George S. Duncan, 19 February 1924. For Machen's own exposition of creation, one that missed the nuances of Warfield, see his *Christian View of Man* (New York: Macmillan, 1937), chaps. 10–12.

8. See Marsden, *Fundamentalism and American Culture*, chap. 16.

chusetts Republicans, Machen opposed the growth and power of the federal government in such initiatives as Prohibition, the Child Labor Amendment, and the creation of a Federal Department of Education. And while Machen was a loyal son of the South, his politics were not that different from another Baltimorean, H. L. Mencken, whose conservative libertarianism poked as much fun at Southern culture as at the polite society of mainstream Protestantism.[9]

Machen's efforts to protect the autonomy and integrity of local institutions and culture from the spread of national government and cultural uniformity made him critical of both fundamentalist and liberal Protestant views of the nation. Northern evangelicals, whether conservative or liberal, desired the preservation of Christian civilization in America even though disagreeing about the means. From Machen's perspective, fundamentalists and modernists were equally guilty of confusing the spheres of the church and the state. In fact, the cruelty and vindictiveness of Yankee aggression toward the South during the Civil War and Reconstruction, Machen argued, as well as Protestant efforts to Americanize immigrants, demonstrated the evils that could result from mixing religion and politics.

Thus, while fundamentalism sprouted in fertile debates about Christian civilization in America during and after World War I, we must look for a different source of Machen's opposition to liberalism. Clues come from his duties as a first-time delegate to the Presbyterian Church's 1920 General Assembly. There Machen heard and reacted strongly against plans produced by the American Council on Organic Union for a union of the largest Protestant denominations. He argued that the plan's theological rationale omitted practically all the "great essentials of the Christian faith" and relegated the Westminster Confession of Faith to merely a denominational affair. This argument turned out to be the essence of his critique of theological modernism in *Christianity and Liberalism*. Hopes for Protestant unity, he argued, exhibited a religious epistemology that possessed all the earmarks of liberalism and ultimately circumvented Christianity's explicit supernaturalism.[10]

Because Machen's opposition to church union was contemporaneous with the rise of fundamentalism, historians have usually linked the two forms of protest. But here a comparison with Canadian develop-

9. On Machen's politics, see D. G. Hart, *Defending the Faith: J. Gresham Machen and the Crisis of Conservative Protestantism in Modern America* (Baltimore: Johns Hopkins University Press), chap. 6.

10. J. Gresham Machen, "The Proposed Plan of Union," *The Presbyterian* 90 (10 June 1920): 8–9. See also "For Christ or against Him," *The Presbyterian* 91 (20 January 1921): 8–9; and "The Second Declaration of the Council on Organic Union," *The Presbyterian* 91 (17 March 1921): 8, 26.

ments is instructive. Like Presbyterians in the United States, conservative Canadian Presbyterians also resisted the ecumenical efforts and liberal Protestant sentiments that in 1925 produced the United Church of Canada. Some of these Presbyterians had fundamentalist sympathies but did not champion the doctrines of inerrancy or dispensationalism. Rather, conservatives took their vows to the Westminster Confession of Faith so seriously that they felt betrayed when other Presbyterians seemed eager to merge their church with non-Presbyterian bodies. Significantly, Canadian conservatives saw Machen as an ally. Machen regularly preached at Knox Church in Toronto whose pastor, John Gibson Inkster, in 1926 recommended Machen for the principalship of Knox College, the Presbyterian theological school at the University of Toronto, an invitation Machen declined.[11]

Christianity and Liberalism, Machen's most popular book, also needs to be read more in the light of Presbyterian rather than pan-Protestant developments. The manuscript stemmed from a speaking engagement sponsored by Pennsylvania presbyteries opposed to church union and summarized Machen's critique of the progressive and cooperative ideals fueling mainstream American Protestantism. While the central argument of the book—that Christianity and liberalism were two entirely different religions—would have broad appeal to fundamentalists, it reads more like a primer in Calvinist theology than a fundamentalist tract. Machen took issue with liberalism not because of defective views of creation, Christ's return, or even the Bible, but because it denied Christian teaching about sin and grace. To be sure, his uncompromising defense of Christian supernaturalism and the historical truthfulness of the Bible, his commonsensical handling of problems in professional biblical scholarship, and his seeming scorn for denominational officials appealed powerfully to Protestants who believed that Christian salvation was primarily individual not social, that the Bible was reliable in scientific as well as religious matters, and that churches were becoming obstacles to the faithful proclamation of the gospel. But Machen was writing with the problems of his own communion in mind. It was, after all, modernist ministers in the Presbyterian Church who had taken vows of subscription to the Westminster Confession of Faith whom he reproached for exhibiting liberalism's worst feature, using theological language equivocally if not dishonestly. Consequently, conservatives who focused only on Machen's apology for the general outline of historic Christianity would be disappointed by the trajectory of his career. Rather than seeking alliances across denominational lines to

11. See N. Keith Clifford, *The Resistance to Church Union in Canada 1904–1939* (Vancouver: University of British Columbia Press, 1985).

resuscitate an earlier evangelical empire, Machen spent the remaining years of his life fighting one denominational battle after another.[12]

The confessional orientation of Machen's arguments became especially clear in the aftermath of the northern Presbyterian Church's bureaucratic efforts to cover up and recover from the instability of the fundamentalist controversy. At three successive General Assemblies, from 1925 to 1927, the church avoided a threatened liberal exodus by appointing committees to study denominational tensions. These studies concluded that the principal cause of controversy was the unfair and unfounded accusations of conservatives, especially of Calvinists associated with Princeton Seminary. This finding led to an investigation and reorganization in 1929 of the institution that many regarded as the West Point of Calvinist orthodoxy. This reorganization shifted the makeup of the seminary's governing boards, putting conservatives in the minority. The public-relations spin that the denomination put on the affair was that the older patterns of governance were ineffective. The reorganization, consequently, was not theological or ideological; it was merely an effort to make the seminary more responsive to the church and society's changing needs. Conservatives, however, had a different impression. They believed reorganization was an unconstitutional effort by tyrannical church bureaucrats to muzzle conservative dissent and, ultimately, obscure the true state of affairs in the Presbyterian Church.[13]

The changes that occurred at Princeton Seminary in 1929 are worth highlighting because they underscore the inadequacy of two-party interpretations of twentieth-century Protestantism. Historians have had difficulty making sense of the Princeton controversy because the struggle was not between liberals and conservatives. Rather, by the light of American Protestant historiography, both sides were conservative. The chief antagonists were Machen, who opposed reorganization, and Charles Erdman, a dispensationalist professor of pastoral theology and coeditor of the *Fundamentals* who supported the changes at Princeton and insisted that the church and seminary were still orthodox. Because liberals were absent, most scholars have reduced the conflict to person-

---

12. See Machen, *Christianity and Liberalism*, 162–72. Machen detested what he called the "sickly interdenominationalism" of fundamentalists. The best way to counteract liberalism, he felt, was not through a union of interdenominational conservatives but through historic Protestant creeds, reinforced by a strong denominational consciousness. While he affirmed "warm Christian fellowship" with fundamentalists, he said his greatest sympathies were with "those brethren, like the Lutherans, who are most insistent upon their ecclesiastical distinctness."

13. See Bradley J. Longfield, *The Presbyterian Controversy: Fundamentalists, Modernists, and Moderates* (New York: Oxford University Press, 1991), chaps. 5–7.

alities. But the transcripts of the Princeton proceedings show that the struggle was indeed theological even if not between liberalism and fundamentalism. Erdman represented the New School version of Presbyterianism, one that smoothed out the sharper angles of seventeenth-century British Calvinism to match the contours of American religion. Machen, in contrast, manifested the traditional theological and ecclesiastical concerns of Old School Presbyterianism, a tradition that had a long history of opposing American Protestant innovations, from Charles Finney's revivals to Wesleyan perfectionism. The Princeton controversy was one more episode in that rivalry. But the two-party interpretation, sensing that both Machen and Erdman were not liberal, misses the shades of Presbyterianism within a place like Princeton.[14]

More importantly, the Princeton reorganization clarified the confessional dimension of Machen's conservatism. For Machen and like-minded Calvinists in the northern Presbyterian Church, the outcome of the Princeton Seminary affair threatened the very existence of Old School Presbyterianism. Since the reunion of Old and New School Presbyterians in 1870, Princeton had been designated an Old School institution. But reorganization forced the seminary to reflect the pluralism of the denomination, thus leaving conservatives without a base. The founding of Westminster Seminary in 1929 was designed to remedy this situation. According to Machen, who spoke at the new seminary's convocation, though Princeton Seminary was "dead," its "noble tradition" was still alive. Westminster would endeavor "to continue that tradition unimpaired" by propagating and defending the Westminster Confession of Faith as true and capable of scholarly defense.[15]

The Point of Being Presbyterian

As the 1930s would show, Machen had more in mind than merely forming a new seminary. He also wanted to create the skeleton of a church so that when conservatives left the mainline denomination they

14. See Lefferts A. Loetscher, *The Broadening Church: A Study of Theological Issues in the Presbyterian Church since 1869* (Philadelphia: University of Pennsylvania Press, 1954), 147; and Longfield, *Presbyterian Controversy*, chap. 7. For a recent assessment of Erdman that ironically regards him the way Machen did, as having more affinities with liberals than conservatives, see Barbara Wheeler, "Henry Sloane Coffin and Charles R. Erdman and Our Search for a Liveable Piety," *Princeton Seminary Bulletin* 21, no. 1 (2000): 24–37.

15. J. Gresham Machen, "Westminster Theological Seminary, Its Purpose and Plan," in *What Is Christianity?* ed. Ned Bernard Stonehouse (Grand Rapids: Eerdmans, 1951), 232–33.

would have a place to go. The missions controversy of the early 1930s provided Machen with the first opportunity to pursue this strategy. The infamous "Layman's Inquiry" published in 1932 raised suspicions about the soundness of the Presbyterian Church's Board of Foreign Missions. After failing to force the General Assembly to investigate the board, Machen decided in 1933 to found his own missions agency, the Independent Board for Presbyterian Foreign Missions. This proved to be the most audacious decision of Machen's stormy career. On the one hand, it split the already small and seemingly insignificant wing of confessionalists in the denomination. Debates about the wisdom and anomaly of founding an independent Presbyterian missions agency eventually forced a showdown at Westminster, an independent Presbyterian seminary, where conservatives such as Clarence Macartney and others in 1935 resigned because of their unwillingness to endorse the Independent Board. On the other hand, the anomaly of an independent Presbyterian institution was equally evident to Presbyterian officials. Even though the new missions agency could muster support for only six missionaries, the northern Presbyterian Church vigorously opposed the Independent Board, eventually trying and suspending board members from the ministry for violating membership and ordination vows. These disciplinary actions led to the founding in 1936 of the Orthodox Presbyterian Church.

The anomalies of the Independent Board can easily obscure the confessional character of that missions agency. On the surface, the board had all the marks of a fundamentalist operation. It was adamantly opposed to the modernism of the Protestant establishment, and above all it was independent. But while other fundamentalists were equally alarmed by modernism within mainstream Protestant missionary endeavors and established interdenominational faith missions free from the encumbrances of denominational creeds and machinery, Machen desired to work along distinctly Presbyterian lines. The Presbyterian identity of the Independent Board proved to be crucial to the last controversy of Machen's life. In the fall of 1936, only four months after the founding of the OPC, the Independent Board held its annual elections of officers and in a surprising move failed to reelect Machen as president, a post he had held since the organization's founding. This election reflected the growing antagonism in the OPC between dispensationalists led by Carl McIntire and confessionalists led by Machen and other Westminster faculty. While the confessionalists controlled the denomination, McIntire sought control of the Independent Board. Machen believed that with this election the board had substituted fundamentalism for true Presbyterianism. Because of McIntire's temerity as well as the Westminster faculty's opposition to dispensationalism, McIntire left the OPC in 1937 to form the Bible Presbyterian Synod.[16]

The 1937 split within the OPC makes little sense from the perspective of the two-party model, but it does shed light on Presbyterian confessionalism. Because both Machen and McIntire were conservative, the standard explanation of the division has been psychological, though historians have highlighted the paranoia of McIntire, not the temperamental idiosyncrasies of Machen. Without denying the influence of personalities—Machen and McIntire had strong and, no doubt, unusual ones—the OPC split is relatively easy to explain when Machen's confessional concerns are taken into account. As George Marsden observed almost thirty years ago, three issues divided orthodox and Bible Presbyterians: theology, morality, and ecclesiology.

The OPC stood for the unadulterated Calvinism of the Westminster Standards and removed chapters on the love of God and missions that the northern church had added in 1903. The Bible Presbyterians, if not all dispensationalists, were clearly sympathetic to the doctrinal glue of popular fundamentalism. The church also split over the issue of Christian liberty. McIntire accused Westminster's faculty of encouraging the consumption of alcohol (rumors circulated that the seminary owned a still) and endeavored to make abstinence the official policy of the church. Confessionalists, however, were unwilling to go beyond the Westminster Standards and ruled that the use of alcohol was a matter of liberty. Just as important for the division was church polity. The OPC wanted to send foreign missionaries who were fully committed to Presbyterian theology and polity. The change of leadership within the Independent Board prompted the OPC to found its own committee on foreign missions. Bible Presbyterians, in contrast, thought that the theological and ecclesiastical concerns of Westminster's ethnic faculty were alien to the tradition of American Presbyterianism.[17]

If this reading of the OPC's identity is correct and if the church's eventual refusal to join the NAE reflects Presbyterian confessionalism rather than fundamentalist separatism, then it is possible to distinguish orthodox Presbyterians from both fundamentalists and liberals. The prevailing difference between confessionalists and other Protestants is the degree to which each group has adapted Christianity to the social and religious environment of the United States. Theologically, the message of mainstream Protestantism, both in its evangelical and

16. See George M. Marsden, "Perspective on the Division of 1937," in *Pressing toward the Mark: Essays Commemorating Fifty Years of the Orthodox Presbyterian Church*, ed. Charlie G. Dennison and Richard C. Gamble (Philadelphia: OPC Committee for the Historian, 1986), 301–23.

17. Marsden, "Perspective on the Division," passim.

liberal forms, has been well adapted to the realities of the American experiment, while confessionalists have generally fought to retain Old World practices. By calling on rational, autonomous individuals to make personal decisions for Christ or to follow the moral example of Jesus, evangelicals and liberals have displayed a higher estimate of human nature than confessionalists, who have been more aware of human sinfulness and look to the institutional church for spiritual sustenance in the ministry of Word and sacrament. Evangelicals, like their Protestant cousins, liberals, have stressed Christianity's ethical demands and have used the criteria of a highly disciplined and morally responsible life as evidence of true faith. For confessionalists, theological distinctions have been crucial. They have equated correct doctrine with religious faithfulness.[18]

Furthermore, confessionalists and other Protestants have disagreed about the nature and function of the church. Evangelicals have not had clear definitions of the church; their communions minimize the distinction between clergy and laity, and they support a variety of parachurch endeavors, both evangelistic and political, that blur differences between religious and social matters. At the same time, liberal Protestant conceptions of the church have stressed ecumenicity at the expense of confessions and creeds. Confessionalists, in contrast, have defended a high view of church office and polity and have regarded preaching, the sacraments, and discipline as the church's essential tasks and as the best response to human suffering. Evangelicals, in this respect, departed from conservative ways by developing a theology and means of outreach that were at home in a nation that made the individual sovereign, regarded hierarchy and the clergy with suspicion, and thrived in the religious free market that resulted from religious disestablishment. While liberal Protestantism has been less individualistic than evangelicalism, its theology and ecclesiology were equally well adapted to the corporate and bureaucratic trends of twentieth-century American society. Conversely, confessionalists have tried to conserve the historic Protestant practices of Christian nurture through catechesis and church schools and by promoting respect and recognition of the need for clergy and for the centrality of Word and sacrament. To be sure, America's religious disestablishment has been beneficial to confessionalists, even to the point of allowing them to outdo the confessionalism of their Old World counterparts who have been constrained

18. See Daniel Walker Howe, "The Evangelical Movement and Political Culture in the North during the Second Party System," *Journal of American History* 77 (1991): 1216–39; and Robert P. Swierenga, "Ethnoreligious Political Behavior in the Mid-Nineteenth Century: Voting, Values, Cultures," in *Religion and American Politics*, ed. Mark A. Noll (New York: Oxford University Press, 1990), chap. 7.

in established churches by the state. But the forces of modernization have ultimately proven to be more favorable to evangelicals and liberals than to confessionalists, who depend on the mediating structures of family, church, and neighborhood for watering the seeds of faith they have tried to plant in the New World.

Theological and ecclesiastical differences have, in turn, made Protestant confessionalists uneasy about the Americanness of evangelical and liberal Protestant religiosity. First, because confessionalists have maintained strict loyalty to creedal and doctrinal expressions from the Reformation or Protestant scholastic eras, they have been suspicious of interdenominational or nondenominational forms of cooperation. Second, confessionalists have manifested a tribal culture, seeking to form an isolated world rather than proselytizing among people with different roots. Third, Protestant confessionalists have been extremely wary of various programs of assimilation into the American religious mainstream, whether the progressivist path of liberal Protestantism or the millennial biblicism of evangelicalism. Fourth, resistance to assimilation has prompted confessionalists to be equally suspicious of their American coreligionists whose practices deviate from Old World norms.[19]

Of course, Machen and his followers in the OPC came out of mainstream and evangelical Protestant backgrounds and so might be expected to display more affinity to fundamentalists than to confessionalists. Indeed, the biggest difference between the OPC and other confessional Protestants in the United States is ethnicity. For most confessional Protestants, immigration and ethnicity nurtured a separate theological and ecclesiastical identity. Yet while Machen himself came from a blue-blood Southern family in Baltimore, and most orthodox Presbyterians were WASP, even if lower-middle class, the ecclesiastical controversies of the 1920s and 1930s combined with the logic of Reformed theology and polity to give the OPC the sense of marginalization and alienation that ethnic confessionalists experienced. Interestingly enough, Machen and his supporters looked to other Protestant confessional groups as their closest allies. The OPC had warm relations with the Christian Reformed Church, so much so that some church leaders talked about merger for a time. And Machen himself regarded the confessional and catechetical rigor as well as the denominational self-consciousness of both the Christian Reformed and the Missouri Synod as models for his own communion. These and other pieces of evidence indicate that

19. James D. Bratt, "Protestant Immigrants" (paper presented at the Pew Charitable Trusts Project on Minority Faiths in the American Protestant Mainstream, Waltham, Massachusetts, June 1993), 2–5.

Machen and the OPC had more in common with Protestant confessionalists than with neo-evangelicals, fundamentalists, or the Protestant establishment.[20]

Even though the OPC had few members whom observers might describe as hyphenated Americans, during its early history, the church formed the kind of ghetto that sustained ethnic confessionalists. Moving to clearly defined neighborhoods was not possible. Starting Christian schools, producing confessional literature, making the home a center of Presbyterian piety, and establishing ecclesiastical ties with like-minded Presbyterian and Reformed communions were the primary means by which orthodox Presbyterians established a separate identity. If one looks at the many controversies that beleaguered the OPC throughout its first ten years, from the secession of the Bible Presbyterians in 1937 to the withdrawal of Gordon Clark and his supporters, what emerges is a steady and deliberate effort to create a church and nurture a piety different from the dominant forms of American Protestantism. While the OPC's ecclesiology resembled the double separatism that fundamentalists championed against the neo-evangelicals, it was decidedly different. Like fundamentalists, the OPC wanted nothing to do with modernism. But orthodox Presbyterians also opposed—maybe not to the same degree—the theology and ecclesiology of fundamentalists and evangelicals. This opposition was rooted in strict Presbyterianism and moved the OPC outside the standard taxonomy of liberal and evangelical into the neglected category of Protestant confessionalism.

The history of twentieth-century American Protestantism, however, has obscured the nuances of Protestant confessionalism. The opposition between fundamentalists and modernists of the 1920s continues to dominate the categories scholars use, with the unhappy result that Pentecostals and Calvinists, because both profess belief in the supernatural, are lumped together like peas from the same pod. A recognition of confessional Protestantism yields a richer and more accurate picture of American Christianity, or as the old chestnut has it, goes to the heart of historical writing, which is to draw "distinctions between things that really differ." In the case of Presbyterian history alone, identifying the concerns of confessional Presbyterians such as Machen makes sense of the seemingly petty and personal acrimony that eventually divided his denomination. This is not to say that Machen was right or that his course was always wise. But exploring the diversity of views in Ameri-

20. On union discussions between the OPC and CRC, see Henry Zwaanstra, *Catholicity and Secession: A Study of Ecumenicity in the Christian Reformed Church* (Grand Rapids: Eerdmans, 1991), 51–56, 116–17.

can Protestantism does afford the opportunity to understand ideas and movements too often flattened in the dominant historiography.[21]

Confessionalism, Ecumenism, and Church History

As interesting or unusual as confessional Protestantism may be and as helpful as confessional concerns are for understanding particular developments within twentieth-century American Protestantism, the $64,000 question still remains. What difference does it make that Machen was a Presbyterian confessionalist rather than a fundamentalist, and why should anyone care?

It may be too much to argue, as Laurence Moore does, that by focusing on the particular identity of these groups and the process by which they forged their identity, the study of confessional Protestantism goes to the heart of the American experience. But acknowledging the particular and even belligerent aspects of Protestant communions such as the OPC does reveal some of the weaknesses of the history of twentieth-century American Protestantism.[22]

For good or ill, the United States has experienced remarkable religious diversity, and Americans have handled this diversity in a variety of ways, some commendable and some deplorable. Historians have generally celebrated America's religious diversity when it has produced harmony and goodwill. The belief of many Americans, religious historians included, has been that tolerance of such diversity will yield national unity and common purpose. In fact, academic historians have been among the greatest advocates of consensus history, a narrative that stresses stability, harmony, and continuity. Yet historians of American Protestantism have generally ignored the larger pattern of human history that shows that heterogenous cultures breed antagonism and division, not consensus and goodwill.[23]

The two-party model of American Protestantism is the direct result of a consensus approach to American religious history. Though the two-party model appears to stress conflict between conservatives and liberals, the record of hostility most often highlights animosity between

21. Grant Wacker, "You Want It on Plain White or Pumpernickel? Reflections on Two Kinds of History" (paper presented at the Institute for the Study of American Evangelicals Consultation on Advocacy and the Writing of American History, Wheaton, Illinois, April 1994), 3.

22. R. Laurence Moore, *Religious Outsiders and the Making of Americans* (New York: Oxford University Press, 1986), vii–xv.

23. See R. Laurence Moore, "Learning to Love American Religious Pluralism: A Review Essay," *American Jewish History* 77 (1987): 316–30.

sectarians and ecumenicals. Thus, the desire for a religious consensus in which ecumenicity, cosmopolitanism, and cooperation prevail prompts historians to reduce religious differences and conflicts to questions of cooperation and separatism. The dominant interpretations of American Protestantism from Daniel Dorchester to Martin Marty have displayed the assimilationist impulse of the dominant WASP culture. Like ethnic groups, religious traditions are welcome if they shed Old World identities and join the mainstream. If not, they are often written off as psychologically defective or temperamentally incapable of adjusting to life in the big city. The failure of religious historians to take seriously the peculiar views of groups such as confessional Protestants stems in part from fear of the hostility that genuine diversity might produce.

Ironically, however, consensus history and the two-party model it has fostered have probably yielded as much resentment, hostility, and misunderstanding as the exclusive and divisive claims made by religious sectarians. As Machen himself argued, conservatives were not nearly as narrow-minded as liberals. Conservatives, by arguing for a division in the church, actually took liberal ideas seriously, so seriously that they perceived such teaching as a real threat to individual souls. But liberals, he explained, by trying to keep both parties united in the same denomination or organization, displayed real intolerance, for their insistence on unity and cooperation revealed a failure to understand the substance of the conservative argument—that liberal and conservative doctrines were fundamentally at odds. This was the reason why Walter Lippmann said that the liberal plea for tolerance and goodwill was the equivalent of telling conservatives to "smile and commit suicide." Some modern-day historians confirm Lippmann's point. The religious tolerance they display often stems more from indifference than high-mindedness. Thus, to the extent that religious historians make cooperation, ecumenicity, and service to the public the criteria by which they include religious groups, individuals, and ideas in the religious history canon, they manifest not so much an admirable outlook as a general indifference to the doctrines and practices that give believers identity.[24]

Finally, an effort to recover the distinctiveness and history of communions such as confessional Protestants is to acknowledge the reali-

24. Machen, *Christianity and Liberalism,* 167–68; Walter Lippmann, *American Inquisitors* (New York: Macmillan, 1928), 65–66; and Moore, *Religious Outsiders,* 205. For the invectives broad-minded historians have hurled at Machen, see Sandeen, *Roots of Fundamentalism,* which refers to Machen's "perverse obstinacy"; and Robert Moats Miller, "A Compleat (Almost) Guide through the Forest of Fundamentalism," *Reviews in American History* 9 (1981): 397, which says Machen was "quite loony."

ties and problems of America's religious diversity. Possible benefits of such study will be greater understanding of different ideas, greater reluctance to dismiss such differences with condescension or ridicule, and perhaps even the rare quality of respecting those with whom we disagree. Yet even if the study of these groups fails to produce virtue, it does provide a candid and bracing view of the American experiment and the nature of religion. As R. Laurence Moore has argued, the American religious system is only working when it is "creating cracks within denominations, when it is producing novelty, when it is fueling antagonism." This antagonism stems not only from the legacy of religious disestablishment but also from the nature of religious conviction itself.[25]

In his obituary of Machen, H. L. Mencken wrote that "religion, if it is to retain any genuine significance, can never be reduced to a series of sweet attitudes, possible to anyone not actually in jail for felony." Rather, religion, he continued, is "something far more deep-down-diving and mud-upbringing." Mencken concluded that Machen had failed to impress this "obvious fact" upon his fellow Presbyterians but was "undoubtedly right." We may not necessarily concur with Mencken's conclusion. But just as Machen reminded Mencken of the profound dimensions of faith, so the study of confessional Protestantism may remind religious historians of the darker and more complex aspects of the subject they study.[26]

25. Moore, *Religious Outsiders*, 208.
26. Ibid.; H. L. Mencken, "Doctor Fundamentalis," Baltimore *Evening Sun*, 18 January 1937.

11

Evangelicals and Catholics Together, Presbyterians Apart

"Evangelicals and Catholics Together" (hereafter ECT) has been hailed by some as a vehicle for promoting greater unity between Protestants and Catholics. While this reading has some plausibility (and may in fact reflect the motives of its authors), the declaration makes the most sense as an index to the growing political/cultural alliance between conservative and post-liberal Catholics and Protestants, an alliance that minimizes the serious theological and ecclesial matters that divide Western Christianity. I take this view not to impugn the motives of the document's authors or signers but in the interests of achieving genuine unity of the body of Christ. Serious doctrinal matters still divide Protestants and Catholics, and the only way of achieving a real consensus is to take account of such difficulties rather than to ignore them. Moreover, I am troubled by ECT's apparent conflation of the political and religious spheres, a tendency that has characterized the religious right as much as the Christian left. And while all aspects of life may be political, as the feminists have instructed us, I still think it is valuable to keep religion and politics as separate as possible.

Because of ECT's political overtones, I read it as essentially a modernist document. To be sure, its modernism is not that of the old social gospel variety. How could it be when many of the declaration's signers have been outspokenly critical of the politics championed by liberals within the Protestant establishment and the American Catholic hierarchy? Still, many of the individuals who have endorsed ECT (especially the evangelicals) have also distinguished themselves not as theologians or churchmen but as respected generals in the contemporary culture wars, thus raising the suspicion at the outset that ECT is more a statement about the perils confronting American society than an effort to heal the centuries-long division between Catholics and Protestants. In fact, ECT shares many features in common with the Roman Catholic and Protestant modernism that surfaced in the late nineteenth and early twentieth centuries. Furthermore, even though I find the politics of ECT's modernism more congenial than the older version, I am convinced that modernism of the right is just as bad for theology and the church as modernism of the left.

Before readers dismiss this point as the mere ranting of a Protestant sectarian, definitions are in order. Historians of Roman Catholicism and Protestantism in America are generally unanimous in pointing to the adaptation of religious ideas to modern culture as the central trait of theological modernism. In Roman Catholic circles, the "modernist impulse" surfaced during the Americanist controversy of the 1880s and 1890s. In fact, the term *modernism*, whether used to describe cultural or theological developments, emerged first in Roman Catholic discussions when church leaders such as John Ireland and John L. Spalding desired to update the church's teachings and practices in the light of America's political and social realities. This goal was no less true of Protestant liberals such as Harry Emerson Fosdick and Shailer Mathews, who insisted that old Protestant ways were irrelevant to modern society and argued for a new understanding of Christianity that would attract the educated and, more importantly, put the church at the forefront of efforts to secure a just and peaceful society.[1]

Added to this demand for greater relevance was modernism's characteristic blurring of theological distinctions and ecclesiastical lines in order for the church to have a greater impact on American society. Rather than being fettered by the specifics of polity and theology, modernists often overlooked religious differences to pursue a particular vision of American society, one they believed stemmed from religious convictions. The greatest example of interdenominational cooperation was the effort by Protestants during the 1920s to form a national federated church. Nevertheless, cooperative endeavors also extended beyond denominational differences between Protestants to include Protestant-Catholic relations. Protestant and Roman Catholic modernists

---

1. See, for instance, William R. Hutchison, *The Modernist Impulse in American Protestantism* (Cambridge: Harvard University Press, 1976); and Jay P. Dolan, *The American Catholic Experience: A History from Colonial Times to the Present* (Garden City, N.Y.: Doubleday, 1985), 304–20.

recognized that difficulties arising from urban-industrial society made the issues of the sixteenth century less important. In turn, they were criticized by conservatives in their respective communions for being too friendly with the other side.

The parallels between modernism of a century ago and ECT do not necessarily prove my point. These similarities could, of course, merely be coincidental. Yet ECT does exhibit many of the features that typified modernism. One such characteristic is the habit of rendering doctrinal statements in a general manner. For instance, as many Protestant critics have noted, the statement on justification by faith—"we are justified by grace through faith because of Christ"—is particularly weak, lacking the precision of older Catholic and Protestant confessions and the discernment of recent Protestant-Catholic dialogues. (It is, indeed, remarkable that the material principle of the Protestant Reformation can be dispensed with in such a cursory way and that some would hail and defend ECT as primarily a theological statement.) This weakness becomes all the more obvious when considerations about missions and evangelism emerge. If, as some Protestants contend, the Roman Catholic understanding of how humans are made right with God is false and therefore that souls under the influence of such teaching are in peril, how can such Protestants agree and not take issue with the statement that it is "neither theologically legitimate nor a prudent use of resources for one Christian community to proselytize among active adherents of another Christian community"? It is one thing to tolerate insufficient or ambiguous theological declarations, but when such statements begin to alter definitions of mission and witness, it appears that a crucial line has been crossed.

But beyond the merit of the specific wording of particular doctrines is the deeper matter of how to interpret the theological portion of ECT. For instance, a straightforward reading of the statement "Jesus Christ is Lord" would probably render it an affirmation of Christ's deity. But in an age of hermeneutical uncertainty, will straightforward readings really do? Beyond the failure of ECT to elaborate specific doctrines with sufficient precision, the document neglects the question of hermeneutics altogether. This is a glaring omission that ignores developments over the past two hundred years within both Protestant and Catholic communions (e.g., theological liberalism), developments that on the basis of higher criticism and the study of comparative religions have made straightforward readings of confessions such as the Apostles' Creed either naive or incredible even within Christian communions. Can the signers really "affirm together" the doctrines sparsely spelled out in ECT without knowing *how* each signer understands these doctrines? Again, this may sound like the objection of a fundamentalist.

But for good or ill, many of the evangelicals who were asked to endorse ECT are not evangelical in the older sixteenth-century (i.e., Lutheran) sense but rather in the way the term came to be used in the twentieth century. And evangelicalism of this variety, with its roots in the fundamentalist controversy, does have a reputation for questioning the meaning of theological affirmations.

I would argue that the reason ECT skirts theological and hermeneutical issues is that its drafters, much like modernists at the beginning of the twentieth century, assume that the crisis in American culture is so grave that Christians in Protestant and Roman Catholic communions need to work together. Indeed, it is the contemporary cultural crisis (which is profound!) that accounts for the relative ambiguity in the theological section of the document and for the specificity on matters pertaining to Christian contention. Like early twentieth-century Protestant modernism, which popularized the refrain "doctrine divides, ministry unites," ECT slights theology but describes the condition of modern American society and the need for public standards of virtue and vice with remarkably clarity. To make this point, one need only notice that ECT addresses the doctrine of justification in one sentence while devoting three paragraphs (fourteen sentences) to abortion.

While abortion and the social policies sustaining it are genuinely perilous to America's collective soul and well-being, they do not compare to *the* problem of the gospel, that is, how sinful men and women are made right with a holy and righteous God and how they are prepared for life in the next world by life in this one. And while it is proper for Protestants and Catholics to contend together in the political sphere against abortion, it is not clear that they need to contend together as Christians. ECT, however, gives the impression that to oppose abortion one needs to subscribe to the document's theology. In other words, it would appear that one should be a Christian to support the mission described in ECT. But what about the flip side of that proposition? Does one—and some older modernists argued this way—become a Christian by supporting a particular social policy or reform? These questions are not meant to make light of the problems that afflict the United States, but they do point out the problems of mixing religious and social concerns. I believe the task of the church is defined more by the issues surrounding the salvation of the individual soul (proclaiming "Christ and him crucified") than by addressing the moral issues that ravage America. By arguing this way, of course, I run the risk of sounding like a fundamentalist. But then again, that may not be such bad company, for the fundamentalists were the ones who opposed the social gospel (though not always consistently) and who stressed the prior commitment of the church to evangelism and missions.

My reading of ECT is actually supported by recent studies of American Christianity that monitor the tensions between Protestants and Catholics. In his widely acclaimed book *Culture Wars*, James Davison Hunter documented the remarkable shift in Protestant-Catholic relations that ECT appears to illustrate. Hunter argued that conservative Protestants, Catholics, and Jews increasingly have more in common with one another than with progressive or liberal members of the same faith, for it is the orthodox party within Protestantism, Catholicism, and Judaism that believes that divine revelation is the source of truth and morality and, hence, that truth transcends time and place. Progressive believers, in contrast, attempt to adjust religious conviction and teaching to the assumptions and circumstances of contemporary life. For this reason, Hunter concluded that the question of truth—whether it is unchangeable and fixed or constantly changing—is the principal issue dividing American culture and religion.[2]

Yet what emerges from Hunter's analysis, if ECT is any indication, is that evangelicals and Catholics are on better terms, not because of any clearly defined theological or even epistemological consensus about revealed truth but because of a common enemy in the cultural and political antagonisms that have surfaced in the United States since the 1960s. To be sure, Hunter would probably put the ECT folk into his orthodox camp. But judging by the theological rationale for Christian unity proposed in ECT (and finding few efforts to bridge the Protestant-Catholic divide beyond the serious but nevertheless obscure discussions between Lutherans and Catholics), Hunter's use of the term *orthodox* to describe this alliance looks ill-advised. This is not to say that the individual signers of the document are not orthodox as defined by their communions. Rather, the point is that ECT leaves orthodoxy surrounded with too much haze to qualify as a particularly good theological statement, which, of course, should be the first criterion for making common cause in the name of Christ.

The way the document is framed only confirms this point. Rather than trying to make headway on the "disagreements and differences" that ECT mentions (most having to do with ecclesiology and the sacraments), the declaration merely lists them, says they cannot be resolved now, pledges to study them more in the future, and quickly moves on to the matter of contending together. For me, this juxtaposition is revealing because it demonstrates how ECT gives more attention to the woes of American society than to the work and ministry of the church (whether Protestant or Catholic). Now, most of the believers in the

2. James Davison Hunter, *Culture Wars: The Struggle to Define America* (New York: Basic Books, 1991), 35–51.

United States may think that the welfare of their country is more important than what happens during the celebration of the Lord's Supper, but this concern does not necessarily make them orthodox.

Mark Noll, one of the signers of ECT, has also suggested a typology for evaluating Protestant-Catholic relations that sustains suspicions that the document is more a product of the current culture wars than a watershed in ecumenical relations. Noll detects three different outlooks within American Christianity that color and steer Protestant-Catholic relations. First, there are New Catholics and New Protestants who believe that Christianity is relative to time and place and that American values (whether on the left or the right) are the surest way to progress. Next come Old Catholics and Old Protestants who affirm the fixity of dogma and who put loyalty to Christian convictions above political commitments. Finally, there are Americanist Catholics and Americanist Protestants, Christians who differ about the permanence or relativity of Protestant and Catholic creeds but hold to the superiority of American values and institutions.[3] Judged by this typology, ECT emerges most clearly as an expression of Americanist Christianity. The document is too critical of moral and epistemological relativism to be compatible with the historicism of New Protestantism or New Catholicism. Yet ECT is too ambiguous in its theological sections to satisfy the demands of Old Catholics or Old Protestants for fidelity to the historic distinctives of the faith. This leaves the category of Americanist Christianity, and I would argue that ECT fits remarkably well here (despite the best intentions of some of its defenders), not by default but because the document pays more attention to America's social ills than to the theological differences between Catholics and Protestants. Indeed, ECT implies that Protestants and Catholics should lay aside disputed points of doctrine to contend and witness together. Again, this may not have been the aim, but those of us who were not part of the discussions that led to the document's ratification and publication have only the text to go by. It is difficult to read ECT, comb through its meager doctrinal substance, compare its theology to its cultural affirmations, look at some of the celebrities who signed it, and not conclude that political motives were as much at work as religious convictions. As Noll warns about Protestant-Catholic relations, "Motives may be Christian, but the arguments actually employed Americanist."[4]

3. Mark A. Noll, "The Eclipse of Old Hostilities *between* and the Potential for New Strife *among* Catholics and Protestants Since Vatican II," in *Uncivil Religion*, ed. Robert Bellah et al. (New York: Crossroad, 1987), chap. 5.
    4. Ibid., 99.

I am an Old Protestant by Noll's standards, and my most serious objection to ECT is that it misconstrues the work and mission of the church. I believe that churches, not individuals, are the final arbiters when determining matters of Christian unity or ecumenicity. Some signers of ECT have claimed that all they hoped to do with this declaration was affirm their unity as brothers and sisters in Christ. The signers may think they have done that. But it is a fairly hollow affirmation of unity that fails to result in the ultimate demonstration of Christian fraternity, namely, partaking of Christ's body and blood in the Lord's Supper. Furthermore, I could not in good conscience recommend ECT to my own church as a standard for membership or as a basis for ecumenical relations with other Christian communions. Nor could I conceive of a church embracing ECT as an adequate statement of its beliefs or mission. In the sphere in which the church is called to minister, what the apostle Paul calls the "things that are unseen and eternal," ECT is sadly deficient. As the apostle also reminds us, it is "one Lord, one faith, one baptism" that unites Christians. Unfortunately, as ECT apparently shows, vague theological affirmations and specific public policies have a greater chance of achieving Christian unity today than careful doctrinal formulations and political agnosticism. I can do no better than reiterate Peter Berger at this point. Neither the religious left's nor the religious right's agenda "belongs in the pulpit, in the liturgy, or in any statement that claims to have the authority of the gospel. *Any* cultural or political agenda embellished with such authority is a manifestation of 'works-righteousness' and *ipso facto* an act of apostasy."[5]

This does not mean that individual Christians are free from social and political responsibilities. The lordship of Christ extends to all points of his creation, and believers are bound to make his rule as evident as possible in all spheres of the created order. But the problem is that we lack sufficient wisdom to know what Christ's lordship should look like in politics, law, and economics, for instance. The Bible does not reveal a blueprint for a Christian society (at least, that is what we keep telling the theonomists). For this reason, Christians who engage in political activities should do so with great humility, recognizing that they do so on the basis of general revelation or the light of nature, that part of God's truth that is also accessible to nonbelievers. It also means that the church, as an institution, must refrain from all political activities. The Bible calls the church to proclaim the Good News about Christ. It also holds the power to bind the consciences of men and women in the areas in which God has revealed himself clearly. To use

5. Peter Berger, "Different Gospels: The Social Sources of Apostasy," *This World* (1987): 13.

that power for purposes that are unclear is, as Berger says, an act of apostasy.

So while I may be faulted for exhibiting a lack of charity in my reading of ECT, I remain convinced that the document is inadequate either for achieving greater Christian unity or for promoting a particular cultural agenda. In the first case, there is too little theology, and in the second, there is too much. And while I sympathize with most of the cultural concerns expressed in ECT, my Christian convictions give me grave reservations about the document's overall purposes and usefulness.

12

What Can Presbyterians Learn from Lutherans?

Celebrating Reformation Day is an activity typically reserved for Lutherans. After all, October 31 marks the day when Martin Luther nailed his Ninety-Five Theses to the cathedral door and launched the Protestant Reformation. James Nuechterlein, a Lutheran historian who now edits the journal *First Things*, recalls that when he was a child, Lutherans "enthusiastically celebrated" October 31. The services he remembers were "unabashed exercises in Protestant triumphalism." Such enthusiastic celebration owed much to the marginal status of the German-Americans who comprised the majority of American Lutheranism. "Protestantism in those days," Nuechterlein explains, "still constituted the vital center of American religious culture." Lutherans, in turn, "were located some distance from the center of that center— which was occupied, more or less in order, by Episcopalians, Presbyterians"—mainline, that is, not Orthodox—"Methodists, and Congregationalists." But on Reformation Day, Lutherans "could escape our marginal status and enter fully into the grand anti-papist communion" of American Protestantism.[1]

In some ways, it is ironic that Presbyterians celebrate Reformation Day, given that it is a day of greater importance to the theological descendants of Martin Luther. Perhaps part of the reason why members of the Orthodox Presbyterian Church (OPC) observe Reformation Day has to do with their own feelings of cultural inferiority. Lutherans may

1. James Nuechterlein, "The Lutheran Prospect," *First Things* 86 (October 1998): 12.

have been at the margins of American Protestantism, but at least they could point to professors of church history, such as Sydney Ahlstrom and Jaroslav Pelikan at Yale, Martin Marty at the University of Chicago, and Lewis Spitz at Stanford, who had moved from the province of Lutheranism into the centers of American learning and mainstream Protestantism. George Marsden, who now teaches at the University of Notre Dame, is the closest the OPC has come to producing a scholar with national recognition in the United States. All the more reason, then, for Orthodox Presbyterians to celebrate Reformation Day with gusto. For one brief day they can go from a denomination in need of explanation to the central current of Western history since the sixteenth century.

The desire to feel important, even if only for one day, may also explain why on Reformation Day Presbyterians often hear glowing and inspiring words about the genius not only of the Protestant Reformation but also of the Reformed tradition more narrowly. Of course, Calvinists trace their lineage back to Luther's initial discovery of the doctrine of justification by faith, a doctrine on which Presbyterians and Lutherans agree and a doctrine that moved the likes of Ulrich Zwingli, John Calvin, and Martin Bucer to initiate even greater reforms in the church. But those greater reforms are the point at which Presbyterians and Reformed begin to part company with Lutherans. Luther, some Calvinists argue, went only so far and not far enough at that. The Calvinist wing of the Reformation, therefore, pushed beyond Luther's initial efforts and reformed all aspects of the church, from its theology all the way to its polity and worship, according to the Word of God. For some Presbyterians and Reformed, this reform effort did not stop with the church. It kept going out the doors of the church and into the markets and city councils of Western Europe, thus transforming the life and culture of the West.

This is how Christopher Dawson described the difference between Calvinism and Lutheranism:

> Behind Democracy there lies the spiritual world of Calvinism and the Free Churches, which is . . . completely different in its political and social outlook from the world of Lutheranism, and which has had a far greater influence and closer connection with what we know as Western civilization without further qualification. . . . The genius of Calvin was that of an organizer and legislator, severe, logical, and inflexible in purpose, and consequently it was he and not Luther who inspired Protestantism with the will to dominate the world and to change society and culture.[2]

So much for Lutheran triumphalism.

2. Christopher Dawson, *The Judgment of Nations* (New York: Sheed and Ward, 1942), 44–45.

Abraham Kuyper rendered a similar estimate of the differences between Calvinism and Lutheranism in his famous *Lectures on Calvinism*, given over one hundred years ago at Princeton Seminary. Kuyper said:

> Luther never worked out his fundamental thought. And Protestantism, taken in a general sense, without further differentiation, is either a purely negative conception without content, or a chameleon-like name which the deniers of the God-Man like to adopt as their shield. Only of Calvinism can it be said that it has consistently and logically followed out the lines of the Reformation, has established not only Churches but also States, has set its stamp upon social and public life, and has thus, in the full sense of the word, created for the whole life of man a world of thought entirely its own.[3]

What then do Presbyterians have to learn from Lutherans? Can they learn merely how to be as enthusiastic in celebrations of Reformation Day as Lutherans used to be? Or could it be that Lutherans have something to teach Calvinists and themselves about the dangers of Protestant triumphalism? What follows are a few observations about the genius of Lutheranism for the purpose of gaining a better understanding of the Reformation's significance. An appreciation of Lutheranism may not only lead to a greater regard for Luther's accomplishments but also help Presbyterians learn that the real spirit of Reformation Day is not pride and celebration but humility and sobriety.

Why Lutherans Might Be Proud

One reason for learning humility from Lutherans has simply to do with statistics. Those in the conservative neck of the Presbyterian woods tend to think of themselves as prominent and gaining even more importance. In some OPC and Presbyterian Church of America (PCA) circles, one even hears talk about transforming the culture. In fact, some discussions about PCA church planting efforts in New York City speak of redeeming the Big Apple, a tall order that might call for a little more restraint. The world may not be the Calvinists' oyster, but sometimes conservative Presbyterians think and act as if they aspire to be power brokers in American life.

And then Calvinists run into the wall of American Lutheranism, a world that is foreign to most Presbyterians, whether conservative or liberal. The OPC, for instance, numbers approximately 22,000 mem-

3. Abraham Kuyper, *Lectures on Calvinism* (Grand Rapids: Eerdmans, 1931), 22–23.

bers, and growth over the past few years has been encouraging. The PCA has roughly 275,000 members, a figure that often tempts Orthodox Presbyterians to break the Tenth Commandment. If we are such a good church, some lament, why is the OPC so small? What is the PCA doing right? But these questions do not make much difference in comparison to statistics for comparable Lutheran denominations. The Wisconsin Evangelical Lutheran Synod, which some Protestant observers say is the Lutheran equivalent of the OPC, has approximately 400,000 members, which means that this virtually unknown denomination is larger than the OPC and the PCA put together. Then there is the Lutheran Church–Missouri Synod, the rough Lutheran equivalent of the PCA, meaning that it is a little more progressive, a little more affluent, and a little more open to evangelicalism than the Wisconsin Synod. The Missouri Synod has a whopping 2.5 million members, which means that even if all the conservative Presbyterian and Reformed denominations that comprised the North American Presbyterian and Reformed Churches (NAPARC) were lumped together, there would be only one conservative Calvinist in America for every five conservative Lutherans. If this comparison extended all the way to include both mainline and conservative Lutherans and Presbyterians, the statistics would not be much more encouraging for American Presbyterianism. The OPC, the PCA, and the mainline Presbyterian Church in the U.S.A. account for only approximately 4 million Americans who identify themselves as Presbyterian. In contrast, membership in the Wisconsin Synod, the Missouri Synod, and the mainline Evangelical Lutheran Church in America weighs in at approximately 8 million, which raises an interesting question about whether America is more hospitable to Lutherans than to Presbyterians.

The point is not that numbers are a good index to the health of a church. Faithfulness matters more than size. The OPC should not compromise its witness, teachings, or worship to gain more members. Still, statistics are telling about what kind of mark conservative Presbyterianism is making on American society. If conservative Presbyterians want to talk about transforming culture and the best they can do is muster only 300,000 members, then Calvinists might want to consider the example of confessional Lutherans in America, who are much less inclined to talk about the transformation of culture and yet outnumber confessional Presbyterians ten to one. Comparisons with Lutherans teach Presbyterians a lesson of humility. (By the way, humility need not be limited to a comparison of church membership statistics. Confessional Lutherans sponsor a number of good universities and colleges, publish a variety of learned theological journals, and count within their ranks Christian scholars who write thoughtfully about most aspects of the Christian life.)

Why Lutherans Should Be Humble

Nevertheless, statistics are not the best source for learning humility from Lutherans. Much more important is the theology of Lutheranism itself. One of the reasons why Lutherans talk less about the transformation of culture, and so talk and act more humbly with regard to their own abilities and accomplishments, stems from the theology of the cross that lies at the heart of Luther's understanding of justification by faith. As much as Luther's doctrine of justification revolutionized Christianity in sixteenth-century Western Europe, his notion of the theology of the cross is perhaps just as pivotal for understanding the gospel revealed in God's holy Word.

The theology of the cross is basically a way of considering how God makes himself known to humans. It stands in direct contrast with the theology of glory. In 1518, Luther wrote, "That person does not deserve to be called a theologian who looks upon the invisible things of God as though they were clearly perceptible in those things which have actually happened." In other words, the man who tries to know God on the basis of nature and the created world will always fail. But, Luther continued, "he deserves to be called a theologian . . . who comprehends the visible and manifest things of God seen through suffering and the cross."[4] Just as Moses could not see the face of God (Exodus 33) but had to content himself with God's back, what Luther called God's rearward parts, so men and women cannot know God except through the cross and suffering of Christ. For Luther, God's ways run directly contrary to the wisdom of the world or the speculations of the theology of glory. Instead of making himself known through the splendor of creation and the power of his sovereign rule over the world, God chooses to reveal himself through what the world considers foolish, base, ignoble, and weak.

The theology of the cross, however, is not simply a way of understanding the way God reveals himself and his purpose in history. For Luther, true knowledge of God could not be separated from a right relationship with God. For this reason, the theology of the cross not only opposes the efforts of humans to know God through creation but also condemns their endeavors to make themselves righteous before God's justice. The theology of glory tempts a person to make a deal with God

4. Martin Luther, "Heidelberg Disputation," in *Martin Luther's Basic Theological Writings*, ed. Timothy F. Lull (Minneapolis: Fortress, 1989), 43.

on the basis of his or her own moral goodness. The theology of glory is in effect a theology of works or self-righteousness. But the theology of the cross undercuts any grounds for self-confidence. Through the theology of the cross, a person moves from trying to earn salvation to leaning on God entirely for redemption. In sum, just as the cross demonstrated the ultimate humility of Christ in his earthly ministry, so the theology of the cross humbles humans by revealing that they cannot know God or be righteous before God apart from the saving work of Christ, which paradoxically uses what is weak, foolish, and poor to triumph over the strong, wise, and rich.

A good way to illustrate how the theology of the cross functioned in Luther's teaching is to look at his commentary on the Magnificat, that is, the prayer the virgin Mary prayed after hearing that she would give birth to the Messiah. In this prayer, Mary begins by praising God for regarding her poor and lowly estate and for making her an instrument of his blessing. She also recounts the mighty deeds that God has done, generation after generation, for those who fear him. God has, she says, "scattered those who are proud in their inmost thoughts. He has brought down rulers from their thrones but has lifted up the humble. He has filled the hungry with good things but has sent the rich away empty" (Luke 1:51–53). This is precisely the sort of paradox that Luther had in mind with the theology of the cross: How God could do great and mighty things by humbling the powerful and making the humble strong. Luther wrote in the introduction to his commentary, "Just as God in the beginning of creation made the world out of nothing, whence He is called the Creator and Almighty, so His manner of working continues unchanged. Even now and to the end of the world, all His works are such that out of that which is nothing, worthless, despised, wretched, and dead, He makes that which is something, precious, honorable, blessed, and living."[5]

In Luther's estimation, nothing better illustrated the ways of God than his selection of Mary to be the human vehicle through which our Lord would be conceived. "Let us make it very plain for the sake of the simple," Luther wrote:

> Doubtless there were in Jerusalem daughters of the chief priests and counselors who were rich, comely, youthful, cultured, and held in high renown by all the people; even as it is today with the daughters of kings, princes, and men of wealth. . . . Even in her own town of Nazareth [Mary] was not the daughter of one of the chief rulers, but a poor and plain citizen's daughter, whom none looked up to or esteemed. To her neighbors and their daughters she was but a simple maiden, tending the

5. Martin Luther, "The Magnificat," in *Luther's Works*, vol. 21, *The Sermon on the Mount and the Magnificat*, ed. Jaroslav Pelikan (St. Louis: Concordia, 1956), 299.

cattle and doing the housework, and doubtless esteemed no more than any poor maidservant today, who does as she is told around the house.[6]

This was hardly the stem and root from which the world would have expected the rod and flower of King David to spring.

It was, of course, incredible that a virgin could give birth to a child—it was equally miraculous for a branch to grow out of a dead tree stump as the prophet Isaiah had predicted. What made the incarnation of Christ through the womb of the virgin Mary all the more remarkable was the utter disparity between mother and son. Luther explained:

> In the days of David and Solomon the royal stem and line of David had been green and flourishing, fortunate in its great glory, might, and riches, and famous in the eyes of the world. But in the latter days, when Christ was to come, the priests had usurped this honor and were the sole rulers, while the royal line of David had become so impoverished and despised that it was like a dead stump, so that there was no hope or likelihood that a king descended from it would ever attain to any great glory. But when all seemed most unlikely—comes Christ, and is born of the despised stump, of the poor and lowly maiden. The rod and flower springs from her whom Sir Annas' or Caiaphas' daughter would not have deigned to have for her humblest lady's maid.[7]

The mother of Christ, then, is a perfect illustration of the theology of the cross. As 1 Peter 5:5 says, "God opposes the proud but gives grace to the humble." This paradox is, according to Luther, the source of the believer's love and praise of God. When we know that God is one who "looks into the depths and helps only the poor, despised, afflicted, miserable, forsaken and those who are nothing," then we will have a "hearty love" for God. And the theology of the cross helps to explain why God acts and reveals himself the way he does. "For this reason," Luther wrote, "God has also imposed death on us all and laid the cross of Christ together with countless sufferings and afflictions on His beloved children." In the depths of suffering and trials, God is our refuge and shows himself "known and worthy of love and praise."[8]

The history of redemption recorded in Scripture illustrates not only the theology of the cross. Luther's insights on the way God uses suffering and affliction also have important repercussions for the way Presbyterians have understood history since the time of the Bible and their place in it. Just as God's salvation comes through weak and lowly

6. Ibid., 301.
7. Ibid., 302.
8. Ibid., 300.

means, so his ongoing work of the church goes forward in the same manner. Instead of displaying riches, power, and glory in this life, the kingdom of God follows a different course. The church, which for Luther is the manifestation of God's kingdom in this life, has means and ends that the world considers foolish and weak, and her members are blessed in the sight of God while in the world's eyes are "the most wretched of all."

One implication of this understanding of the church is the Lutheran doctrine of the two kingdoms. Just as there are two kinds of righteousness according to the theology of the cross and the theology of glory, so the two kingdoms, that of the church and that of the state, have two standards for good conduct. Christian righteousness is rooted in faith that is the work of the Holy Spirit. Only those who trust the promises that God makes in the gospel of Jesus Christ are righteous before him. Civil righteousness, in contrast, stems from a code of human conduct that all citizens are capable of maintaining, whether Christian or not. The norms for the church are faith and love, but the standards for public order are reason and justice. Consequently, the doctrine of the two kingdoms teaches that while one may be righteous before the eyes of men, the same individual is unrighteous in the sight of God unless clothed in the imputed righteousness of Christ, received by faith alone. One kingdom, that of the state, is earthly and temporal, but the kingdom of God is spiritual and eternal. As the Apology of the Augsburg Confession (1531) puts it:

> Christ's kingdom is spiritual; it is the knowledge of God in the heart, the fear of God and faith, the beginning of eternal righteousness and eternal life. At the same time it lets us make outward use of the legitimate political ordinances of the nation in which we live, just as it lets us make use of medicine or architecture, food or drink or air. The Gospel does not introduce any new laws about the civil estate, but commands us to obey the existing laws, whether they were formulated by heathens or by others, and in this obedience to practice love. (Art. 16)

A Reformed World-and-Life View

At this point some Presbyterians might begin to object to Luther's doctrine of the theology of the cross. The doctrine of the two kingdoms, you see, is supposed to be an idea foreign to Calvinism. In his classic book *Christ and Culture*, H. Richard Niebuhr contrasted the Reformed and Lutheran understandings of the relationship between Christ and culture precisely at this point of the doctrine of the two kingdoms. Niebuhr said that Lutherans hold to the model of "Christ and culture in paradox." According to this perspective, a person is "seen as subject to two moralities, and as citizen of two worlds that are not only discontinuous with each other but largely opposed. In the *polarity* and *tension* of Christ and culture life must be lived precariously and sinfully in the hope of a justification which lies beyond history."[9] The last stanza of "A Mighty Fortress" echoes this conception of the Christian life.

> That Word above all earthly powers,
> No thanks to them, abideth;
> The Spirit and the gifts are ours
> Through him who with us sideth;
> Let goods and kindred go,
> this mortal life also;
> The body they may kill:
> God's truth abideth still;
> His kingdom is forever.

For Luther, the kingdom of God does not depend on earthly rulers or believers' prosperity in this world. God's kingdom is otherworldly and will gain the victory in the end, even though his people may in the meantime be forced to live without "goods" or "kindred."

The Calvinist worldview, according to Niebuhr, stands in contrast to the Lutheran outlook. Instead of "Christ and culture in paradox," the Reformed view is "Christ the transformer of culture." Niebuhr wrote that Calvin, more than Luther, "looks for the present permeation of all life by the gospel." In addition to his understanding of vocation, the relationship between church and state, human nature, and the resurrection of the body, Calvin's idea of God's sovereignty "leads to the thought that what the gospel promises and makes possible, . . . is the transformation of mankind and all its nature and culture into a kingdom of God in which the laws of the kingdom have been written upon inward parts."[10] Rather than looking for salvation in the world to come, the Calvinist looks for evidence of redemption in this world, not only in the sanctification of individuals but in the transformation of all spheres of life.

Whether or not Niebuhr was entirely accurate, the contrast he drew between Lutheranism and Calvinism raises serious concerns, especially if Presbyterians begin to think too highly of their contribution to human history. One obvious concern is pride. The other is confusing the ways of the church with those of the world. Both problems are evi-

---

9. H. Richard Niebuhr, *Christ and Culture* (New York: Harper, 1951), 43.
10. Ibid., 218.

dent in the words of one of the all-time great Calvinist transformers of culture, Abraham Kuyper. Kuyper was the Dutch Calvinist minister and theologian who became a journalist, founded a university, led in the formation of a new church, began a political party, and ruled as prime minister in the Netherlands at the beginning of the twentieth century. If anyone could legitimately claim to speak of the transformation of culture, Kuyper could, and Kuyper's articulation of the Reformed world-and-life view has inspired countless Calvinists to go into all walks of life, pursue them to the glory of God, and show the difference that Calvinism makes not simply for religion but for all spheres of life. Here is how Kuyper explained the Reformed world-and-life view:

> Everything that has been created was, in its creation, furnished by God with an unchangeable law of existence. And because God has fully ordained such laws and ordinances for all of life, therefore the Calvinist demands that all life be consecrated to His service, in strict obedience. A religion confined to the closet, the cell, or the church, therefore Calvin abhors. . . . God is present in all life, with the influence of His omnipresent and almighty power, and no sphere of human life is conceivable in which religion does not maintain its demands that God shall be praised, that God's ordinances shall be observed, and that every *labora* shall be permeated with its *ora* in fervent and ceaseless prayer.[11]

As inspiring as Kuyper's vision of Calvinism may be, it has at times fostered pride that seeks to attribute all the advances of Western civilization to the Reformed tradition. According to Kuyper, "The history of the Netherlands, of Europe and of the world would have been . . . painfully sad" without the influence of Calvinism, which has made that history "bright and inspiring." Aside from fostering an overly high estimate of the Calvinist contribution to culture that other Christian traditions would certainly dispute, Kuyper's idea of the Reformed world-and-life view nurtures a tendency to look to worldly accomplishments rather than theological, liturgical, or ecclesiastical faithfulness as marks of Calvinism's success. It was not enough that Calvinism reformed the church and her teaching. For Kuyper, what proved the truth of Calvinism was its "indomitable energy" that fermented in "every department of human activity" and "imparted a new impulse for an entirely new development of life to the whole of Western Europe."[12]

Kuyper's effort to rehabilitate Calvinism, as admirable and rigorous as it was, was at least indirectly responsible for the misunderstanding of the Reformed tradition that has most recently plagued the Christian

11. Kuyper, *Lectures*, 53.
12. Ibid., 73.

Reformed Church. In this case, being Reformed has less to do with the five points of Calvinism and the teachings of the Heidelberg Catechism, Belgic Confession, and Canons of Dort and more to do with a Reformed world-and-life view about all spheres of life, from agriculture to quantum physics. For instance, one writer said that to be Reformed means extending the sovereignty of God in personal salvation to all of life. "We want everything around us to be brought into conformity with Jesus' plan to make all things new. . . . We are not shy about poking our noses into every nook and cranny of the world. . . . We Reformed Christians are not content to confine the Lord to our hearts."[13] The application of the Reformed worldview to all of life has progressed so far that is it now possible to be Reformed without being a Calvinist. This is what happens when you begin to give the Reformed world-and-life view priority over the Calvinist understanding of sin and grace. If being Reformed means that "creation has priority over salvation, that salvation is not the escape from or elevation above creation but the *restoration* of creation,"[14] then life in this world begins to look more important than preparation for the life to come. Again, Kuyper may have introduced this problem into Reformed circles by insisting that Calvinists needed to go beyond Lutherans. The Reformed could not be content with salvation or the church; they had a holy duty to transform their society according to God's revealed principles. According to Kuyper, salvation of souls was not enough. Real Calvinism had to change society.

If Calvinists were more Lutheran, would they be less inclined to yield to the temptation of triumphalism and social Christianity that afflicts the Reformed tradition? Obviously, the humility taught by the theology of the cross and the doctrine of the two kingdoms puts a strong brake on conceiving of Christianity as the transformation of culture. Lutheranism especially teaches that God is gaining the victory not through human accomplishments in making a better world but through the suffering and turmoil of our pilgrimage here. Could it be, in fact, that the aggressiveness associated with the Reformed world-and-life view is a form of the theology of glory to which the Corinthian church aspired? The Corinthians wanted a return to the glory days of Israel and could not see that God had actually accomplished far more through the cross of Christ—foolishness to the Gentiles—than through all the glories of David or Solomon. The cross, as Paul taught, reverses all human expectations and shows, through the eyes of faith, that when Christians are weak God is strong, when they are poor God is rich, and when they are defeated God triumphs. This is a lesson that Presbyterians could well

13. John Suk, "Alien Transformers," *The Banner* 129 (21 March 1994): 2.
14. Ibid.

learn from Lutherans. It would not only keep them humble but would also teach them how to regard the present earthly life.

But Presbyterians may not have to go to Lutherans only to learn this lesson. Ironically, they can learn it from Calvin, who was closer to Luther's theology of the cross than Kuyper's theology of cultural transformation. According to Calvin, the Christian life is a pilgrimage filled with suffering and defeat. He wrote:

> Then only do we rightly advance by the discipline of the cross, when we learn that this life, judged in itself, is troubled, turbulent, unhappy, in countless ways, and in no respect clearly happy; that all those things which are judged to be its goods are uncertain, fleeting, vain, and vitiated by many intermingled evils. From this, at the same time, we conclude that in this life we are to seek and hope for nothing but struggle; when we think of our crown, we are to raise our eyes to heaven. For this we must believe; that the mind is never seriously aroused to desire and ponder the life to come unless it be previously imbued with contempt for the present life. Indeed, there is no middle ground between these two: either world must become worthless to us or hold us bound by intemperate love of it.[15]

Calvin's teaching suggests that the theology of the cross is not foreign to the Reformed tradition but actually flows directly from a proper understanding of justification and sanctification. His attitude toward life in this world is clearly not the one usually associated with the Reformed worldview, but it was not an aberration in Calvin's thinking. It was constantly on display in all his expressions of piety.

For instance, in the hymn "I Greet Thee Who My Sure Redeemer Art," commonly attributed to Calvin, we see a sober estimate of the trials and suffering of this life coupled with the reassuring hope of salvation through Jesus Christ, our only comfort in life and death. The last stanza reads:

> Our hope is in no other save in thee;
> Our faith is built upon thy promise free;
> O grant to us such stronger hope and sure;
> That we can boldly conquer and endure.

Here is a different picture of Calvinism, not one of the triumphant crusader conquering the world for Christ and his kingdom but rather one of the suffering pilgrim who endures pain and persecution, just as the

---

15. John Calvin, *Institutes of the Christian Religion*, ed. John T. McNeill, trans. Ford Lewis Battles (Philadelphia: Westminster, 1960), III.ix.1–2.

Savior did, who hopes for the life to come, and whose hope for victory lies only in what God has done to conquer sin and death through the suffering and death of Christ.

In closing, then, let one of the prayers that Calvin wrote be a reminder of the humility that all Christians, whether Lutheran or Calvinist, need to keep close at hand. Its theme of suffering, endurance, and hope for the world to come is precisely what Presbyterians need to learn, whether from Luther or from Calvin. Its lesson comes closest to capturing the real significance of the Protestant Reformation, a reform movement that on its best behavior boasted not in the glories and might of human effort but in the merits and benefits of a suffering Savior. Calvin wrote:

> Grant, Almighty God, that as you try us in the warfare of the cross, and arouse most powerful enemies whose barbarity might justly terrify and dishearten us, were we not depending on your aid,—O grant, that we may call to mind how wonderfully you did in former times deliver your people, and how seasonably you did bring them help, when they were oppressed and entirely overwhelmed, so that we may learn at this day to flee to your protection, and not doubt, that when you become propitious to us there is in you sufficient power to preserve us, and to lay prostrate our enemies, how much soever they may now exult and think to triumph above the heavens, so that they may at length know by experience that they are earthly and frail creatures, whose life and condition is like the mist which soon vanishes; and may we learn to aspire after that blessed eternity which is laid up for us in heaven through Christ our Lord. Amen.[16]

---

16. John Calvin, *Devotions and Prayers of John Calvin,* ed. Charles E. Edwards (Grand Rapids: Baker, 1960), 79.

Part 5

WORSHIP AND REVIVAL

13

The Irony of American Presbyterian Worship

Observers of the current religious scene in the United States should not be faulted if they sometimes lose track of that ever present but always elusive dividing line between liberal and evangelical Protestants. Without a scorecard, identifying the players on each side is tricky, especially when it comes to matters of liturgy and worship. The evasive quality of Protestant divisions, for instance, was recently on display in the pages of *First Things*, a journal that leans to the cultural, political, and Roman Catholic right. On one page, in a short review of Donald Miller's new book on Calvary Chapel and the Vineyard Movement, the churches that have done much to popularize Praise and Worship forms of worship (hereafter P & W), the reviewer lauds these movements as the wave of the future for American Protestantism. Although he admits that these evangelicals are antiritualistic, anti-creedal, and anti-intellectual, he gives them credit for emphasizing personal accountability and obedience to biblical norms. Their search for simplicity, accordingly, makes them the odds-on favorite to beat those churches "dominated by eighteenth-century hymns, routinized liturgy, and bureaucratized layers of social organization."[1] A few pages later, in a review of Gertrude Himmelfarb's book, *One Nation, Two Cultures*, the analysis continues to be upbeat regarding the cultural and religious right that contemporary evangelicalism has become. The reviewer notes that

---

1. Walter Sundberg, review of *Reinventing American Protestantism: Christianity in the New Millennium, First Things* 98 (December 1999): 59–60.

Himmelfarb believes America is experiencing yet another Great Awakening and that this will provide a "modest reformation" of the "elite cultural revolutions of this century."[2] The impression conveyed by *First Things*, then, is that evangelical Protestantism in the form of the charismatic renewal is an ally of cultural traditionalists in the contemporary culture war.[3] What these reviewers fail to notice, along with the authors of the books under review, is that the cultural sensibility of evangelicals that is embodied in contemporary worship is at odds with the traditionalism, formalism, and cultural standards advocated by cultural conservatives, whether Protestant, Roman Catholic, Jewish, or secular. For that reason, perceptive readers of *First Things* must have been reaching for Dramamine to calm stomachs upset by the sudden shift in perspective.

Let me explain. People with strong ethical beliefs are, according to books such as those by James Davison Hunter and Gertrude Himmelfarb, supposed to be on the conservative end of the cultural spectrum. That supposition puts evangelicals squarely on the cultural right. In contrast, the mainline churches, whose morals many think are loose, are supposed to be on the liberal side of the culture wars. But the worship wars are another matter altogether. When it comes to order of worship and liturgical forms, evangelical Protestants turn out to be about as conservative as the script writers for the *Simpsons* television show. Meanwhile, mainline Protestants have emerged as the chief advocates of traditional worship and liturgy. Furthermore, the worship wars confuse most of the categories used to assess the culture wars. If the cultural left and right are supposed to have different ethical standards, with the left leaning toward relativism and the right advocating strict moral standards, what does it say about evangelical morality that proponents of contemporary worship seem to disregard the first table of the Decalogue? After all, these commandments have a fair amount to say about worship. In other words, the cultural and religious left in American Protestantism turns out to be the liturgical right, and the cultural and religious right is actually the chief force behind liturgical liberalism. Hence the difficulty in keeping track of cultural conservatism among Protestants in the United States.

Why few have yet to note these inconsistencies and reversals is not as much the concern here as it is simply to acknowledge the significant error of equating the culture and worship wars. Such an acknowledg-

2. Anonymous, review of *One Nation, Two Cultures, First Things* 98 (December 1999): 64.

3. See James Davison Hunter, *Culture Wars: The Struggle to Define America* (New York: Basic Books, 1991).

ment is necessary if those who cherish and wish to perpetuate the distinctive character of Reformed worship are to make any headway within their own congregations or discern genuine allies in the wider culture. The same ambiguities that hamper interpreters of the worship and the culture wars also plague those who try to make sense of contemporary American Presbyterianism. Ever since the exodus of J. Gresham Machen and his small band of followers from the northern Presbyterian Church, the premise guiding most studies of twentieth-century Presbyterianism has been that the mainline church is liberal and the sideline churches are conservative. Of course, the conservative-vs.-liberal shorthand does not receive unanimous approval. But regardless of the rubric used, whether sectarian vs. ecumenical, dogmatic vs. broadminded, or traditional vs. progressive, most Presbyterians have an innate sense that a substantial divide separates the Presbyterian Church, U.S.A. from either the Orthodox Presbyterian Church or the Presbyterian Church in America and that this division corresponds in large measure to the former's discomfort with being right-wing and the latter two denominations' fears about liberalism.

This premise regarding the left and right wings of American Presbyterianism would suggest that anyone looking for traces of John Calvin's liturgy would have a better chance of finding it in those denominations that look to the past for examples of faithfulness rather than in those that have endeavored to adapt Christianity to modern times. But such a seeker would be sadly misinformed because more congregations in the PCUSA are likely to follow the Genevan order of service than those in the OPC or the PCA. If this judgment sounds fanciful, consider that at the same time the PCUSA was releasing a new hymnal that featured as complete a psalter as any Presbyterian hymnal of the twentieth century other than those of the covenanters, the crusty OPC was phasing out its traditional hymnal while flirting with the publication of a praise-song/chorus book for congregational use in worship. The circumstance that saved the OPC from this liturgical nightmare had less to do with the collective wisdom of the saints than with reports that the proposed songbook did not include the best of the recent products from the Christian Contemporary Music (CCM) industry. Which is to say that making sense of the different parties in American Presbyterianism is as difficult as spotting the fault line between liberal and evangelical Protestants.

The following observations are designed to lend some clarity to the murkiness surrounding contemporary Reformed worship as practiced by American Presbyterians. A look at two notable books on worship by Presbyterians is followed by analysis that reveals eighteenth-century precedents for the current confusion in Presbyterian circles about Reformed worship and how the divisions of the 1920s and 1930s furthered this disarray. The hope is that even if the ensuing argument does not persuade advocates of P & W to exchange their overhead projectors for psalters, it may provide a clearer understanding of the genius of Reformed worship and its organic connection to Reformed theological convictions.

The State of the Art

The best way to examine the health of contemporary Reformed worship is by looking at two books published during the 1980s and 1990s that represent developments in the mainline and sideline Presbyterian worlds. The first, published in 1984 and entitled *Worship That Is Reformed according to Scripture,* comes from Hughes Oliphant Old, who wrote this book while a pastor of a PCUSA congregation. He now teaches homiletics at Princeton Theological Seminary. The second, *Worship in Spirit and Truth,* published twelve years later, is by John M. Frame, who taught at Westminster Seminary (both campuses) for approximately twenty-five years and now teaches at Reformed Seminary in Florida. He wrote this book as part of his experience as a pianist and song leader for a PCA congregation.[4] The differences between the two books stand out based on a cursory glance at the table of contents. Old organizes his book around the traditional elements of Reformed worship, devoting separate chapters to baptism, the Sabbath, praise, the Word, prayer, and the Lord's Supper. Frame, however, approaches the matter inductively, gearing his argument toward specific issues in contemporary debates. He starts with biblical teaching on worship, the order and tone of the service, the dialogical character of worship, and the place and function of music. In fact, in the one chapter in which Frame addresses the idea of "elements," something Old assumes, the Reformed Seminary professor concludes that Scripture nowhere gives warrant for the parts of worship drawn up by the Westminster divines in chapter 21 of the Westminster Confession.[5] This may explain why Frame's discussion of baptism occurs on two pages in comparison to Old's chapter-length treatment, or why Frame devotes as much space to "liturgical drama" (which he does not advocate but does approve) as

4. Hughes Oliphant Old, *Worship That Is Reformed according to Scripture* (Atlanta: John Knox, 1984); John M. Frame, *Worship in Spirit and Truth* (Phillipsburg, N.J.: Presbyterian and Reformed, 1996).

5. Frame, *Worship,* 53. References to the Westminster Confession throughout this essay will be to the pre-1903 revised version, which thanks to added chapters threw off the numbering of chapters.

he does to the sacraments in general.[6] In the "liberal" PCUSA, if Old's book is any indication, the traditional elements and rites of historic Reformed liturgy are firmly in place. But in the "conservative" PCA, using Frame as a guide, the conventional pieces of Reformed worship are in flux.

The innovative and traditional expressions of contemporary Presbyterian worship are particularly evident in the concluding chapters of each book. Frame ends with a description of the typical service he used to lead in a Southern California PCA congregation, the implication of which is that such a service follows from the preceding arguments. An elder opens with announcements and an expression of welcome to visitors, followed by a reminder to those gathered that their purpose is to worship God ("We rarely have a formal call to worship," Frame writes).[7] Next comes a prelude, an introduction from the pastor, two songs on overheads, and then a prayer of adoration and confession. This sets the stage for a fifteen-minute period of song—a mix of classic hymns and soft praise songs. During such singing, the leadership encourages people "to clap, whistle, tap tambourines, or to otherwise use their gifts to enhance the worship."[8] A prayer of intercession follows this round of song, which leads to another song that allows children time to leave for children's church. Then comes the sermon. Once a month the Lord's Supper follows the sermon, though Frame prefers Calvin's argument for weekly observance; songs accompany the distribution of both elements. Following the sacrament, ushers take the collection while the choir sings an anthem, and then the entire congregation sings the doxology. A formal benediction concludes the service, though Frame cautions that "ceremonial sentences" may become "empty forms over time."[9] Frame's order of service, then, goes something like this: introduction, song, prayer, song, prayer, song, sermon, the Supper, collection, doxology, and benediction. This liturgy may not reinforce the centrality of the Word, but at least Frame's congregation learns how to sing.

Old takes a different approach in his concluding chapter. He closes with several comments on the contribution that Reformed liturgies can make to contemporary Protestant worship. The first concerns preaching and the value of the Reformed habit of expository sermons as well as "systematic preaching through one book of the Bible after another."[10] The second point concerns prayer, and here Old advocates

6. Frame, *Worship*, 92–94, 96–98.
7. Ibid., 146.
8. Ibid., 148.
9. Ibid., 152.
10. Old, *Worship*, 172.

older Reformed practices of praying the psalms accompanied by an appreciation of the way Reformed liturgies provide a "full diet of prayer," including praise, confession, thanksgiving, supplication, and intercession.[11] The third contribution of Reformed worship is evident in the observance of and teaching about the Lord's Supper. Old notes how the Reformers rediscovered this sacrament as a form of communion of the saints while also retaining its Eucharistic character. He also highlights the epiclectic and diaconal aspects of Reformed sacramental teaching. Fourth, Old emphasizes the links between baptism and covenant theology in Reformed worship, the way baptism undergirds sanctification, and the sacrament's place in a system of catechetical instruction. Fifth, he returns to Reformed teaching on prayer to recommend a daily service of morning and evening prayers, as well as its importance for family worship. Finally, Old concludes where the Shorter Catechism begins: "The greatest single contribution which the Reformed liturgical heritage can make to contemporary American Protestantism is its sense of the majesty and sovereignty of God, its sense of reverence, of simple dignity, its conviction that worship must above all serve the praise of God."[12] It would be difficult to miss Old's indebtedness to the Shorter Catechism's answer 88 in the way he emphasizes the Word, sacraments, and prayer as means of grace.

Still, one could explain Old's traditionalism by the early date of his book's publication, a time when P & W had not yet become popular. For instance, if he had written ten years later, Old may well have stressed music in the way that Frame does by giving over one-fourth of his book to the new genre of worship songs. (Two years later Frame also wrote a sequel that defended "contemporary" Christian music.)[13] In fact, one of the telltale signs that Frame was writing for a different era is the primacy of music in his considerations. Nevertheless, Old displays an awareness of the kind of arguments Presbyterians have used to replace older orders of worship with the simple (some might say unimaginatively limited) pattern of song, prayer, and sermon. For instance, in his introduction, Old shows some familiarity with recent attempts to make worship pleasing, but he is not impressed by these horizontal concerns. "We are often told," he writes, "that we should worship in order to build family solidarity: 'the family that worships together stays together.'" But Old adds that the Canaanite fertility cult offered a similar sentiment. "True worship," Old states, "is distinguished

11. Ibid., 173.
12. Ibid., 176–77.
13. John M. Frame, *Contemporary Worship Music: A Biblical Defense* (Phillipsburg, N.J.: Presbyterian and Reformed, 1997).

from all of these in that it serves above all else the praise of God's glory."[14]

Similarly, at the conclusion of the book, Old gives every impression that he would not have succumbed to the seeker orientation of modern worship. In what remains the best illustration for explaining what has happened to Presbyterian worship since the publication of this book, Old prophetically dismisses all "contemporary" efforts to make worship user-friendly.

> In our evangelistic zeal we are looking for programs that will attract people. We think we have to put honey on the lip of the bitter cup of salvation. It is the story of the wedding of Cana all over again but with this difference. At the crucial moment when the wine failed, we took matters into our own hands and used those five stone jars to mix up a batch of Kool-Aid instead. It seemed like a good solution in terms of our American culture. Unfortunately, all too soon the guests discovered the fraud. Alas! What are we to do now? How can we possibly minister to those who thirst for the real thing? There is but one thing to do, as Mary the mother of Jesus, understood so very well. You remember how the story goes. After presenting the problem to Jesus, Mary turned to the servants and said to them, "Do whatever he tells you." The servants did just that and the water was turned to wine, wine rich and mellow beyond anything they had ever tasted before.[15]

It would be difficult to imagine that Old wrote without sufficient knowledge of the changes transforming Presbyterian liturgy in the early 1980s.

Perhaps the most dramatic of those changes has come in the element of song, and Old's chapter on the ministry of praise demonstrates the same theocentric emphasis that characterizes the book. Even though Old is clearly a traditionalist, he does not emerge as an ally of covenanters and other exclusive psalmody advocates. He clearly recognizes the centrality of psalms to the ministry of congregational song and is well aware of Calvin's and later the Puritan's practice of singing from the psalter exclusively. But Old prefers the liturgies of the first Reformed churches in Constance and Strasbourg that used both hymns and psalms. What is more, Old goes so far as to claim that Isaac Watts "exemplifies the Reformed doxological tradition at its best" with its blend of psalmody and hymnody.[16] To be sure, Old has a point in faulting contemporary proponents of exclusive psalmody with musical wooden-

14. Old, *Worship*, 2.
15. Ibid., 177.
16. Ibid., 55.

ness. Still, he does not appear to pay full heed to his own estimation of the psalms when, following Calvin, he writes, "The psalms lead us in the right manner of offering the sacrifice of praise to God. . . . In the psalms we hear of God's mighty acts of creation, providence and redemption." What then could be a better way of expressing "the sense of awe and wonder which we have when we enter the presence of God"?[17] But even if Old ends up departing from Calvin here by kindly rejecting exclusive psalmody, he strives mightily to ensure that congregational singing be first and foremost a means of exalting the name of God.

Frame's discussion of music, however, takes off in a decidedly different direction and bears all the marks of the recent worship wars, with the author nonchalantly siding with the rebels. Frame begins where Old ends. He agrees that the preeminent function of worship is to honor God and that music must fulfill this requirement. But by a sleight of hand, Frame turns song as praise into music that attracts. Music, he argues, "enhances God's word by making it more vivid and memorable," and this vividness and memorability drive the Word into believers' hearts, motivating them to praise and obedience.[18] Frame even suggests that a worship service consisting entirely of music would be a good thing. Music also makes worship intelligible. This, in fact, is perhaps the chief point of Frame's book. From his perspective, 1 Corinthians 14 teaches that worship must be intelligible, even to nonbelievers. It is little wonder then that Frame spends almost a quarter of his book on music and that he sides with the advocates of contemporary forms of worship. Contemporary praise songs, guitars, rock 'n' roll, dance, the lifting of hands, and clapping are all legitimate means for reaching new converts and keeping teenagers in the church. Frame even thinks that instrumental music without singing is a legitimate part of Reformed worship. His rationale is that "God wants his people to be transformed in every area of their lives." The form of emotional communication and emotional edification that instrumental music provides "is as important in worship as intellectual communication."[19] Such a brief for music not only ignores the centrality of the Word that has characterized Reformed theology and liturgy but also upsets the Calvinist preoccupation with directing all parts of the service to the praise and glory of God.

As great as the differences are between Frame and Old concerning song in worship, they are merely manifestations of a deeper discrepancy, one that is filled with irony because it goes to the heart of what

17. Ibid., 53, 40.
18. Frame, *Worship*, 112.
19. Ibid., 130.

it means to be conservative and liberal. Frame and Old write with two distinct purposes. Frame is concerned to find a way for Presbyterian traditionalists to worship in novel ways. His prefatory remarks are revealing. "I hope to state the fundamental Reformed principles," he writes, "and I hope to justify, on the basis of these principles, some forms of worship that *are not typical of the Reformed tradition.*" Frame adds that his study reflects the recognition that some Christians prefer not to worship according to Reformed practices because "there are real problems in the traditional Presbyterian view."[20] This recognition does not weaken his regard for the Reformed tradition. Frame insists that he affirms the theology of the Westminster Standards. But the Puritan theology of worship, which he thinks is minimal in the confession and the catechisms, is too narrow and does not allow sufficient flexibility for congregations like his. Frame's effort is to retain the Reformed faith without the Reformed practice of worship because he sees no inherent connection between the theology of Reformed churches and their liturgies.

Old's intention, in contrast, is to recover and perpetuate the Reformed tradition of worship, and as much as he writes with the simple goal of explaining the tradition, Old does not hide his deep appreciation for older Reformed liturgies and practices. This point should be obvious from his conclusion. Unlike Frame, Old does not regard this tradition as a burden that restricts liturgical experimentation but rather as a fitting way to conduct the gathering of the saints before the God of Abraham, Isaac, and Jacob. This does not mean that Old wants simply to reproduce older patterns of worship. He cautions against both "archaeological reconstruction" and "liturgical romanticism." "A certain amount of adaptation" is always necessary. Nevertheless, Old is unabashed in his love and respect for Reformed worship. "We recognize [the Reformers] as great because they were great! . . . At the center of their reform was a concern for the reform of worship, and they had a profound insight into the nature of worship."[21] This is the reason, Old concludes, for being interested in what they had to say.

Of course, Frame's and Old's perspectives on the Reformed tradition are not unique. Plenty of people think Reformed concerns about right worship are excessive, and others, perhaps fewer in number, see great spiritual insight and beauty in Reformed worship. But what makes these authors' views poignant is the ecclesiastical affiliation of each man. If sideline Presbyterian denominations such as the PCA and the OPC were as conservative about the Reformed tradition as they regard

20. Ibid., xv (emphasis added).
21. Old, *Worship*, 162–63.

themselves, then we would expect Old's book to have come from a PCA or an OPC minister and to have been published by a conservative Presbyterian press. Moreover, if the mainline Presbyterian denomination was as liberal as its conservative detractors insist, then it would make more sense for Frame's book to have come from a PCUSA officer and publishing house. Yet the opposite is the case. The conservatives have turned modernist, if by modernism we mean the self-conscious adaptation of the faith to modern times.[22] Just as unlikely, the modernists have become the chief defenders of the historic Reformed faith, at least in its liturgical aspects, against efforts to preserve the kernel while refashioning a modern husk. The question is how to account for this reversal of conservative and liberal Presbyterian roles.

The American Presbyterian Predicament

Any explanation of the anomalies within contemporary Presbyterian worship has to start with history. Ever since the beginning of the eighteenth century, American Presbyterianism has struggled between formal and experiential shades of liturgy. Some of that struggle reflects the lessons that seventeenth-century English Puritans and Scottish Presbyterians learned during their contests with the Church of England. But even more crucial to the instability of American Presbyterian worship was the formative influence of revivalism and the First Great Awakening. The victory of the pro-revivalist New Side Presbyterians during the first two generations of American Presbyterian history ensured that the Olds of the tradition would always have the Frames of the New World with them.

On many levels the revivals championed by colonial Presbyterian revivalists such as Gilbert Tennent and Jonathan Dickinson undermined the liturgies of John Knox, Martin Bucer, and John Calvin. Formally, the practice of revivalism made liturgical concerns practically unnecessary or, at least, a minor consideration. This is clearly the impression that George Whitefield gave in his accounts of traveling and speaking in the American colonies. The English revivalist never stopped to consider whether his setting was Anglican, Presbyterian, Reformed, Quaker, or mixed. He preached the same way for all denominations and especially enjoyed interdenominational gatherings. In November of 1739, while preaching in German Town, Whitefield noted that there were "no less than fifteen denominations of Christians" present, and yet "all

---

22. See William R. Hutchison, *The Modernist Impulse in American Protestantism* (Cambridge: Harvard University Press, 1976).

agree in one thing, that is, to hold Jesus Christ as their Head, and to worship Him in spirit and in truth."[23] If so many denominations showed up to hear Whitefield, the service he used must have reflected a liturgical minimalism in which the traditions and forms of different Protestant groups became trifling details.

The Anglican's journals confirm this conclusion when time and again he records that the basic order of service was to read prayers and preach. An entry from 1739 is especially revealing because it concerns worship among colonial Presbyterians:

> Set out for Neshaminy (twenty miles distant from Trent Town), where old Mr. Tennent lives, and keeps an academy, and where I was to preach to-day, according to appointment. We came thither about twelve, and found above three thousand people gathered together in the meeting-house yard, and Mr. William Tennent preaching to them, because we were beyond the appointed time. When I came up he soon stopped, and sung a psalm, and then I began to speak. At first, the people seemed to be melted down, and cried much. After I had finished, Mr. Gilbert Tennent gave a word of exhortation. At the end of his discourse, we sung a psalm, and then dismissed the people with a blessing. Oh, that the Lord may say Amen to it![24]

Obviously, this Thursday afternoon service was not necessarily representative of Sunday worship, though it is interesting to see how its order of song, sermon, and prayer resembles contemporary worship's configuration of elements. This example does suggest, however, that revivalism was not good for Reformed worship because it turned the service almost exclusively into the sermon, with song and prayer being ancillary. What is more, revivals provided no place for the invocation, corporate confession and absolution, the sacraments, or Scripture lessons. Colonial Presbyterians may have received a full diet of liturgical elements on the Lord's Day, but the popularity of Whitefield and the Tennents soon made the old liturgies look uninspired, which they were compared to the revivalists' charisma.

Reformed worship was not prepared to compete with the new revivalistic services, not simply because of the eloquence (and perhaps manipulation) of preachers such as Whitefield but also because of the experience such sermons were designed to produce. Whitefield's journals constantly make reference to the reactions of hearers, and these re-

23. *George Whitefield's Journals (1737–1741)*, with an introduction by William V. Davis (Gainesville, Fl.: Scholars' Facsimiles and Reprints, 1969), 354. On the revolutionary character of Whitefield's revivals, see Harry S. Stout, *The Divine Dramatist: George Whitefield and the Rise of Modern Evangelicalism* (Grand Rapids: Eerdmans, 1991).

24. *George Whitefield's Journals*, 350.

sponses demonstrated, at least to the itinerant evangelist, that his preaching was effective. The common reaction of a revived hearer was tears: "Most wept at the preaching of faith." But silence was another indication of a truly moved soul. "I believe there were nearly two thousand more present to-night than last night," Whitefield wrote. "Even in London, I never observed so profound a silence."[25] But just as important was the experience of the preacher himself. Upon hearing Tennent's searching sermons, Whitefield was convinced "that we can preach the Gospel of Christ no further than we have experienced the power of it in our hearts." He added that because of Tennent's conversion the Presbyterian revivalist had "learned experimentally to dissect the heart of a natural man."[26] Revivalistic preaching was geared toward experience and especially the experience of conversion. None of the other elements of worship was capable of producing such effects. Furthermore, revivals became the standard for worship. What individuals needed to show to prove they had been converted became the norm for public gatherings. If the service was not moving, it would not likely encourage genuine faith and devotion.

Of course, the exaltation of experience has never been pronounced in American Presbyterian directories for worship, and this is especially true of the eighteenth century. Though the proposed directory of 1787 and the one approved in 1789 by the General Assembly departed from that of the Westminster Assembly, the American directory was, according to Stanley R. Hall, "generally less restrictive" on prayer, the sacraments, and preaching.[27] As such, the American revisions of Westminster's *Directory* did not obviously stem from the experientialism and antiformalism inherent in revivalism. Still, whatever liturgical boundaries Presbyterians established formally in their directory, the piety that had once informed Reformed practice in worship had changed dramatically thanks to revivalism. The observations of Leigh Eric Schmidt concerning Reformed spirituality are especially salient.

> What the Reformed Church offered in the place of the old calendar and the traditional festivals was a spiritual life of sustained discipline and devotion. . . . Day-in, day-out, Sabbath after Sabbath, the Reformed saints were to strive after joyful, harmonious communion with their God and their fellow Christians.[28]

25. Ibid., 339.
26. Ibid., 344.
27. Stanley Roberston Hall, "The American Presbyterian 'Directory for Worship': History of Liturgical Strategy" (Ph.D. diss., University of Notre Dame, 1990), 163.
28. Leigh Eric Schmidt, *Holy Fairs: Scottish Communions and American Revivals in the Early Modern Period* (Princeton: Princeton University Press, 1989), 17.

Schmidt adds that the steadfastness and perseverence of Reformed piety proved to be too difficult for most people. And so, the "hope for a community of saints who year-round were diligent, self-controlled, sober, prayerful, and devout within their families and outside them" eventually gave way to the intense and extraordinary experiences of revivalism.[29] In other words, the liturgy that sustained Reformed piety, as much as it assumed such devotion, was no longer adequate for the demands of conversion and holy living that revivalism promoted and promised.

The tensions between Presbyterian liturgy and revivalistic piety did not become immediately evident. By the nineteenth century, however, the discrepancy between the evangelical system of preaching, conversion, and revival and the order and decency of Reformed liturgy began to play itself out in important ways. In the process, revivalism provided the dominant metaphor for the way that Presbyterians conceived of the Christian life, thereby calling into question the rigorous and subdued piety that Reformed worship made plausible. In fact, this is one of the arresting conclusions that follows from David B. Calhoun's two-volume history of Princeton Seminary.[30] Among the fascinating stories he tells about members of Princeton's faculty is the recurring tale of boys who were baptized, reared in the church, and catechized and who attended weekly services on the Lord's Day but still sensed by the time they went off to college that they were not genuine believers and so set off in pursuit of conversion through the now common means of revival.

The classic case is that of Charles Hodge, who said that as a boy he had the habit of thanking God for everything, avoiding curse words, and praying regularly.[31] Even discounting Hodge's recollections of his boyhood and what may have been an overbearing self-righteousness, it is likely that his mother, pastor, and elders were raising young Charles as a child of the covenant. But it was not until he went off to the College of New Jersey and sat under Archibald Alexander's preaching that Hodge could finally make a profession of faith, and the occasion for that decision was the revival Alexander led in the winter of 1814–15. One of Hodge's peers who learned of the conversion told a professor excitedly of the news in the following words: "[Hodge] has enlisted under the banner of King Jesus!"[32] As this comment suggests, observers of young Charles presumed that a boy who had been baptized and who

29. Ibid., 18.
30. David B. Calhoun, *Princeton Seminary*, vol. 1, *Faith and Learning, 1812–1868* (Edinburgh: Banner of Truth Trust, 1994); and idem, *Princeton Seminary*, vol. 2, *The Majestic Testimony* (Edinburgh: Banner of Truth Trust, 1996).
31. Calhoun, *Princeton Seminary*, vol. 1, 106.
32. Ibid., 108.

prayed, tried to live a godly life, and knew that all his life depended on his heavenly Father was actually an enemy of Christ. A moment of decision was necessary. Thus, the elements of Reformed worship that naturally fit into the churchly and familial pattern of covenant children growing up and making a credible profession of faith were all for naught without the crisis of conversion. It should be noted that Hodge may not have been entirely comfortable with the legacy of revivalism, for in his *Constitutional History* he identified many of the emotional displays of the conversion experience with mental disorders and criticized the New Side for abandoning the good order of Presbyterianism.[33] But once his surrogate father, Archibald Alexander, whose own roots were in the revivals of eighteenth-century Virginia, took issue with Hodge's critique, the junior Princeton professor recanted and gave his blessing to the New Side, attributing to the revivals of Whitefield, Edwards, and the Tennents "the religious life which we now enjoy."[34]

One of Hodge's contemporaries who saw with unparalleled insight the effects of revivalism on American Presbyterianism was John Williamson Nevin. Nevin, of course, who taught for Hodge while the latter studied in Germany, eventually left the Presbyterian Church when he began teaching for the German Reformed seminary at Mercerberg. Over the course of his pilgrimage, he would come to an assessment of Reformed liturgy and sacramental theology that differed from that of his former classmate at Princeton. Nevin's own recollections of his youth are worth quoting at length because they capture so well the enormous changes in Presbyterian church life that transpired in the wake of the First and Second Great Awakenings.

> Being of what is called Scotch-Irish extraction, I was by birth and blood also, a Presbyterian; and as my parents were both conscientious and exemplary professors of religion, I was, as a matter of course, carefully brought up in the nurture and admonition of the Lord, according to the Presbyterian faith as it then stood. . . . That the old Presbyterian faith, into which I was born, was based throughout on the idea of covenant family religion, church membership by God's holy act in baptism, and following this a regular catechetical training of the young, with direct reference to their coming to the Lord's table. In one word, all proceeded on the theory of sacramental, educational religion, as it had belonged properly to all the national branches of the *Reformed* Church in Europe from the beginning. . . . The system was churchly, as holding the Church in her visible character to be the medium of salvation for her baptized children, in the sense of that memorable declaration of Calvin (Inst 4.1.4), where,

33. Ibid., 254.
34. Quoted in ibid., 255.

speaking of her title, *Mother,* he says: "There is no other entrance into life, save as she may conceive us in her womb, give us birth, nourish us from her breasts, and embrace us in her loving care to the end."[35]

That was the old Presbyterian order with Reformed liturgy linked directly to the means of grace as a way of building up church members in the faith. But when Nevin went from the Scotch-Irish community of central Pennsylvania to the predominantly Puritan institution, Union College, he found no support for the churchly system in which he had been reared.

> It was my very first contact with the genius of New-England Puritanism, in its character of contradiction to the old *Reformed* faith, as I had been baptized into it, in its Presbyterian form. . . . It is hardly necessary to say, that circumstanced as I then was, I had no power to withstand the shock. It brought to pass, what amounted for me, to a complete breaking up of all my previous Christian life. For I had come to college, a boy of strongly pious dispositions and exemplary religious habits, never doubting but that I was in some way a Christian, though it had not come with me yet (unfortunately) to what is called a public profession of religion. But now one of the first lessons inculcated on me indirectly by this unchurchly system, was that all this must pass for nothing, and that I must learn to look upon myself as an outcast from the family and kingdom of God, before I could come to be in either in the right way. Such, especially, was the instruction I came under, when a "revival of religion," as it was called, made its appearance among us, and brought all to a practical point.[36]

Nevin went on to describe his conversion as inferior compared to the others produced by the "torture" of revivalism's "anxious meetings" and "mechanical counsel." And it was based on the idea that regeneration had nothing to do with the church, baptism, and catechesis. In fact, revivals supposed that the churchly system of Presbyterianism was "more a bar than a help to the process," because conversion came only through "magical lapse or stroke from the Spirit of God." In sum, an "intense subjectivity" took the place of the "grand and glorious *objectivities* of the Christian life." Nevin concluded his reflections on his feeble conversion with a lament that indicates the power and riches of the Reformed liturgical system:

> My own "experience" in this way, at the time here under consideration, was not wholesome, but very morbid rather and weak. Alas, where was

35. John Williamson Nevin, *My Own Life: The Early Years* (Lancaster, Pa.: Historical Society of the Evangelical and Reformed Church, 1964), 2–3.
36. Ibid., 8–9.

mother, the Church, at the very time I most needed her fostering arms? Where was she, I mean, with her true sacramental sympathy and care? How much better it had been for me, if I had only been properly drawn forth from myself by some right soul-communication with the mysteries of the old Christian Creed.[37]

Nevin's reflections bring home the point about the tainted history of American Presbyterian worship. Well before the church had gained sufficient stability to transplant Old World customs to the New World, American Presbyterians drank the strong brew of revivalism and have been under the influence of an alien devotion ever since. To be sure, the Presbyterian sense of decorum and order has kept alive an interest in the practices of Reformed Protestantism, and therefore the American Presbyterian tradition has never been without its Hughes Oliphant Olds, who see the organic connection between Reformed theology, liturgy, and piety. For these Presbyterians, Reformed worship is the natural way to embody the teachings of the Reformed wing of Protestantism. But at the same time, the American Presbyterian tradition has manifested a longing for extraordinary outpourings of the Spirit that revivalism supposedly provides. This longing, which came to prominence among New Side Presbyterians and has contributed the most to the low-church tendencies of the American church, could not be satisfied by the simple and formal liturgy of the Reformed tradition. To borrow Nevin's vernacular, the demand for subjectivities made nonsense of the Reformed elements' objectivities.

The Twentieth-Century Legacy of the Presbyterian Predicament

Still, even in light of the history of American Presbyterianism, it was not a given that today's Presbyterian denominations on the conservative side of the divisions of the 1920s and 1930s would automatically abandon liturgical worship and leave the field to their theological rivals. Here certain tendencies that are commonly associated with liberal and evangelical Protestantism may help to explain the anomalies of contemporary Presbyterian worship. One has to do with evangelism, the other with the implications of biblical inerrancy.

To be sure, anyone who concludes that conservative Protestants, as opposed to the liberal mainline church, have a monopoly on evangelism would be guilty of caricature. Yet one of the factors that led to the fundamentalist controversy was the level of the northern Presbyterian

---

37. Ibid., 10–11. Thanks go to Thomas Boeve, a Ph.D. candidate at Princeton University, who brought this section of Nevin to my attention.

Church's commitment to the social gospel. Some moderates advocated soul winning in addition to societal redemption, but the missions controversy of the 1930s contributed to the impression that the mainline denomination, in the words of Pearl S. Buck, did not believe in hell and therefore lost the motivation for the missionary enterprise. At the same time, the statistics of American Protestant foreign missionaries gathered after the publication in 1932 of *Re-Thinking Missions* confirmed this impression. The number of mainline missionaries declined while fundamentalists and evangelicals continued to send out more. Consequently, the Protestant mainstream bore the reputation, caricature though it may have been, of preaching a social gospel, while conservative Protestants proclaimed a message of heaven and hell.

Conservative Presbyterians emerged from the 1930s clearly committed to evangelism and regarded their evangelistically minded evangelical peers as allies because of this commitment. For this reason, when conservatives consider worship, whether its purpose or its execution, they invariably make evangelism prominent. This conclusion finds support in Frame's book. He repeatedly justifies the use of contemporary forms and popular music by appealing to the principle of intelligibility. Worship must be God-centered, but in an interesting twist, worship that does not welcome outsiders or is beyond the comprehension of church members does not glorify God. Frame writes:

> In worship, we should not be so preoccupied with God that we ignore one another. . . . So, worship has a horizontal dimension as well as a vertical focus. It is to be God-centered, but it is also to be both edifying and evangelistic. Worship that is unedifying or unevangelistic may not properly claim to be God-centered.[38]

With this subtle shift, Frame is free to dismiss the historic forms and liturgies of Presbyterians and Reformed. "We should avoid slavish imitation of older practices," he argues, "without attention to the matter of communication," which is only to say that "our fundamental task" in worship is the Great Commission. "That divine mandate, rather than any human traditions, must ultimately guide our decisions about the order of worship."[39] Frame appears to be unaware that the traditional elements of Reformed worship, such as the reading and preaching of the Word, in the words of the Shorter Catechism, are "effectual means of convincing and converting sinners" (Ans. 89). Indeed, his logic is one of the best examples of how evangelistic aims have trumped the purpose of worship in conservative Presbyterian circles.

38. Frame, *Worship*, 8.
39. Ibid., 67.

Without the burden of always having to evangelize, mainline Presbyterians have been freer to hold on to a liturgical tradition that never made worship into the handmaid for evangelism. Old's book clearly demonstrates this point. "We worship God because God created us to worship him," Old writes. "Worship is at the center of our existence; at the heart of our reason for being." In fact, any discussion of worship, he argues, must begin with the basic principle that God created humans to reflect divine glory. "Worship must above all serve the glory of God." But Old shows he is even more emphatic about the God-centered character of worship when he offers a brief exposition of the first table of the Decalogue. He declares, "Not only did God create us to worship him, but he also commanded us to worship him."[40] This does not mean that Old considers intelligibility unimportant. Rather, his conviction is that God will use faithful worship to accomplish his ends. Old states this emphatically when he discusses Calvin's homiletical method.

> What surprises the modern reader of Calvin's sermons is the simplicity of his sermons. We find no engaging introductions, no illustrative stories nor anecdotes, no quotations from great authors, no stirring conclusions. . . . So confident is the Reformer that God will make his Word alive in the hearts of his people, that Calvin simply explains the text and draws out its implications. The simplicity and directness of his style is based in his confidence that what he is preaching is indeed the Word of God.[41]

It may be unfair to suggest that Frame, with his concern for intelligibility, lacks Calvin's confidence, but it can be asserted with certainty that a significant difference between Frame's and Old's understanding of Reformed liturgy and worship stems from the degree to which worship must serve the purpose of evangelism.

Another important difference concerns the Bible. Again, conservatives no doubt caricature mainline Presbyterians when they argue that liberals do not believe the Bible is infallible and authoritative. Even so, important differences do exist between mainline and conservative Presbyterians concerning the nature of biblical authority, as conservative insistence on inerrancy and statements such as the Confession of 1967 attest. And these different understandings of biblical authority have since the 1930s had important implications for worship. To summarize as succinctly as possible, conservative Presbyterians congenitally regard tradition with suspicion because it appears to put human wisdom on a par with the Bible. In contrast, mainline Presbyterians, perhaps

40. Old, *Worship*, 1–2.
41. Ibid., 75–76.

because they stress the humanity of Scripture, are more comfortable with the work that humans do in the service of God. The obvious inference for Reformed liturgy is that conservatives are biblicists and want to find a direct command for everything they do in worship, forgetting what the Confession of Faith says in chapter 1 about the good and necessary consequence of Scripture. Mainline Presbyterians, however, do not find it necessary to test everything against the Bible and therefore are freer to accept the traditions handed down in Reformed liturgies.

This difference is also evident in the books by Frame and Old. Perhaps the best indication of it in Frame's book is found in his discussion of the Puritan regulative principle of worship. There Frame corrects what he perceives as a fault in the Puritan view. Instead of saying that the Bible governs the corporate life of the church, especially its liturgy, while allowing liberty for persons and families in their private affairs, Frame extends the Puritan notion by applying it to all of life. "In all areas of life, we are subject to biblical commands," he writes. "Human wisdom may never presume to *add* to its commands. The only job of human wisdom is to *apply* those commandments to specific situations."[42] This understanding of the regulative principle prompted Frame to write in defense of biblicism, an argument that has a natural tendency toward theonomy because it supports the view that biblical teaching applies to all spheres, including that of the state. But aside from this implication, Frame's biblicism allows considerable freedom in worship, to the point at which he can find general principles that make dancing, juggling, and drama legitimate. The reason for this liberty is that the Bible nowhere reveals a set liturgy. As Frame puts it, "Unfortunately, it is virtually impossible to prove that anything is divinely required specifically for official services."[43] What biblicism giveth, it quickly taketh away. For conservatives that subtraction has typically involved anything approximating historic Christian liturgy.

Old, however, is not as squeamish about tradition. As pointed out earlier, he concludes his book with an extended discussion of the contribution that the historic forms of Reformed liturgy can make to contemporary American Protestant worship. But for Old the Reformed tradition is most useful for those who continue to regard themselves as Reformed. He argues that maintaining the Reformed tradition is valuable simply for maintaining "contact with our roots" and because it "contains material of lasting value."[44] From a biblicist's perspective,

42. Frame, *Worship*, 43.
43. Ibid., 44.
44. Old, *Worship*, 164–65.

those reasons might seem fairly weak or arbitrary. But Old's reply is important.

> A tradition which gets radically changed every generation is not really a tradition. For tradition to be tradition it must have a considerable amount of permanence and changelessness. Tradition can only become tradition when it is passed from one generation to another.[45]

But just as in the case of Frame's biblicism, which promised restriction only to yield license, Old's argument for tradition gives more than it initially promised, namely, being biblical. The reason for following the Reformed tradition in worship, Old writes, is because it "witnesses to the authority of Scripture." "Above all the leadership of both the Fathers and the Reformers is to be found in the fact that they understood Scripture so well."[46] In contrast to Frame, for whom worship boils down to a choice between tradition and the Bible, Old contends that the Reformed tradition is biblical, and therefore, Frame's choice is a false one.

These factors by no means exhaust the reasons for divergence among contemporary Presbyterians in worship. But the history of Presbyterian developments in the United States cannot be discounted. Ever since the eighteenth-century revivals, led and promoted by New Side Presbyterians, American Presbyterianism has had a significant crack in the foundation of its liturgy, thanks to the experiential piety that revivalism encouraged. The twentieth-century division between mainline and conservative Presbyterians fed theological tendencies that have reinforced certain liturgical predispositions among these groups, with the mainstream branch providing a better context for the maintenance of historic Reformed worship and the smaller streams being susceptible to constant innovation. But this explanation in no way diminishes the irony of theological conservatives being liturgical relativists and theological liberals being liturgical traditionalists.

Presbyterian Worship in a Wesleyan Culture and Pentecostal Age

As ironic as the travails of contemporary Presbyterian worship may be, and whatever the merits of the explanation for these difficulties offered here, in the end the point is not the irony of it all. The point, rather, is, What needs to be done to recover the genius of Reformed

45. Ibid., 162.
46. Ibid., 169.

worship, whether in the mainline or the sideline churches? Specifically, can Presbyterians in North America retrieve the sensibility that produced statements such as the following from John Calvin? When asked about forms for prayer and specific rites in worship, he replied that he "highly approved" of them. His reasons tapped sentiments that are generally foreign in contemporary Presbyterian circles: First, some ministers are unskilled in leading worship; second, forms and rites ensure uniformity among the churches; and finally, they prevent "capricious giddiness and levity" from surfacing in worship.[47] To that end, Calvin recommended a catechism and stated forms for prayer and the sacraments.

The Geneva Reformer's liturgical outlook is clearly foreign to American culture, in which egalitarianism, individualism, and informality prevail. Indeed, one of the major obstacles to Reformed worship in the United States is the failure of Presbyterians to be discerning about the common idiom of American culture. According to David Martin, a British sociologist of religion, American culture is inherently Wesleyan.

> The difference between America and England is the American insistence on sincerity and openness rather than on form and privacy. The whole American style was, and is, "Methodist" in its emphases, whereas in England the culturally prestigious style remained Anglican. "Enthusiasm" of all kinds, religious, cultural and personal, became endemic in America; in England enthusiasm remained intermittent and the object of some mild curiosity.[48]

Of course, the low-church style of many Presbyterians in the United States makes it difficult to place Presbyterianism on Martin's formal/informal spectrum, not to mention that the Presbyterian tradition did not distinguish itself in England. Still, most would agree that Presbyterian theology does not inherently breed enthusiasm. If Martin is correct, American Presbyterians are faced with a dilemma. To make worship accessible to persons for whom informality is as common as the air they breathe is to gut Reformed worship of its reverence, dignity, and simplicity. But to do justice to the rigor of Calvinist worship is to burn fire that may please God but certainly smells foul to residents of the United States. American Presbyterians have tried to dodge that dilemma for almost two centuries, and the consequences have not been

47. Quoted in Charles W. Baird, *Presbyterian Liturgies: Historical Sketches* (1855; reprint, Grand Rapids: Baker, 1957), 23.
48. David Martin, *Tongues of Fire: The Explosion of Protestantism in Latin America* (Cambridge, Mass.: Blackwell, 1990), 21.

propitious for the propriety, uniformity, and dignity that Calvin believed should characterize Reformed worship.

One other significant consideration is related to the first. If the informality of American culture is not fitting for Presbyterian worship, neither are the efforts to package Reformed convictions in Pentecostal and charismatic forms. In a foreword to an evangelical book on worship, the Southern Baptist scholar on hymnody, Donald P. Hustad, offers a telling warning that applies to any liturgical tradition but that Presbyterians should especially take to heart:

> Charismatic believers have a right to develop their own worship to match their own theology and exegesis, and they have done this well. Non-charismatics should not thoughtlessly copy or imitate their worship formulae, unless they expect to enter the same "Holy of Holies" in the same way. Instead, they should develop their worship rationale based on their scriptural understanding, and then sing up to their own theology.[49]

Though Hustad's comments are directed toward song, they apply equally well to the other elements of worship. To use his infelicitous phrases, Presbyterians have a "worship rationale" based on their "scriptural understanding." It is embodied in the treasures of the various Reformed liturgies that serious Calvinists have produced since the sixteenth century. What is more, it cannot be embodied in the forms of worship that emerge from different theological traditions. Hustad knows what Calvin knew: You cannot separate form and content.

One American Presbyterian turned German Reformed who saw the connection between liturgy and theology was John Williamson Nevin. He also knew how alien Reformed liturgy was becoming in the United States. Nevertheless, the alternative with which he left his readers at the end of his pamphlet, *The Anxious Bench,* may turn out to be the same choice confronting contemporary American Presbyterians. Nevin closed this piece by asserting that two rival systems were vying for the church's attention: revivalism, represented by the anxious bench, and the Reformed faith, embodied in the catechism. Of the latter he wrote, it "stands the representative and symbol of a system, embracing its own theory of religion, and including a wide circle of agencies, peculiar to itself, for carrying this theory into effect."[50] One of those agencies necessary for carrying out the Reformed system of religion is Reformed liturgy. What American Presbyterians need, and have always needed, is

---

49. Donald P. Hustad, foreword to Barry Liesch, *The New Worship: Straight Talk on Music and the Church* (Grand Rapids: Baker, 1996), 10.

50. John Williamson Nevin, *The Anxious Bench* (Chambersburg, Pa.: Weekly Messenger, 1843), 56.

Nevin's sense of the organic nature of their religion, that liturgy and theology and polity are not like the parts of an automobile that can be changed for newer or better ones but in fact are connected like the branches, trunk, and roots of a tree. Take a limb away, damage the trunk or roots, and a tree either dies or if grafted with branches from another species produces alien fruit. Reformed theology needs Reformed liturgy just as Reformed worship makes no sense without Reformed theology. For that reason, the Reformed tradition will never be healthy if any aspect of its system is neglected or isolated from the whole. The history of American Presbyterian worship proves as much.

14

Revived and Always Reviving

Was the Protestant Reformation a revival? If we define revivalism as a dramatic increase in new converts and an increased zeal on the part of believers to live godly lives, then the Reformation was at least an urban revival in the sense that it took root and changed church life in a number of Northern European cities. If we add that genuine revivals usually include a recovery of the gospel in the context of a church that has substituted human wisdom for God's Word, then again the Protestant Reformation qualifies as a revival. Looking at the Reformation as a revival may explain why most contemporary histories of evangelicalism trace its historical roots first to Martin Luther and John Calvin, then to seventeenth-century pietism and Puritanism, then to the revivals of the First and Second Great Awakenings, and finally to the urban revivalism of Dwight L. Moody, Billy Sunday, and Billy Graham. To be sure, interpreters of evangelicalism would want to differentiate among the efforts of Martin Bucer, George Whitefield, and Charles Grandison Finney. But on the whole, modern evangelicalism has been shaped by the Reformation and revivalism. In other words, reformation and revival are at least compatible if not complementary.

Calvinist evangelicals would, of course, want to qualify the evangelical narrative. Reformation and revival were mutually supportive, they might argue, up to the nineteenth century, when revivalism's theology soured. Up until Finney and the "new measures," revivalists were predominantly Calvinistic, George Whitefield being exhibit A of evidence for the defense. In addition, throughout the nineteenth century, Calvinists, as David Calhoun's two-volume history of Princeton Theological Seminary proves, continued to profit from, pray for, and promote revivals. One of the striking features of Calhoun's valuable work is that it shows how many of Princeton's Old School Presbyterian professors were converted in revivals even after, in many cases, having been reared as covenant children. From a Calvinist perspective, revivals are not inherently defective. They only turn bad when Arminian people run them.

This selective approach to revivalism—welcome when Calvinists preach but nefarious when Arminians manipulate—reveals an inherent weakness in Reformed self-awareness. The standard Reformed assessments of revivalism consider only sound doctrine or the content of preaching. Yet good reasons exist for questioning the compatibility of revivalism and the Reformation, reasons that have to do with the very definitions of the words *reform* and *revive*. Recently, historians of the First Great Awakening have raised important questions about the way the methods of revivals, even when conducted by Calvinists, undercut the work and ministry of the visible church. But even more harmful is the way the term *revival* inherently skews conceptions of the Christian life and how to discern it. Before contrasting the significance of the words *reformed* and *revived*, a brief foray into revivalist history is in order.

Effective Preaching

Gilbert Tennent would no doubt be a worthy candidate for ministry in most Presbyterian churches today. A strong adherent of the Westminster Standards, long-time successful pastor of a prominent Philadelphia congregation, and fierce opponent of liberalism and hypocrisy in the ministry, Tennent is usually considered one of the good guys of colonial American Presbyterianism. But even good guys can go bad under the influence of revivalism. In 1741, during a heated controversy among Presbyterians over Whitefield's itinerant preaching, Tennent added fuel to the fire with his sermon "The Danger of an Unconverted Ministry." He insinuated that opponents of Whitefield's preaching were unregenerate, or just like the Pharisees—that is, leaders in the church who had not been born again. Furthermore, Tennent argued that God would bless only the ministry of converted pastors. "These foolish builders," he exclaimed, "do but strengthen Men's carnal Security, by their soft, selfish, cowardly Discourses." These false ministers pointed the unregenerate to their duty to obey God's law, as if such obedience would "recommend natural Men to the Favour of GOD, or entitle them to the Promises of Grace and Salvation."[1] Tennent insinu-

---

1. Gilbert Tennent, "The Danger of an Unconverted Ministry," in *The Great Awakening*, ed. Alan Heimert and Perry Miller (Indianapolis: Bobbs-Merrill, 1967), 78.

ated not only that he could identify a converted minister but also that, according to his logic, only regenerate ministers could produce sound and true preaching. An unregenerate pastor automatically preached false doctrine.

To be sure, the ideal pastor is one who has truly trusted in Christ for salvation. But Tennent's conception of the ministry appears to have little room for the views expressed in the Second Helvetic Confession (1561). In the first chapter on Scripture, Heinrich Bullinger, Ulrich Zwingli's successor in Zurich, wrote that when the Word of God is preached by pastors "lawfully called, we believe that the very Word of God is proclaimed, and received by the faithful" (chap. 1). Such a high view of preaching even applied to unfaithful pastors, "for even if he be evil and a sinner, nevertheless the Word of God remains still true and good" (chap. 1). And just in case Reformed believers missed the point, Bullinger added in chapter 18 on the ministry that "we know that the voice of Christ is to be heard, though it be out of the mouths of evil ministers," in the same way that sacraments are sanctified "by the institution and the word of Christ" and are effectual to the godly, even if "administered by unworthy ministers" (chap. 1). In contrast to Tennent's argument that only the preaching of converted ministers would be effectual, Bullinger taught in the Second Helvetic Confession that God would bless even the preaching of wicked ministers.

Tennent's sermon and the Second Helvetic Confession represent different ideas about effective preaching. Tennent indicates a view widely prevalent in evangelical circles that locates effectiveness in the soul or salvation of the minister; if the minister does not believe what he preaches, then his sermons will lack power and conviction. This understandable desire for a believing pastor can lead to the excesses of modern evangelicalism in which the minister's charisma, personality, and charm determine whether his ministry is successful. (This is not to say that pastors should be poor speakers, unlearned, and dull.) The Second Helvetic Confession, in contrast, states that the effectiveness of a sermon depends on God alone, not the spiritual (or natural) abilities of the minister. Even in the extreme case in which the sermon comes out of the mouth of an unregenerate minister, those in the congregation still hear the very Word of God. (This is not to say that we should ignore the profession of faith of a candidate for gospel ministry.) Yet the contrast here can be drawn too starkly. As a good Calvinist, Tennent would not deny the necessity of God's power for preaching to lead to repentance and conversion, or mercy and comfort. Nor would Bullinger deny the importance of godly and therefore believing ministers. Still, the difference between the Reformed and revivalistic conceptions of the ministry is evident in Tennent and the Second Helvetic Confession. The Reformers knew that only God could turn the Word preached into a means of salvation and sanctification, while revivalists acted as if the actions and affects of men were necessary for a work of God to occur.

The modern upshot of revivalism's influence is the triumph of the subjective over the objective elements of the Christian religion. Because of revivalism's concern for the internal state of the preacher or the convert, it fostered an attitude that places a premium on the sincerity and assurance of Christian profession. At the same time, it nurtured disregard for the necessity and importance of external forms, whether in liturgy, creeds, or church polity. As long as the heart is in the right place, as long as methods lead to conversion and repentance, then the forms of religiosity do not matter (do the worship wars come to mind?). In contrast, the Reformed tradition refused to separate the internal from the external aspects of Christian faith and practice. Even though the subjective state of the soul is important, the objective expressions of Christianity are no less important. Worship, confession, and government, the external forms by which we judge the faithfulness of churches, matter not only because God desires true worship, faithful teaching, and right order in his church but also because these objective forms are the means he has ordained to minister to human souls. Consequently, while for revivalists effective preaching was that form of communication that showed the presence and power of God in the life of the preacher, for the Reformed it was a sermon that conformed to the truth of God's Word regardless of whether the pastor believed or conversions followed from it. Unfortunately, because of revivalism's triumph since the eighteenth century, the older reformational synthesis of the external and the internal has been neglected.

"O Be Careful Little Mouth"

Perhaps a better way of showing these differences is to contrast the words *revive* and *reform*. These words connote the same difference already noted between Tennent and the Second Helvetic Confession. The word *revive* suggests an effort to recover genuine spiritual existence and vitality in the lives of believers and to introduce nonbelievers to the eternal life that comes through Christ. A revival cuts through the forms and "vain repetitions" of established and hypocritical religion and goes to the heart to cause and nurture genuine conversion and real repentance. Revivalism thrives on the desire for authentic religion, and its aim is individualistic. To be sure, the more people revived, the better the church may be. But revival stresses individual conversion and personal morality.

The word *reform*, however, suggests a restructuring of a specific order. A reform takes an existing organization or body and makes it conform to a correct or true standard and norm. While revivals aim at generating or deepening spiritual life in individuals, reformations strive to impart a more faithful shape to the visible church in its corporate life, in doctrine, worship, and government.

Though these meanings of *revive* and *reform* do not come from Webster's dictionary, they are implicit in the arguments used to defend both revivalism and reformation. If a revival occurs, its defenders argue that spiritual life has been imparted. In other words, the Spirit of God has been at work. This was true in the eighteenth century, and it is true today. Tennent, for instance, not only thought that ministers who supported Whitefield's revivals were regenerate—after all, he assumed that Whitefield's opponents were dangerous because unconverted—but also presumed that the revivals of his day were a work of God. More recently, Iain Murray has followed a similar logic. Though he has not gone as far as Tennent in questioning the regeneration of individual ministers, Murray is convinced that the First Great Awakening was a work of God. He believes revivals are occasions in which God blesses the ordinary means of grace in an extraordinary way, but he is not reluctant to conclude that the Great Awakening of the eighteenth century was the result of the work of the Spirit. Murray's conclusion should not be surprising. Calvinists believe that only God can give spiritual life to the unregenerate, and therefore, a revival ipso facto has to be a work of God. But that begs the epistemological question of whether we can know for sure where and when God's Spirit is active.

The interpretive stakes are not quite as high, however, when it comes to telling whether reformation has taken place. The marks of the church, according to the Reformers, serve as one important way to discern where the gospel is. Unlike revivalism, which encourages the evaluation of things that are invisible, namely, the human soul, a reformation promotes the search for phenomena that can be observed by the human senses. In the words of the Belgic Confession, Article 29, "The marks by which the true church is known are these: if the pure doctrine of the gospel is preached therein; if she maintains the pure administration of the sacraments as instituted by Christ; if church discipline is exercised in punishing of sin; in short, if all things are managed according to the pure Word of God." In other words, to look for reformation is to evaluate visible or external forms. To look for revival is to make judgments about things invisible and internal.

The "reformed" and the "revived," therefore, make different determinations when they look for reformation and revival. Proponents of revival make claims that should be reserved for God, for example, whether a soul has truly come to new life in Christ. To be sure, the "revived" look for evidence in visible and external things such as profession and deed. But to say that a revival occurred is to determine that God actually regenerated a remarkable number of souls. The parable of the sower suggests the need for less certainty in making such a determination. The "reformed," however, do not pretend to look into the state of souls or to make judgments about God's intervention in human history. Yes, they do use the language of "true" and "false" churches, which is a form of evaluation that connotes eternal significance. Still, they make no claims about the spiritual state of individuals. And in the context of sixteenth-century Europe, one did not need to be a believer to spot a Reformed church. A professing Roman Catholic would have seen an extraordinarily different liturgy in a Protestant church and would have known that this congregation had been "reformed." The difference, of course, was that a Protestant would have called such visible changes true, while the Catholic believer would have regarded them as false.

The lesson taught by the differences implicit in the words *reformed* and *revived* is not simply that we should be careful about claiming to know things we cannot. It is also that our assessment of Christian expressions and practice will always be limited to forms. We cannot see into the human heart and therefore must judge whether the words and deeds of an individual believer's life are credible and whether the liturgy, teaching, and government of a congregation are reformed according to the Word. In other words, we are limited to the world of appearances, and our conclusions should always reflect a caution befitting the limits of our knowledge. For this reason, professing believers who cherish the Reformed faith might want to delete the words *revival, revived,* and *revive* from their vocabulary. If you are Reformed, you should know that detecting the pulse of spiritual life in a convert or the hand of God in human history is work that only God, who surpasses human understanding, can do.

15

The Inevitability of Liturgy

One of the common ways of configuring the world of American Protestantism is to divide it along the lines of worship practice. Accordingly, there are liturgical and nonliturgical churches. The former would most likely include Episcopalians, Lutherans, and in some cases Methodists. These communions are considered liturgical because they use prayer books and set forms for worship, their ministers dress in garb different from the congregation (gowns or robes), an occasional processional and recessional begins and ends the service, their ministers preach homilies rather than sermons, they observe the Lord's Supper weekly, and the mood in worship is generally sober and dignified. The nonliturgical group includes everyone else, but evangelicals are most typically seen as having perfected the nonliturgical worship service. Evangelicals are nonliturgical because they refrain from the elements that characterize liturgical worship. They pray extemporaneously, they avoid routine or prescribed orders of worship, their ministers dress in suits or sometimes even less formal attire, they do not use a special festivity to mark the beginning or end of a worship service, their ministers preach a lengthy sermon beginning in almost clocklike fashion at the middle of the service, they occasionally celebrate the Lord's Supper (monthly or bimonthly), and their services have a casual atmosphere.

For readers curious about where to place Presbyterian and Reformed denominations, it might be tempting to designate a liturgical no-man's-land. In some ways, Calvinists look to be clearly on the side of the nonliturgicals. They are the ones, after all, who rejected almost every element of worship that smacked of Roman Catholicism. Out went the set liturgies, the mass, the practices that turned pastors into priests, the church calendar, and the homily. Calvinists overhauled worship, making it more accessible to the laity, less ritualistic, less formulaic, and more dominated by the Word of God. Thus, Calvinists put the Bible front and center in worship not only by making the preaching of it the centerpiece of worship but also by using Scripture for prayers sung and read and for the opening and close of the service (the invocation and the benediction). Yet Calvinists held on to the gravity and the sobriety that characterizes liturgical worship. To be sure, Reformed worship is much simpler and, Calvinists would argue, more spiritual than liturgical worship, in the sense that it follows Christ's command in John 4 to worship God in spirit and in truth. Presbyterians and Reformed also have a high view of ordained ministry, even if the pastor is not a priest. The pastor is the one who speaks for God and to God for the people. In some Reformed communions, pastors still wear the Geneva gown to designate the special task to which they are called.

The divide between liturgical and nonliturgical churches is too simple, for at the most basic level, any service is liturgical if by that we mean having a set order of worship. In other words, whenever a church prints a bulletin that lists even the simplest arrangement of the service, it has a liturgy, or a set order of when the prayers will be said; the hymns, psalms, or praise songs sung; and the sermon, homily, or inspiring message given. Conceived in this way, "praise and worship" is just as liturgical as Anglo-Catholicism. In fact, a church cannot help but have a liturgy if it wants to have a worship service with any order to it. As long as everyone is expected to be engaged in the same element, whether prayer, preaching, sacrament, or praise, at the same time, a church needs and therefore has a liturgy.

Nevertheless, these caveats aside, it is still accurate to see evangelicalism as hostile to liturgy, that is, to a form of worship that is restrained, dignified, and austere. Worship that manifests these characteristics, according to many evangelicals, stifles the free movement of the Holy Spirit. Even worse, formality and control in worship are telltale signs of spiritual deadness. If Christians are excited about the things of the Lord, and if the Holy Spirit is really present in worship, the service will hardly be able to contain such vitality. Churches that insist on a certain order and decorum in worship, from an evangelical perspective, are guilty of reining in the spontaneous operations of God. Indeed, one of the reasons for the triumph of so-called contemporary forms of worship is their close affinity to the charismatic movement, which has become since 1960 the most popular Christian idiom. This also suggests that much of the confusion about worship within Protestant circles is bound up with confusion about the nature and work of the Holy Spirit.

The Liturgy of the Great Commission

But evangelical hostility to liturgy, in the sense of balking at formality, decorum, and sobriety in worship, came well before the rise and appeal of charismatics. One of the first threats to accepted patterns of worship, whether Lutheran, Reformed, Episcopalian, Quaker, or Anabaptist, occurred during the triumph of revivalism and mass evangelism. This victory did not happen with the crusades of Charles Finney during the Second Great Awakening (1820s and 1830s)—Finney merely built on assumptions about worship that had been forged almost a century earlier. Rather, the origins of mass evangelism can be traced to the efforts and practices of George Whitefield and his supporters during the First Great Awakening (1740s). Few historians of that revival study Whitefield's liturgy and for good reason. The meetings at which Whitefield spoke, whether in a field, a market, or a church (the latter were rare because church buildings could not accommodate large crowds), were not services of worship. Instead, they were vehicles designed to move individuals to an experience of converting grace. Whitefield's audiences may have sung praise, he may have led them in prayer and confession of sin, and he may even have begun with an invocation, but the chief reason people came was to hear his message, not to worship God. For this reason, the modern-day equivalent of Whitefield's revivals is not a church service but rather the mass meetings sponsored by Promise Keepers.

Of course, we cannot blame the excesses of revivalism on Whitefield, whose theology was Calvinist in outline. Charles Finney codified the standard feature of a revival, the lone evangelical contribution to liturgy, namely, the altar call (though Methodist circuit riders could rightly claim this innovation for themselves). But while the altar call used to be reserved for the revival meeting and is still the way Billy Graham closes his services, it eventually became a regular part of evangelical worship. It became a standard practice for evangelical ministers to conclude their sermons with an invitation to come forward to accept Christ or rededicate oneself to a holy life. Rather than following the sermon with the celebration of the Lord's Supper, in which believers come forward to a table or a rail to receive Christ in the elements of bread and wine, evangelicals follow it with an invitation to come forward to meet Christ in the form of the altar call. As T. David Gordon has argued, the evangelical practice of calling people to receive Christ at the close of the service was in some ways wholesome because the sermon should make ultimate claims on the individual soul. But the problem is that evangelicals replaced the Lord's Supper, the very means God gave his church to call believers to repentance and commitment, with the altar call, a manipulative practice designed to generate a quick decision for Christ.

Revivalism was just as destructive in reconfiguring the purpose of worship. Worship in evangelical circles is oriented primarily to reaching the lost rather than to ascribing power and glory to God. Once the gathering of the saints and the proclamation of the Word become chiefly a way to reach the lost, worship moves from its properly God-centered orientation to one in which pleasing men and women, preferably the lost (or in today's lingo, "seekers"), becomes the overarching goal.

Worship as Homeroom

While revivalism upended Protestant patterns of worship wherever it went, thus making evangelicals hostile to accepted liturgies and re-defining the meaning of worship, it also proved to be destructive to a proper understanding of the work of the church. One of the curious features of the relatively recent novelties associated with church growth is the decline in the use of the altar call in churches desiring to reach unchurched Harry and Harriet. This is curious because the first seeker-sensitive ministers and churches were those who took an active interest in the work of revivals. Revivals, after all, were the way to reach the lost. But in an era of refined consumer tastes and sharp competition for market share, altar calls do not appear to be effective anymore. Why would the owners of a half-a-million dollar home in the suburbs want to subject themselves to the embarrassment of walking down the aisle to pray a prayer of conversion in a place where they are strangers? These same homeowners would probably be just as reluctant to walk down to the front at the end of a PTA meeting to volunteer to assist with the school lunch program. Such an act is too uncomfortable and exacting for consumers who want the comforts of faith without the commitments.

Consequently, many churches that want to grow and make an impact (or "transform the culture," in Reformed coinage) sponsor a variety of programs designed to meet the felt needs of residents in the vicinity. This way of growing the local church has had a profound effect on worship and says volumes about the way evangelicals regard the task of the church. If the real work of the church is the ministry that all the saints perform for each other throughout the week, whether in a

Christian aerobics class, a story hour for preschoolers, classes on parenting for first-time fathers and mothers, or even the more legitimate evening Bible study, then the weekly gathering of the saints on the Lord's Day takes on a much different character and purpose. Word, sacrament, and prayer, the traditional marks and purposes of the church and, as the Westminster Shorter Catechism describes them, "the outward and ordinary means whereby God communicates to us the benefits of redemption" (Ans. 88), become less important. Ministry is no longer defined by these means of grace but rather by all the things that believers do in times of fellowship and support groups. (This is not to say that fellowship and support are unimportant. But fellowship and support are things that spheres such as the family and the neighborhood also provide and may not be at the heart of the church's ministry.) In the process, worship becomes not a time for the proclamation of the Word in preaching and sacrament but a time to rally support for all the programs of the church. In other words, worship in the "successful" church becomes homeroom.

Homeroom, as all graduates of public high schools know, is that time usually at the beginning of the school day during which the logistics of the educational enterprise are addressed. The teacher takes attendance, pupils say the Pledge of Allegiance, and administrators or teachers make announcements about upcoming school events and programs. In many churches, this is exactly what worship has become. The attendance pads at the ends of pews provide a record of individuals present for church. Praise songs projected overhead are the equivalent of the Pledge of Allegiance. And the announcements that come in a variety of forms perform the function of—well—announcements. It is interesting to note the many ways in which announcements are given in evangelical worship. Ministers or various heads of committees talk about upcoming events in the church. Testimonies become plugs for a specific program in the church. Then there is the time for recognizing or even commissioning various workers in the church, whether Sunday school or Vacation Bible School teachers, which also draws attention to church programs and the need for more laborers.

The significant differences between evangelical worship and public high school homeroom are the collection of the offering and the pastor's message. Public schools rely on real estate taxes and therefore have no need to pass the plate in homeroom. Public schools also have the sense to put lectures in real class time rather than mixing them with the details of operating the school. But the message in evangelical worship does allow the pastor to give a pep talk that will inspire church members to become involved in the weekly activities of the congregation, much like the high school principal's pleas for volunteers during homeroom. In the process, the means of grace become the means of motivation. Rather than regarding the proclamation of the Word as the way of "convincing and converting sinners and of building them up in holiness and comfort" (WSC Ans. 89), preaching is a tool for inspiring believers to become involved in the real work of the church—that is, all the activities and programs throughout the week. As a result, preaching and the other elements of worship, indeed, the entire liturgy, suffer. People no longer see them as the means of being nurtured in the faith but instead perceive "special ministries" as the ways of reaching out, growing the church, and making members more devout.

Spiritual Positivism

The mention of devoutness raises the question of what counts for devotion in evangelical circles. This question also has important implications as to why evangelicals do not care for liturgy, whether in the sense of an ethos of formality and sobriety or in the sense of using prayer books, hymnals, Scripture lessons, and exegetical preaching, for the way that evangelicals have come to judge whether devotion or piety is genuine stems from a faulty view of religious experience.

Evangelicals have for almost three centuries distrusted the formal and the routine in worship. They discount forms in worship because they insist that genuine piety or faith must be expressed in an individual's own words. A believer who uses the language of the Westminster Confession of Faith to express his or her own faith or uses prayers written by dead Christians is going through the motions and has not experienced a real outpouring of grace, which would automatically express itself in personal and intimate language. Thus, evangelicals often ridicule the elements of various liturgies as dead and boring. Real Christian experience comes alive in new and different words, and the more emotional and intimate those words are, the better. Evangelicals are also suspicious of routine in worship for similar reasons. Order or set patterns of worship restrict or confine the movement of the Holy Spirit. It does not seem to matter that these elements may be precisely the means that God uses to bring people to himself. If some people do not respond well to the various elements of worship, such as the unchurched, then we need to find new ways of worship that will allow seekers to be moved by the Spirit.

The irony, of course, is that even the most seemingly spontaneous and informal worship can be just as formal and routine as the highest of Anglo-Catholic services. Anytime there is an order of service (e.g., thirty minutes of praise songs, thirty minutes of talking by the pastor, and twenty minutes for prayer, announcements, and offering), then worship is not spontaneous. Also, what evangelicals so often fail to remember is that outward expressions of piety, whether the hymn "A Mighty Fortress" or the praise song "Majesty," do not guarantee or determine the state of the singer's heart. A participant in the most charismatic of services can fake speaking in tongues and being slain in the Spirit just as much as a Presbyterian can fake recitation of the Nicene Creed, praying the Lord's Prayer, and paying attention to the sermon. None of us can see into the human heart. All we have to go on are outward appearances or a credible profession of faith. Worshiping in a particular manner does not indicate the state of the soul. Once this truth is conceded, once it is a given that all worship will be formal in some sense because we cannot help but use forms in worship (again speaking in tongues is as much a form as a corporate prayer of confession), the question then becomes, Which forms of worship does God reveal to us? The answer to that question is not announcements, testimonies, and special music. Rather, the elements or forms of worship revealed in Scripture are the reading and preaching of the Word, prayer, singing of praise, and the administration of the sacraments.

But these forms are not satisfying to evangelicals, hence their hostility to liturgy. These forms are dissatisfying because evangelicals want absolute certainty in knowing who is and who is not a real Christian. Because forms are not good barometers of the state of the human heart, evangelicals have looked for other clues. The clue that seems to be the most convincing is experience, especially a religious experience that testifies to a dramatic and immediate work of God in an individual's life. Conversion filled the bill for a long time. But then came the second blessing of perfection and with it speaking in tongues and, most recently, holy laughter. Whatever the manifestation, evangelicals want direct proof of God's activity. This activity has to be visible, a dramatically changed life or an extraordinary display of piety. Thus, evangelicals, despite their seemingly mystical stress on experience, are really closet positivists. They need a physical manifestation of grace to be convinced that it has occurred and are not content with expressions of grace that may be formal, routine, restrained, and conventional. This conclusion only confirms David Bebbington's suggestive observation that evangelicalism originated at the same time as the Enlightenment and adopted criteria for spiritual truth that were remarkably similar to the standards for truth that scientists used in the natural world. Both Enlightenment philosophers and evangelical itinerant preachers demanded that truth be empirically discernible. Such a move was disastrous for Christianity. It repudiated what Scripture teaches about the inscrutability of God's dealings with humankind and the hiddenness of the human heart. It also denied the importance of the work of the church in providing a body of believers and a pattern of devotion in which an individual's faith is disciplined and nurtured.

Liturgical Renewal?

Of course, some evangelicals are beginning to rediscover liturgy. A successful megachurch will often have not only a P & W service but also one with robes, choirs, and read prayers. But these dabblings in liturgy are not the genuine article. They display once more the entrepreneurial instinct of evangelicalism, another way to attract the unchurched, this time the ones with tastes too refined and minds too intelligent to be satisfied with the MTV-like worship that characterizes many evangelical services.

The solution, of course, is not for evangelicals to rediscover the value or appeal of liturgy. Rather, evangelicals need to take stock theologically of what constitutes biblical worship, the real purpose and ministry of the church, and genuine Christian piety. But that kind of stock-taking would undo evangelicalism, for it would send evangelicals off to the riches of the Reformed, Lutheran, and Anglican traditions in which these matters have been defined and articulated and in which worship is the logical extension of a congregation's confession of faith and lies at the heart of the church's mission. And it would get rid of those awful praise songs. Keep that thought.

16

Twentieth-Century American Presbyterian Hymnody

Arguably, one of the best books ever written on congregational and liturgical song is Thomas Day's *Why Catholics Can't Sing*.[1] If not the best, it is the funniest. For example, Day describes that memorable scene of his friend trying to pass the peace to an elderly woman who was absorbed with her rosary beads during the mass at Philadelphia's Cathedral. The response from the woman to "May the peace of the Lord be with you" cannot be found in any Christian liturgy, nor is it repeatable in polite company.[2] But it wonderfully captured the problem Day set out to explain, namely, why Catholic congregations' participation in the liturgy, especially in congregational singing, was about as warm as this hoary Catholic woman's response to the handshake of peace. Here is how Day described the difficulty: "Today, a large number of Roman Catholics in the United States who go to church regularly—perhaps the majority—rarely or barely sing any of the music. . . . This stands out as a most curious development in the history of Christianity."[3]

What is interesting about Day's book for what follows is the contrast Day draws between Catholics and Presbyterians. While in graduate school, Day worked as a substitute organist, playing in Catholic and Presbyterian churches. The difference between the two services, espe-

1. Thomas Day, *Why Catholics Can't Sing: The Culture of Catholicism and the Triumph of Bad Taste* (New York: Crossroad, 1990).
2. Ibid., 6.
3. Ibid., 1.

cially given that the congregations sometimes sang the exact same hymn, was in Day's estimate amazing. "Why," Day asked, "did the small Presbyterian church make such a joyful noise, while the Catholics sounded almost in pain?" It was not because Presbyterians alone are such good singers. Day also acknowledged that he had been in Episcopalian churches in which fifty church members produced "more volume than three hundred Roman Catholics."[4] From Day's perspective, this indicated that Protestants are healthier than Catholics. "When hundreds of parishioners packed into a church do not even make an attempt to sing *Silent Night* . . . you have a religious, social, and cultural breakdown of astounding proportions."[5]

The history of Presbyterian hymnody and their twentieth-century hymnals might prompt Day to revise his assessment of Protestant singing. To be sure, Day is correct to observe that Presbyterians, both mainline and sideline, sing well, often, and with gusto. But after examining their thick hymnals with short shelf lives along with Presbyterian writing about corporate worship, one could legitimately ask whether Presbyterians know why they sing. In other words, the volume of singing alone may not be a reliable index of liturgical well-being, just as the consumption of large quantities of food does not make one a gourmet. What believers sing is just as important. And the history of Presbyterian hymnals in the last century indicates that the liturgical heirs of John Calvin and John Knox have acquired an undiscriminating taste for congregational song. At the same time, Presbyterians do not complain much. Whatever hymns their denominational committees offer, Presbyterians are likely to sing.

This may not in itself be a lamentable condition, and it is by no means one that Presbyterians bear alone. But it does provide a useful gauge to measure the direction of Presbyterian worship practices. In fact, recent developments in Presbyterian hymnody indicate the liturgical thin ice on which American Presbyterians tread every time they gather for worship. Over the last 250 years, Presbyterianism, and the Reformed tradition more generally, has not distinguished itself as fertile ground for the making of hymns, especially compared to other Protestant traditions. Lutherans have Bach, Episcopalians have Vaughn Williams, Methodists have Charles Wesley, and Pentecostals have Jack Hayford. The closest Presbyterians have come to making a contribution to Protestant hymnody is Louis F. Benson, perhaps the twentieth-century's leading student of hymns but not much of a producer of song for corporate worship. Part of the trouble for Calvinists is the legacy of ex-

4. Ibid., 4, 1.
5. Ibid., 3.

clusive psalmody. As Benson himself put it in the Stone Lectures he gave at Princeton Seminary in 1927, the musical bind in which Presbyterians historically have found themselves is as old as the Christian church. "Has the Church a right," he asked, "to supersede or even enlarge the hymn book that is of canonical authority? Is it not audacious to supplement inspired Psalms with hand-made hymns?" Benson then went one step farther. "Even if it be lawful" to replace psalms with hymns, "is it expedient?" This was, in his estimation, even as late as the 1920s, well after mainline American Presbyterianism had introduced hymns into corporate worship, "the issue" not just for Benson's fellow Presbyterians but for all Christians.[6]

As it turns out, what for Benson was "the issue" has not been much of a factor for Presbyterians and the hymnals they have produced. If their books of song show anything it is that Presbyterians sing a lot but do not have much of an idea why they sing what they do. What follows is an analysis of the most popular hymns (i.e., the most frequently published) in twentieth-century Presbyterian hymnals, both mainline and sideline, with some attempt to explain these preferences.[7] This study shows that so-called conservative and liberal Presbyterians, contrary to the oft-repeated claim that "theology matters," have roughly the same favorite hymns, still pay deference to the tradition of psalmody, and sing hymns mainly for pedagogical or homiletical reasons. The explanation for these similarities has as much to do with liturgical developments in the seventeenth and eighteenth centuries as with the particulars of twentieth-century American Presbyterianism. Whatever Presbyterian hymnals reveal about the liturgical health of the Reformed tradition in the United States, the Presbyterian experience illustrates perhaps the most important lesson taught by evangelical hymnody over the last cen-

6. Louis F. Benson, *The Hymnody of the Christian Church* (1927; reprint, Richmond: John Knox, 1956), 57–58.

7. The hymnals surveyed here run chronologically as follows: General Assembly of the Presbyterian Church in the U.S., *The New Psalms and Hymns* (Richmond: Presbyterian Committee of Publication, 1901); General Assembly of the Presbyterian Church, U.S.A., *The Hymnal*, rev. ed. (Philadelphia: Presbyterian Board of Publication and Sabbath-School Work, 1911); General Assembly of the Presbyterian Church, U.S.A., *The Hymnal* (Philadelphia: Presbyterian Board of Education, 1933); Presbyterian Church, U.S. et al., *The Hymnbook* (Richmond: John Ribble, 1955); Committee on Christian Education, Orthodox Presbyterian Church, *The Trinity Hymnal* (Philadelphia: Great Commission Publications, 1961); Joint Committee on Worship, *The Worshipbook* (Philadelphia: Westminster, 1972); Great Commission Publications, *The Trinity Hymnal* (Philadelphia: Great Commission Publications, 1990); and Westminster John Knox, *The Presbyterian Hymnal* (Louisville: Westminster John Knox, 1990). There is one additional hymnal, the PCUSA's 1927 *Presbyterian Hymnal*, that was not included in this survey because its indexes are so poor and because its editors failed to attribute hymn texts to biblical (e.g., Psalm) sources.

tury: The trend that encourages greater ecumenicity through song also functions as a generic solvent of historic liturgical and theological traditions.

Presbyterian Song before Benson

The eight hymnals that Presbyterians have produced over the last century for corporate worship must be regarded first in the context of Calvin's Anglo-American heirs' inexperience with hymns.[8] Here it is important to remember that American Presbyterians did not create their first hymnal until 1831, and they were among the first in the Reformed tradition to do so. In other words, only after 125 years of Presbyterian history in the New World did the Reformed branch of the Protestant Reformation officially embrace hymnody. By 1831, American Presbyterians apparently felt the need to make up for lost time and produced nine different hymnals during the rest of the nineteenth century. With the addition of eight more during the twentieth century, American Presbyterians have since 1831 gone through seventeen official denominationally sponsored hymnals for use in corporate worship. That pattern averages out to a staggering rate of a new Presbyterian hymnal every decade.

One of the major reasons American Presbyterians have apparently rushed into the business of making many hymnals may be that, coming out of the Protestant Reformation, the prospects for Presbyterian hymnody were grim. The gravity of worship and the fear of blasphemy made the Calvinist wing of the Reformation extremely wary about what went on during the course of a service. As a result, two positions emerged, one propounded by the churches in Zurich under the direction of Ulrich Zwingli and Heinrich Bullinger, the other articulated by the churches in Geneva, led by John Calvin. Although Zwingli was likely the best musician among the Reformers, he removed song from worship, in part because of its potentially destructive power and also because he found no biblical warrant for singing in worship. He acknowledged that the apostle Paul did in fact teach Christians to sing (e.g., Col. 3:16) but countered that this instruction did not necessarily address corporate worship. In fact, Paul's meaning was for believers to sing "in their hearts," not necessarily with their mouths. Consequently, aside from removing organs from Zurich's churches, Zwingli went one better and left song out of Reformed worship. Nowhere is this liturgical point more evident than in the Second Helvetic Confession, written by

---

8. Nine, counting the 1927 *Presbyterian Hymnal*, which goes without saying hereafter.

Zwingli's successor, Bullinger, who made congregational singing optional. Chapter 23 of the confession reads, "If there be any churches which have faithful prayer in good manner, without any singing, they are not therefore to be condemned, for all churches have not the advantage and opportunity of sacred music" (iv).

In Geneva, things were not as austere for worshipers gifted with good voices. Calvin did eliminate organs, like Zwingli, not because he despised music but because he understood its attraction and potential for abuse, especially without words. But Calvin departed from Zwingli's spiritualizing of the Pauline writings about song. Believers should really sing, both with voice and heart. The question, then, was what to sing. Calvin's answer was simple—the psalms. He believed this was the pattern of the early church, which picked up the practice of worship in the synagogue. Calvin also thought that songs functioned in worship as a form of prayer. What better words to use in praying to God than the ones he had inspired? Calvin's understanding of song prompted the Geneva churches to commission the production of a psalter from Clement Marot; Theodore Beza, who supplied the verse; and Louis Bourgeois, who wrote the tunes. The Geneva Psalter went through seven editions in Calvin's lifetime (1539, 1541, 1543, 1545, 1551, 1554, and 1562), with the final one including all 150 psalms, with 125 tunes and 110 different meters.[9]

For Presbyterians and Puritans (Reformed also, for that matter) who sided with Calvin over Zwingli, the way to sing in congregational worship was from a psalter. Indeed, the seventeenth century witnessed little deviation from Calvin's norm, whether in the Church of England, the Church of Scotland, or the dissenting Protestant churches. For Anglicans, Sternhold and Hopkins, a psalter produced during the reign of Edward VI, and Tate and Brady's version published in 1696 were the only psalters authorized for use in public worship.[10] The Scottish Kirk produced a psalter as early as 1564, before Andro Hart issued another in 1615, which in 1635 was reissued and updated by Hart's heirs.[11] When Presbyterians began in the early eighteenth century to show up in the North American British colonies in numbers large enough to merit a denomination, they carried their psalters with them. In fact, the Old Side/New Side controversy that led to the first rupture of American Presbyterianism in 1741 may have been as much about rival psalters as

9. Paul Westermeyer, *Te Deum: The Church and Music* (Minneapolis: Fortress, 1988), 153–58.

10. Robert Stevenson, *Patterns of Protestant Church Music* (Durham, N.C.: Duke University Press, 1953), 120.

11. Erik Routley, *The Music of Christian Hymnody* (London: Independent Press, 1957), 42.

about George Whitefield's revivals and subscription to the Westminster Confession of Faith and Catechisms. The stodgier Old Side used *The Psalms of David in English Meter*, prepared in 1643 by Francis Rous, a Presbyterian turned Independent and member of the Westminster Assembly, or that of another Puritan, William Barton's *Book of Psalms in Metre* (1644). The more innovative New Side preferred Tate and Brady.

The introduction of a new type of song into churches in which metrical psalms had been the norm also contributed to the Old Side/New Side struggle. The source of this novelty was Benjamin Franklin's publication in 1729 of the first American edition of Isaac Watts's *The Psalms of David Imitated*. To be sure, Watts's songs were not full-blown hymns like the ones he had written for *Hymns and Spiritual Songs* (1707), which were compositions based on scriptural thoughts as well as the fullness of biblical revelation in the New Testament. In his imitations of the psalter, Watts was simply trying to present psalms in a way "accommodated to modern Gospel worship."[12] Even so, Watts's Christianizing of the psalms was an explicit break with the tradition of metrical psalmody that had prevailed among Presbyterians and Reformed since Calvin.

Watts's renovated psalmody slowly gained a foothold among colonial Presbyterians during the revivals for which George Whitefield became the cause celebre. The initial publication of Watts in 1729 would have to wait until 1741 for a second edition.[13] The New Side, who supported Whitefield, tended to buy copies of Watts's gospel psalms. As early as 1746, Whitefield's Presbyterian sympathizers in Newburyport began to use Watts, and soon thereafter the Presbytery of Boston followed suit.[14] Whitefield himself actively promoted Watts's *Hymns* and *Psalms*, which, according to Henry Wilder Foote, the revivalist "greatly admired." Foote also states that Whitefield prompted Jonathan Edwards to introduce Watts into public worship at his Northampton church.[15] In the South, Samuel Davies, an itinerant evangelist in Virginia as early as 1752, introduced not only Watts's psalms but also his hymns. When Davies left Virginia to preside over the newly founded College of New Jersey, a New Side institution, his successor, John Todd, petitioned his presbytery to approve the use of Watts's psalms and hymns, because the churches "have received great advantage"

12. Louis Fitzgerald Benson, *The English Hymn: Its Development and Use* (Philadelphia: Presbyterian Board of Publication, 1915), 101.
13. Westermeyer, *Te Deum*, 204.
14. Benson, *English Hymn*, 180.
15. Henry Wilder Foote, *Three Centuries of American Hymnody* (Cambridge: Harvard University Press, 1940), 147–48.

from the writer's "excellent compositions, especially his sacramental hymns."[16]

During the seventeen years during which the Old Side Presbyterian Church ministered separately from the New Side, Watts's imitations never became an issue, and the ethnic composition of the Old Side helps to explain this absence. As a communion that was predominantly Scotch-Irish, the Old Side churches were devoted to Rous's version of the psalms and fully prepared to resist innovation. So adamant could the Scotch-Irish be in their opposition to new songs that in 1756 New York's "Scotch Church" withdrew from the Synod of New York (a New Side body) to align with the Associate Presbytery, a communion composed of secessionist churches from the Church of Scotland. By 1765, after the reunion of the Old and New Sides, the issue was hardly settled. In a dispute over the proper content of song in worship, the Synod of New York and Philadelphia ruled that "the inspired Psalms in Scripture" were "proper matter to be sung in Divine worship, according to their original design and the practice of the Christian churches." At the same time, the Synod refused to "forbid" those "whose judgment and inclination lead them to use the imitation of psalms."[17]

From 1765 until 1831, American Presbyterians were truly conflicted over congregational song. Watts gained in popularity as his work came out in newer and better editions. At the same time, many Presbyterians continued in their attachment to Rous's version. Even though a denominationally approved hymnal would have to wait until the fourth decade of the nineteenth century, the first General Assembly of American Presbyterians in effect settled the controversy when in 1789 it adopted its first *Directory for the Worship of God*. Instead of saying that the "duty of Christians was to praise God publiquely by singing Psalms," as a first draft stated, following the lead of the Westminster Assembly's *Directory*, the General Assembly said instead that the duty of believers in public praise was to sing "psalms and hymns."[18] Because for Presbyterians in the new nation the words "hymns" and "Watts" were synonymous, Watts's *Hymns*, as Benson put it, "may be called the first hymn book of American Presbyterians."[19] Until 1831, Presbyterians used Watts's and Rous's texts in corporate worship.

The primacy of Watts and metrical psalmody, then, is the best framework for trying to make sense of the many hymnals Presbyterians have published. The Anglo-American liturgical descendents of John Calvin

16. Benson, *English Hymn,* 182.
17. Ibid.
18. Ibid., 191.
19. Ibid., 193.

have felt a duty to show allegiance to metrical psalms even while possibly preferring to sing the Christianized verse of Watts. The first official Presbyterian hymnal of 1831 reflected this tension. It began with an entire metrical psalter but also included 531 hymns, 199 of which were by Watts.[20] Although the numbers have changed, twentieth-century Presbyterian hymnals display a similarly high proportion of psalms and hymns by Watts. This is true even after accounting for theological differences among mainline and sideline Presbyterians. Whether Presbyterians are sympathetic to J. Gresham Machen or Eugene Carson Blake, chances are their hymnals look similar to that of their Presbyterian great-grandparents. In other words, twentieth-century theological conflicts and ecclesiastical separations among Presbyterians in the United States have done little to change the pattern established when American Presbyterians first chose to add Watts's imitations to the metrical versions of King David's psalms.

Presbyterians Prefer Watts

In his book on Protestant church music, Robert Stevenson makes the astute observation that Isaac Watts is the favorite of Presbyterians, Charles Wesley is the favorite among Methodists, and the Anglican High Churchman John Mason Neale is the choice of Episcopalians.[21] In fact, Stevenson's calculations are accurate even if his method of using them slightly misrepresents the numbers. Watts is undoubtedly the most frequently included author in Presbyterian hymnals. In the eight hymnbooks produced in the twentieth century, Watts accounts for 155 titles. These titles make up 295 of the total number of hymns in Presbyterian hymnals (which is roughly 6 percent of the 4,871 total). The runners-up to Watts are Charles Wesley with 137 hymns in all the hymnbooks; Catherine Winkworth, whose hymns show up 119 times; Neale, whose translations and hymns show up 109 times; and the Scottish Free Church minister Horatius Bonar, who has 80 hymns in the 8 hymnals. Another way of putting it is to say that the average twentieth-century Presbyterian hymnal has 37 hymns by Watts, 17 by Wesley and Neale, 15 by Winkworth, and 10 by Bonar. A sampling of other Reformed, Lutheran, and Episcopal hymnbooks backs up Stevenson's contention that Presbyterians prefer Watts. In these other non-Presbyterian collections, Neale is the most popular, accounting on av-

20. James Rawlings Sydnor, "Sing a New Song to the Lord: An Historical Survey of American Presbyterian Hymnals," *American Presbyterians* 68 (1990): 4.
21. Stevenson, *Patterns*, 139.

erage for 18 hymns per hymnal. Next is Wesley, who averages 17, followed by Watts at 16, Winkworth at 15, and Bonar at 7.

These numbers represent for the twentieth century something of a decline in Watts's popularity compared to nineteenth-century patterns. For instance, as early as 1834, Watts accounted for one-third of the hymns in the German Reformed Church's *Psalms and Hymns*. A survey of 750 hymnbooks in 1891 revealed that two-fifths of the hymns printed were written by Watts. Seven years later a study of the 32 most popular English hymns included 5 by Watts. These statistics may explain the composition of the first two Presbyterian hymnbooks of the twentieth century, the southern Presbyterian Church's *New Psalms and Hymns* (1901) and the northern Presbyterian Church's 1911 revision of *The Hymnal* (1895). Southern Presbyterians had 127 Watts hymns from which to choose in contrast to the 49 available to northern Presbyterians. By 1990, when Great Commission Publications revised *The Trinity Hymnal*, the favorite among the sideline denominations, the Presbyterian Church in America and the Orthodox Presbyterian Church, Watts was still holding strong with 36 hymns, while the mainline Presbyterian Church, U.S.A.'s hymnal of the same year contained only 13 Watts hymns (7 behind the most frequent author, Neale). One of the obvious reasons for Watts's decline during the twentieth century was the growing awareness of Christian hymnody and efforts by denominations to reflect an ecumenical posture in congregational song. This also accounts for the disparity of Watts hymns between the northern and the southern churches' hymnbooks of 1901 and 1911. The northern church's 1911 hymnal relied on the efforts of Louis F. Benson, whose knowledge of the variety of hymns was vast. Therefore, he did not feature Watts to the same degree as did his peers to the south.

Despite the steady decline of Watts's hymns throughout the twentieth century, he continues to receive the most attention from Presbyterian authors writing about worship. According to Hughes Oliphant Old, a mainline Presbyterian pastor and professor of homiletics at Princeton Seminary, Watts "exemplifies the Reformed doxological tradition at its best." His "hymnody springs from the psalmody," and its "devotional quality" is "unsurpassed."[22] Old's comments are worth highlighting because they come from a book that may well rank as one of the most thoughtful arguments for historic Reformed worship written in the last 150 years. And yet even among the proponents of liturgical conservation, what were innovative practices by sixteenth- and

22. Hughes Oliphant Old, *Worship That Is Reformed according to Scripture* (Atlanta: John Knox, 1984), 55.

seventeenth-century standards now provide the best resources for congregational song.

The affinity between Watts and twentieth-century liturgical traditionalists finds additional support in the work of Horton Davies, longtime professor of religious history at Princeton University and a Congregationalist minister. In his monumental study of Puritan worship, Davies curiously presents Watts as the culmination of psalmody among the Puritans. By Watts's "brave defence of the right to paraphrase the songs of the Old Dispensation in the interests of the New," Davies asserts, "he was delivering the Puritans from the Bibliolatry of the literalists." Davies even goes so far as to say that Watts's hymns and paraphrases "are the finest flowers of Puritan piety."[23] Considering how long it took for Watts to gain a following among the Puritans' Presbyterian and Congregationalist heirs, Davies's attempt to hitch the father of English hymnody to the wagon of traditional metrical psalmody could arguably be deemed a stretch. But after two centuries of Presbyterian congregational singing, trying to tell the difference between Watts and historic Reformed practices in congregational song has become almost impossible. This may explain Stevenson's biting remark that "in our day Calvin's precepts on church music are more honored in the breach than in the observance."[24] More winsome but equally apt is Benson's remark, "That the hymns of this innovator should thus become a badge and symbol of orthodoxy and conservatism in the churches that once disputed his way is an illustration of personal influence not easy to parallel."[25]

Davies's and Old's evaluations may reflect a certain form of Presbyterian naivete about Protestant hymnody, but Benson, perhaps the leading student of hymns and a Presbyterian in his own right, provides ample justification for Watts's importance to Presbyterians. Benson did not always regard Watts's hymns as the best and, in fact, argued that the English Independent's popularity may have retarded the development of Presbyterian hymnody. During the early nineteenth century, for instance, when revivals spawned "fresh" and "new types" of hymns, Presbyterians remained stuck with Watts, which, according to Benson, seemed "like a step backward."[26] Even so, the contribution of Watts was in its context "so glaringly original" that Benson, in his lectures at Princeton Seminary in 1927, gave Watts a place equal to that of the

23. Horton Davies, *The Worship of the English Puritans* (1948; reprint, Clear Spring, Md.: Soli Deo Gloria, 1997), 178–79.

24. Stevenson, *Patterns*, 13.

25. Louis F. Benson, *Studies of Familiar Hymns* (1903; reprint, Philadelphia: Westminster, 1921), 129.

26. Benson, *English Hymn*, 195–96.

early church, Greek and Latin hymns, Luther, and Calvin. "The fetters, whether of obligation, or of prudence, or of use and wont, that held the Church's songs so close to the letter of Scripture," Benson summarized, "were in the minds and habits of English-speaking Christians finally severed by Dr. Watts."[27] In a backhanded way, Benson explained the appeal of Watts to Presbyterians. The quality of his hymns may not have been as good as other authors, but by inaugurating a new era of congregational song, especially for communions that sang only metrical psalms, Watts became for Presbyterians the way to justify singing hymns, a justification that would always tip the scales in favor of Watts's compositions.

The popularity of Watts, however, did not prevent the Wesley brothers, especially Charles, from establishing a discernible presence in twentieth-century Presbyterian hymnals. In fact, of the ten hymns to appear in every Presbyterian hymnal produced over the last century, Charles Wesley wrote twice as many as Watts. The most popular Wesley hymns among Presbyterians have been "Christ, Whose Glory Fills the Skies"; "Hark! The Herald Angels Sing"; "Come, Thou Long Expected Jesus"; "Ye Servants of God, Your Master Proclaim"; "Rejoice, the Lord Is King"; and "Love Divine, All Loves Excelling." The three by Watts in every hymnal are "Our God, Our Help in Ages Past"; "Joy to the World, the Lord Is Come"; and "When I Survey the Wondrous Cross." Rounding out the top ten Presbyterian hymns of the twentieth century is Horatius Bonar's "Here, O My Lord, I See." In the category of hymns to appear in all but one of the Presbyterian hymnbooks, Watts wrote two ("Alas! And Did My Savior Bleed" and "From All That Dwell Below the Skies"), and Wesley wrote one ("O For a Thousand Tongues to Sing"). The third most popular group of hymns, that is, the ones to appear in all but two of the hymnals, totaled six. Wesley wrote four of them ("Jesus, Lover of My Soul"; "Soldiers of Christ, Arise"; "Jesus Christ Is Risen Today"; and "Lo! He Comes, with Clouds Descending"), Watts one ("Jesus Shall Reign Wher'ere the Sun"), and Bonar one ("Blessing and Honor and Glory").[28] Part of the explanation for Wesley's popularity among lovers of Watts is the sheer volume of the Methodist's hymns, which numbered more than six thousand, compared to Watts's combined effort of approximately seven hundred hymns and psalm imitations.[29]

27. Louis F. Benson, *The Hymnody of the Christian Church* (1927; reprint, Richmond: John Knox, 1956), 88, 93.

28. The 1927 *Presbyterian Hymnal* does not include "Jesus Christ Is Risen Today" or "Blessing and Honor and Glory."

29. On the number of hymns Watts and Wesley wrote, see Benson, *English Hymn*, 114–16, 245.

Still, the Presbyterian use of Wesleyan hymnody is one of those liturgical curiosities that deserves some comment, especially considering that many of Charles Wesley's hymns pertain to the Christian life and that Calvinists and Wesleyans disagree fairly vigorously on sanctification. Benson contends that the reception of Wesley's hymns was gradual over the course of the nineteenth century. The reason had to do with the nature of the Methodist movement itself. While Watts "moved on the social uplands of English Noncomformity," Wesley worked "behind the hedges," and therefore Methodists were regarded as "schismatics," "ranters," "sentimentalists," and "sensationalists."[30] So great was the isolation of Methodism and its hymnody from other Protestants that, according to Benson, when Wesley's hymns began to appear in the nineteenth century, compilers often printed them anonymously or attributed them to other authors. Even though John Mason Neale was an accomplished student of hymns, in 1850 he could not identify the author of "Hark! The Herald Angels Sing," attributing it instead to Philip Doddridge.[31] Benson, perhaps being overly charitable to fellow Calvinists, did not believe such mistakes were evidence of a conspiracy. "There was a common ignorance concerning Charles Wesley and his work," Benson explained. Even so, all's well that ends well, and in Benson's estimation, once other Protestants realized the extent of Wesley's contribution, they also recognized the "large area of Christian truth and feeling which all the Churches hold in common."[32]

This happy spin, however, could not overcome the tension that Benson himself recognized in the experiential quality of Wesley's hymns, and this tension points to the unstable compound produced when mixing Presbyterian doctrine and Wesleyan piety. For instance, in his discussion of "Jesus, Lover of My Soul" for *Studies in Familiar Hymns*, Benson could not help asking whether "a lyric so tender and deeply felt should be used in public worship or reserved for private devotion." He went on to quote an English bishop who thought it "inexpressibly shocking" to put such sentiments "into the mouths of a large and mixed gathering of people." Benson even noted that "actual investigations" found this hymn to be one of the three favored by "English tramps." To the defensive response of noting that the apostle John, who lay on the bosom of the Lord, could have penned these lines, Benson replied, "We are not all St. Johns."[33]

30. Ibid., 258.
31. Ibid., 259–61.
32. Ibid., 261.
33. Louis F. Benson, *Studies of Familiar Hymns*, second series (1923; reprint, Philadelphia: Westminster, 1926), 43.

This line of criticism dovetailed with Benson's general assessment of Wesley's "hymnody of the Methodist revival." Unlike Watts, who broke the back of the psalter's reign within congregational singing, Wesley made a twofold contribution, aside from raising a new literary standard for hymnody. First, he introduced the genre of evangelistic hymn "as we use that term to-day."[34] These hymns were designed "to bring the unchurched and unsaved within the sound of the gospel" and lead to conversion. For Benson, this explained why the first section of the original collection of Methodist hymns was entitled "Exhorting and Entreating to Return to God." Second, Wesley turned hymnody in the direction of Christian experience. In fact, Benson thought Wesley conceived of hymnody primarily as a "manual of spiritual discipline." The experience Wesley charted may too often have been his own, and Benson had reservations about the autobiographical nature of the Methodist's hymns, namely, whether the individual author's experience was "fitted to be a norm of Christian experience in general," or whether such expression made the one singing guilty of "religious insincerity." Nevertheless, Wesley's hymns charted "with firmness and precision" the entire scope of "the operations of the Spirit in the heart."[35]

Although Benson appeared to be assessing Wesley more from the perspective of his own study (and possibly preferences) as a hymnologist rather than as a Presbyterian churchman, his objections may in fact help to account for the Presbyterian adoption of Wesleyan hymnody. Ever since the First Great Awakening, the division between Old and New Side Presbyterians in 1741, and their subsequent reunion in 1758, American Presbyterians have embraced the revival as beneficial for reaching new converts and invigorating old ones.[36] In other words, Presbyterians in the mainstream American denominations would not necessarily have objected in principle to the evangelistic purposes or experiential piety involved in Wesley's hymns. Presbyterians did take a while to include his compositions in their hymnals, but even if their confession and catechisms articulated a piety that was oriented more toward the objective character of Christianity than to the subjective experience of the Christian, Presbyterian history from 1750 to 1900 made Presbyterians susceptible to Wesley's intimate and soul-wrenching sentiments.

Even so, the attraction of Wesley for Presbyterians may have stemmed from their reliance on Watts. Indeed, Watts's hymns of "di-

34. Benson, *English Hymn*, 252, 248.

35. Ibid., 248, 249, 250, 249.

36. See Leonard J. Trinterud, *The Forming of an American Tradition: A Re-examination of Colonial Presbyterianism* (Philadelphia: Westminster, 1949).

vine love" delved into matters of the heart in ways that many of his contemporaries and later commentators would find unprecedented, thus paving the way for Wesley's emotionalism. For instance, John Wesley, who omitted his brother's "Jesus, Lover of My Soul" from the Methodist Collection of hymns, wrote that Watts offended him "in a more gross manner than in anything which was before published in the English tongue." He faulted Watts especially for inserting "coarse expressions" in "spiritual hymns." "How often," Wesley complained, "in the midst of excellent verse, are lines inserted which disgrace those that precede and follow."[37] Robert Stevenson more recently commented on the amorous quality of the English dissenter's verse, such as when Watts refers to Christ's "sweet Lips" and "Heavenly Look" that "seek my kisses and my Love." Stevenson also noted that Watts's use of the word "die," such as in a line about the believer dissolving in the arms of Christ like "the Billows [that] after Billow rolls to kiss the Shoar, and Dye," had perhaps not the most fitting of connotations in the context of eighteen-century romantic poetry.[38]

Explaining Bonar's popularity among twentieth-century Presbyterians is less difficult than accounting for Wesley's because the appeal turns out to be similar. A minister in the Free Church of Scotland, first in Kelso and later in Edinburgh, Bonar was, at least by Benson's reckoning, "the greatest of Scottish hymn writers."[39] He was also, according to Benson, the only answer to the charge that Presbyterians had not written hymns of lasting value for congregational song.[40] That attribute in and of itself may explain the number of Bonar's hymns found in twentieth-century Presbyterian hymnals. Although it is just as likely that Benson was correct when he asserted that the denominational identity of hymn writers is insignificant. "We choose our hymns for what they are," he wrote, thus making "the modern hymn book" the best expression of "church unity so far achieved."[41]

Just as likely an explanation of Bonar's appeal to twentieth-century Presbyterians is the emotional character of his lyric. According to Ben-

---

37. John Wesley, *The Works of the Rev. John Wesley* (New York, 1856), II, 443, quoted in Stevenson, *Patterns*, 105.

38. Isaac Watts, *Horae Lyricae, Poems Chiefly of the Lyric Kind* (London, 1706), 80, 83, quoted in Stevenson, *Patterns*, 106.

39. Benson, *Studies of Familiar Hymns*, second series, 209.

40. Ibid., 218. Benson adds the following names to the list of Presbyterian hymn authors of note: from Scotland, "Bruce, Logan, Morison, J. D. Burns, Norman MacLeod, Matheson, Miss Borthwick and Mrs. Findlater, Brownlie, Mrs. Cousin and the Duke of Argyll"; from Canada, Robert Murray; and from the United States, "Davies, J. W. Alexander, Duffield, Dunn, Hastings, Mrs. Prentiss, Wolfe, Hopper, March, Mrs. C. L. Smith, and van Dyke" (219).

41. Ibid., 219.

son, one bishop in the Church of England thought Bonar's hymns belonged "to the class known as 'subjective hymns' or 'hymns of inward experience.'" [42] Benson himself concluded that Bonar was more like the "writers of the Evangelical Revival" than any other group, though in this case the theology was of a sterner Calvinistic sort. Actually, Bonar's premillennialism may account for the predominance of pilgrimage as a theme in his hymns. For instance, in his most popular hymn, "I Heard the Voice of Jesus Say," Christ is a source of comfort to the weary pilgrim, offering him rest, water, and light. The world, accordingly, offers no delights of its own, nor does God work through his creation to meet the needs of his children. Instead, Bonar's piety is absorbed with the immediate ministry of Christ as an escape from the toil, tedium, and darkness of this life. Bonar's verse, according to Benson, was so escapist that one "High Church lady" thought the Scottish hymn writer was actually a medieval saint.[43]

Bonar's appeal, then, like that of Wesley and Watts to a lesser degree, confirms the legacy of revivalism for Presbyterian hymnody. The authors most frequently included are those who either gained prominence during revivals or whose verse evoked the piety of revivalism. It might even be fair to claim that if it had not been for the First and Second Great Awakenings, Presbyterians would still be singing the songs that Calvin prescribed, namely, the psalms. In fact, during the twentieth century, the one period in American Protestantism that lacked a clearly identifiable awakening comparable to those of the eighteenth and nineteenth centuries that split the Presbyterian Church, metrical psalmody made a comeback, and Presbyterian hymnals bear that out.

The Return of the Psalter

As much as Watts continues to be a dominant influence on Presbyterian congregational song, another chapter of the story of twentieth-century hymnbooks is the recovery of psalm singing, though this development was largely a post–World War II phenomenon. During the first half of the twentieth century, metrical psalmody represented a small percentage of the songs available for Presbyterian congregations. In the southern Presbyterian Church's 1901 hymnal, for instance, 102 of the

42. Ibid., 216.
43. Ibid., 211. Bonar has not received much attention in the historical literature, but Kenneth R. Ross, "Calvinists in Controversy: John Kennedy, Horatius Bonar, and the Moody Mission of 1873–1874," *Scottish Bulletin of Evangelical Theology* 9 (1991–1992): 51–63, is helpful for placing Bonar's views about revivalism and thus adds another link connecting hymns and evangelistic piety.

715 hymns could be classified as metrical psalms.[44] But of these psalms, 64 were by Watts, meaning that only 38 came from other sources and authors. Most of these songs were like those of Watts, paraphrases of the psalms by such authors as James Montgomery, Henry Lyte, and John Newton. Indeed, few of the 1901 hymnal's psalms came from old psalters. The health of metrical psalmody was even worse in the northern Presbyterian Church, where the revision of 1911 contained only 47 psalms out of 734 total hymns, 23 of which were paraphrases by Watts. In 1933, the northern church's hymnal contained 41 psalms out of 513 total hymns, 12 by Watts. The all-time low in psalm output came with the ill-fated 1972 *Worshipbook* by the northern Presbyterian Church. Of the 373 hymns, a manageable size but arranged mechanically in alphabetical order, 33 were fashioned after the psalms, with Watts the source of 6.

The 1972 hymnal, however, was the exception among post-1950 Presbyterian collections. Prospects for metrical psalms brightened considerably with the 1955 *Hymnbook*, an initiative of the southern Presbyterian Church that enlisted cooperation from the northern Presbyterian Church as well as the Associate Reformed Presbyterian Church, the United Presbyterian Church of North America, and the Reformed Church in America. This hymnal included 83 psalms, only 9 of which were from Watts, out of the 600 total hymns. In 1961, the Orthodox Presbyterian Church kept up the pace in its *Trinity Hymnal*, which contained 146 psalms out of 730 total hymns, 15 of which were Watts's paraphrases. The revision of this hymnal in 1990, sponsored jointly by the OPC, the Presbyterian Church in America, and Great Commission Publications, included the most psalms of all twentieth-century Presbyterian hymnals: 154 out of 742 total hymns, with 15 by Watts. For some in the OPC and the PCA, the new hymnal did not have enough psalms, and in 1991, Great Commission Publications issued the *Trinity Psalter*, a condensed version of the Reformed Presbyterian Church in North America's psalter, containing all canonical psalms without music.[45]

But arguably, just as significant for the recovery of psalm singing among American Presbyterians was the 1990 *Presbyterian Hymnal*, which features a section much like older psalter hymnals designated

44. For this study I counted as metrical psalms only those in which the attribution for the song explicitly mentioned a psalm or portion of one, as opposed to the later custom in many hymnals of quoting a line of Scripture at the very top of the page that the hymn is supposed to be reinforcing or teaching. The scriptural indexes to many hymnals include these biblical references even when the hymn itself is not a versification of the cited text.

45. See *Trinity Psalter: Psalms 1–150: Words Only Edition* (Pittsburgh: Crown and Covenant, 1994).

for metrical psalms. Unlike many of those earlier hymnals, however, the psalms follow a section of hymns for use during the Christian year. Even though the total number of psalms, 96 out of 564 total hymns, is not as great as in the new *Trinity Hymnal*, the *Presbyterian Hymnal* uses fewer paraphrases of Watts (5) and new metrical versions of the psalms, many of which were commissioned by the hymnal committee.[46]

Part of any explanation for the twentieth-century recovery of metrical psalmody has to include the *1912 Psalter*. This project began in the late nineteenth century under the efforts of the United Presbyterian Church of North America, which invited all Presbyterian and Reformed denominations to cooperate in the compilation of a new psalter. Nine denominations accepted the invitation—only the southern Presbyterian Church and the German Reformed declined—and the *1912 Psalter* became, in the words of Emily R. Brink, "the most widely used and influential metrical psalter of the twentieth century."[47] It became the official psalter of the United Presbyterian Church, and the Christian Reformed Church used it as the basis for its 1914 *Psalter*. How the other Presbyterian denominations used it is unclear because individual congregations are free to choose whatever songs they prefer. None of the other denominations adopted it officially, however.

Even if the hymn-singing denominations initially slighted the *1912 Psalter*, by 1955 it had emerged as the reliable source for recovering metrical psalmody. Of the 83 psalms in *The Hymnbook* (1955), 53 came from the *1912 Psalter*. The OPC's *Trinity Hymnal* (1961) selected 84 psalms out of its total 146 from the *1912 Psalter*. And the revised *Trinity Hymnal* used 70 from the 1912 collection out of its total 154 metrical psalms. Only in the *Presbyterian Hymnal* (1990) does the influence of the *1912 Psalter* begin to subside. Twenty of its 96 psalms come from the earlier book of praise. Part of the reason for this decline was a concerted effort by the PCUSA to find metrical versions of the psalms from within the denomination.[48] Even so, the UPCNA's *1912 Psalter* arguably deserves the most credit for reviving the tradition of metrical psalmody.

Of the psalms sung (at least printed) with the most frequency, perhaps the biggest surprise is Psalm 103, which appeared twenty-five

46. See Linda Jo H. McKim, *The Presbyterian Hymnal Companion* (Louisville: Westminster John Knox, 1993).

47. Emily R. Brink, "Metrical Psalmody in North America: A Story of Survival and Revival," *The Hymn* 44, no. 4 (October 1993): 21.

48. On the metrical psalms commissioned by the PCUSA, see McKim, *Presbyterian Hymnal Companion*, 159, 164, 177. Some of the other psalters used in the recovery of metrical psalmody were the United Presbyterian *1871 Psalter*, the Associate Reformed Presbyterian *1931 Psalter*, and the Reformed Presbyterian *1940 Psalter*.

times in the hymnals, only five times fewer than the ever popular Psalm 23. The first lines of the three most popular versions may indicate the reason for Psalm 103's popularity. Watts's version, "O, Bless the Lord, My Soul," and the *1912 Psalter*'s "O, Come My Soul, Bless the Lord" make this psalm an easy one to use in that part of the service calling for praise. At the same time, "The Tender Love a Father Has," from the later verses in the psalm, as rendered in the *1912 Psalter*, make it an attractive way to sing of God's faithfulness, much like Psalm 23. Psalm 119 was the third most frequently used, though its length may explain part of its appeal, as well as the general Protestant high regard for God's Word, the subject of the psalm. Psalms 84, 19, 72, and 100 appeared twenty, nineteen, eighteen, and seventeen times respectively. The theme of these metrical psalms are diverse, from the Lord's house to the law of God, the reign of Christ, and God's sovereignty, and serve a variety of purposes in worship. Of the last three psalms rounding out the ten most frequently printed, 46, 91, and 148, all appearing fourteen times, the only surprise may be that Psalm 46, originally versified by Luther as one of the great hymns of the Reformation, did not inspire more metrical versions. The other two, Psalms 91 and 148, treat God's faithfulness and the work of creation. Drawing any conclusions about the theological or liturgical preferences from this top-ten list of metrical psalms would be ill-advised, though it is important to consider which psalms do not appear in any of the hymnals. Twenty-four in all (Psalms 7, 21, 26, 28, 35, 49, 52, 53, 54, 57, 58, 59, 64, 70, 74, 75, 81, 101, 105, 109, 111, 112, 120, and 140) have not been available for Presbyterians to sing. The likeliest explanation for a number of these is their imprecatory nature.

The one conclusion that may be drawn responsibly, aside from noting the recovery of metrical psalmody among twentieth-century Presbyterians, is a point made by Benson during his Stone Lectures. The modern Presbyterian disposition of the question of what to sing in corporate worship is "the natural result of its own experimenting with the double standard of 'Psalms and Hymns' set up by Dr. Watts."[49] To be sure, American twentieth-century Presbyterians still reserve a great deal of space for Watts even while adding a bevy of other hymns to their repertoire. And the most recent generation of Presbyterians appears to be willing to sing more psalms than its grandparents. Nevertheless, the staples of Presbyterian congregational singing, if twentieth-century hymnals are any indication, are Watts and King David as advocated by Calvin. In the words of James Rawlings Sydnor, "The two men who had the most profound influence on Presbyterian congregational song"

49. Benson, *Hymnody*, 91.

were Calvin and Watts.[50] Twentieth-century Presbyterian hymnals prove that point.

Why Presbyterians Sing

The continuing preponderance of Watts's songs and the recovery of psalmody are no doubt reassuring to Presbyterians and outsiders who might think them odd. Watts may not be the greatest of hymn writers, but he is certainly not the worst. Furthermore, metrical psalms have the advantage of antiquity as well as the appeal of being native to the Reformed tradition. The Presbyterian rediscovery of the psalter, therefore, has a laudable nostalgic ring to it. Yet as reassuring as the results of this survey are, several other factors need to be kept in mind that are less flattering about Presbyterian liturgy and hymnody.

As suggested above, Presbyterians are drowning in a tsunami of hymns and metrical psalms. Mainstream and sideline Presbyterian denominations have produced hymnals roughly every twenty-five years, the average length of which has been 621 hymns. The northern church's revised hymnal of 1911 was the longest at 734 hymns, and the PCUSA's 1972 *Worshipbook* was the most brief with only 373 selections. These figures do not include hymnals that the denominations sponsored for evangelistic purposes and youth activities. Nor do they take into account the individual congregations that choose to use a hymnal other than the one provided by the denomination.

What such variety and numbers indicate is that contrary to the popular perception that hymns are a great way to learn theology (more below), the size of Presbyterian hymnals and the frequency with which they are produced may actually hamper such instruction. For instance, it would take a congregation almost four years to sing through its hymnal only once (e.g., if a congregation sang three new hymns per week, it would learn only roughly 150 hymns per year, which is one-quarter of the average number of hymns in each hymnal). After the congregation had sung through the hymnal six times, the members would have to adjust to the next hymnal produced by denominational officers. On the positive side, the size of Presbyterian hymnals and the frequency with which they are produced help to cut down on controversy over songs. A long, new hymnal makes it difficult to notice when an old favorite is missing.

Many think the diversity of hymns and the number of hymnals are a sign of musical vitality and ecumenical zeal. To be sure, Presbyterian

---

50. Sydnor, "Sing a New Song," 1.

hymnals reflect a pattern among all denominational hymnals, namely, that they increasingly lack liturgical or theological particularity and look the same. In the words of James F. White, denominational hymnals "have become an anomaly, the contents becoming more and more identical with each revision. . . . Denominational labels are no longer important."[51] Morgan F. Simmons thinks Presbyterians "are richer for sharing in the wealth of expression that comes from all branches of Christendom."[52] James Rawlings Sydnor concurs, adding that "the quality and scope" of Presbyterian hymnals has "improved and expanded."[53]

Others, however, see such diversity as harmful. Benson, who may have started the trend of including more hymns from diverse sources, concluded his Stone Lectures with the observation that "the church hymnal has become cumbersome . . . too encyclopedic and utilitarian to appeal to the heart." The problem is that pastors require "all sorts of hymns for all sorts of purposes," and thus, hymnals have been padded "with so much that is dull." "This encyclopedic range," Benson concluded, "may be a pastoral convenience but it is a spiritual blunder."[54] Erik Routley also expressed reservations about the virtue of variety in hymns. Contrary to the notion that Lutheran hymnody is superior to Presbyterian congregational song because of its longer history of development, Routley suggested that a quantitative increase of chorales among Lutherans had the opposite effect. It introduced a "sorry confusion" that detracted from the "original clarity" of Lutheran song, while the original canon of the Genevan psalms "propagated" a healthy species in Britain and America.[55] Routley's comments concern the music of hymns, but they may be equally applicable to the text, especially if, as so many claim, the value of hymns is their pedagogical function.

One way to illustrate this confusion is to look at the placement of some of the most popular hymns. For instance, Watts's "Our God, Our Help in Ages Past" could likely be placed in any section covering the attributes of God or God's love and faithfulness. This is the general way the hymnals situate Watts's hymn, but they also reflect uncertainty about the author's meaning. Three of the hymnals (1911, 1933, 1955) place this hymn in the section on God's love and fatherhood, two (1961, 1990a) put it in the section on God's eternity, and one (1901) places it in a section on the father-

51. James F. White, "Public Worship in Protestantism," in *Altered Landscapes: Christianity in America, 1935–1985*, ed. David W. Lotz (Grand Rapids: Eerdmans, 1989), 113.

52. Morgan F. Simmons, "Hymnody: Its Place in Twentieth-Century Presbyterianism," in *The Confessional Mosaic: Presbyterians and Twentieth-Century Theology*, ed. Milton J. Coalter et al. (Louisville: Westminster John Knox, 1990), 183.

53. Sydnor, "Sing a New Song," 12.

54. Benson, *Hymnody*, 276.

55. Routley, *Music*, 35.

hood of God. (The other two give it no topical placement; 1972 arranged everything alphabetically, and 1990b situated it in the metrical psalm section.) Even greater uncertainty surrounds the placement of Wesley's "Love Divine, All Loves Excelling." Three (1933, 1955, 1990b) place this hymn in a section on life in Christ, though two (1933, 1955) of these hymnals further divide this section into the various aspects of such life, putting Wesley in the love group. Meanwhile, three hymnals (1901, 1961, 1990a) include this hymn in the section on sanctification. Finally, one hymnal (1911) places Wesley's hymn in the section on forgiveness of sins. Bonar's "Here, O My Lord, I See" is more straightforward and is usually sung in connection with the Lord's Supper, which is the category in which five of the hymnals (1901, 1911, 1933, 1955, 1990b), all mainline Presbyterian, put it. But the OPC and the PCA editors responsible for the editions of the *Trinity Hymnal* (1961, 1990a) placed it in the section on the opening of worship.

Despite such ambiguity about the instruction of individual hymns, Presbyterians continue to insist that the primary purpose of congregational song is instructional. This is most evident in the way Presbyterians organize their hymnals. With the exception of two, all the hymnals arrange the songs according to a thematic structure that begins with God, the Trinity, and his attributes, moves to the church, and then concludes with different themes from the Christian life and special occasions. The two exceptions are the 1972 *Worshipbook*, again with its alphabetical arrangement, and the 1990 *Presbyterian Hymnal*, which includes a section on the church year and metrical psalms before moving to the conventional Presbyterian topical arrangement. Such thematic patterns follow the arguments made in most Presbyterian writing on worship, hymns, and congregational song. According to Sydnor, "People absorb a great deal of Christian truth from the hymns which they sing," namely, "the great foundation doctrines of our faith."[56] Even more emphatic is a PCA church musician, Leonard R. Payton, who insists that the biblical role of singing is as a partner to preaching. Hymns, accordingly, "teach" and "admonish."[57]

Perhaps if Presbyterians had not been historically so liturgically wooden, they might recognize the other purposes for which song is legitimately used. Calvin, for instance, argued that corporate worship consisted of three elements, Word, sacrament, and prayer, and regarded song as a form of prayer.[58] Likewise, Benson distinguishes

---

56. Sydnor, "Sing a New Song," 18.

57. Leonard R. Payton, "Congregational Singing and the Ministry of the Word," *Reformation and Revival* 7 (1998): 121.

58. See Charles Garside, Jr., *The Origins of Calvin's Theology of Music: 1536–1543* (Philadelphia: American Philosophical Society, 1979).

among three categories of hymns, those of praise, edification, and liturgy. The first are designed for praise of God, the second for the nurture of the singers, and the third for use in the church's order of worship.[59] In his history of the English hymn, Benson places Presbyterians via Watts squarely in the second category, namely, the tradition of doctrinal hymnody that edifies by reinforcing the sermon. Watts "designed his hymns to meet the demand from the pulpit for hymns that would illustrate and enforce the sermon themes." It is no wonder that Presbyterians preferred Watts, especially since his hymns were, in Benson's words, "Calvinistic in tone and often in detail."[60] This may also explain the variety and size of Presbyterian hymnals because sermons vary according to biblical text and theme. But the homiletical purpose of Presbyterian congregational song is vulnerable to replacement by superior forms of theological reinforcement, such as skits, readings, or even the sacraments. In addition, poetry has not been the way the church has usually taught propositional truth. Catechisms were considered a better form of instruction. And if the congregation does not understand a hymn, or even that singing hymns is part of the church's pedagogy, song in corporate worship threatens to become little more than a time for worshipers to stretch their legs and lungs.

At this point, Presbyterians might well learn from their liturgical Christian counterparts who use set forms and defend them as laudable. Communions that use set liturgies or books of prayer have an easier time figuring out what song does because it performs a specific function in worship, usually as a response to the means of grace. It is, in other words, a way for the congregation to express praise, petition, or thanksgiving to God. Liturgy, then, undergirds congregational song. With a clear sense of what the order of worship does and how the pieces fit together, figuring out which hymns to sing and why becomes a much easier task. As Paul Westermeyer puts it, "When the public liturgical bones of communal worship are dismissed, the church's song is left in a free fall."[61] What is more, liturgical coherence could help to reduce the volume of songs in Presbyterian hymnals. To be sure, Lutheran and Episcopalian hymnals are by no means lean, but they are published less frequently because these traditions are less hostile to the notion of repetition and ritual. Presbyterians, however, ever since the debates and fights in seventeenth-century Britain over the Book of Common Prayer, have avoided liturgy as a sign of either episcopal tyranny or dead formalism. As such, the number of hymns and hymnals available to Pres-

---

59. Benson, *Hymnody*, lect. 4.
60. Benson, *English Hymn*, 208–9.
61. Westermeyer, *Te Deum*, 209.

byterians in the twentieth century was inversely proportional to the number of Presbyterian church members. Which is another way of saying that the liturgical confusion reflected in Presbyterian hymnals may be a factor in the loss of Presbyterian identity both within churches and among individual members.

In *Why Catholics Can't Sing,* Thomas Day saw the connection between liturgy, hymns, and religious identity. In his closing advice to priests and parishes, Day wrote, "Good congregational singing begins with a sense of beloved familiarity and the best way to develop that familiarity is with an outstanding hymnal/service book which will stay in the pews for more than a generation."[62] Day's logic would not seem to work for Presbyterians because they sing well despite the constant change of hymnals. But for Day, good congregational singing is not just about volume but also liturgical good sense. Repetition, familiarity, and habit, even in congregational song, humbles the minister and the congregation by instilling the idea that corporate worship is bigger than any single individual or faction in the church.[63] Musical variety, in turn, may encourage the idea that worship is more about the style or taste of a church than about serving God. Day's point is that liturgical uniformity and a limited range of songs keep the emphasis of worship on the Creator rather than his creatures. After all, Christian worship historically has been chiefly about serving God, not the ones involved in the service. One would think that Presbyterians, whose Shorter Catechism states that man's chief end is to glorify God, would understand the direction and purpose of worship. Ironically, it may very well be their hymnals, which are supposed to teach doctrine, that have helped to obscure this basic point.

62. Day, *Why Catholics,* 170.
63. Ibid., 140–44.

Afterword

The Case for Observant Protestantism

"But are Presbyterians evangelical?" That was the question that kept coming back to me during breaks at a conference at a prominent Presbyterian church where I was speaking on the Holy Spirit in Reformed theology. The emphasis in my talks over the course of the weekend was that American evangelicalism so dominated Protestant understandings of the Spirit that most evangelicals wondered whether Calvinists actually believed in the Third Person of the Trinity. I noted how the Reformed tradition has usually had a different notion, for instance, of conversion and sanctification. Because of this difference between Reformed teaching and evangelicalism, Calvinists have gained a reputation opposite those Christians known for being Spirit-filled. My task, accordingly, was to try to correct these misunderstandings, show that the Reformed tradition has taught a great deal about the importance of the Holy Spirit's ministry, and suggest that evangelical notions about being Spirit-filled might need revision. But during breaks over coffee and over meals in the fellowship hall, these Presbyterians wanted to know if they were evangelical. My way of dodging the question was to say that there would be time for questions and answers during the last session, and I would try to give a definitive response then.

Clearly, I had my work cut out for me. I did not want to offend people who had not only been gracious enough to invite me to speak at their fall retreat but also dutiful enough to attend sessions that competed with the pennant race and the start of the college football season. What is more, these were good, devout Presbyterians for whom the word *evangelical* stood for something true and wholesome. Trying to give the term more precision and to show the complexities of its development were not what got these godly folk out of bed in the morning. Evangelicals had stood unequivocally for the faith once delivered during the troublous times of twentieth-century Protestantism, and there was no need for criticism. In other words, *evangelical* stood for conservative Protestantism, and the real issue was not where evangelicalism differed from the Reformed faith but rather whether Presbyterians had the courage to stand up and be counted among the ranks of evangelicals.

The point of my remarks during the weekend was that evangelicalism's reputation for defending the biblical and supernatural character of Christianity had obscured important teachings of Reformed theology. At the same time, many of the doctrines affirmed in the Reformed faith about the Holy Spirit were of great importance for the way believers lived their daily lives. So even by submitting to the question "Are Presbyterians evangelical?" I sensed that I was having to concede too much. The issue for me was not whether Presbyterians measured up to evangelical standards but simply that evangelicalism functioned as a foil by which I could highlight the distinctive ideas of Reformed Christianity on the work of the Holy Spirit.

The question and answer session on the final day of the conference began on a good note. Because I had spent some time talking about Pentecostalism, the charismatic movement, and the practice of speaking in tongues, a form of piety foreign to these Presbyterians, most of the questions centered on trying to understand better what the Bible meant when it talks about the gifts of the Spirit. Although this taxed my own knowledge of Pentecostalism, it was better than having to answer the $64,000 question, the one, to mix metaphors, that would force me to put my cards on the table. Finally, however, the moment came. A man on the pastoral staff stood up and asked if Presbyterians are evangelical. He inquired not to put me on the spot but because that was the question on most people's minds. I could not duck it any longer, even though I would have gladly tried to bluff my way through 1 Corinthians 14 for the rest of the hour.

Christian Faith and Churchly Practice

Rather than answering the question, I did what most academics do in difficult situations—I tried to rephrase the question. So I responded that the better question to ask may be, "Are evangelicals Presbyterian?" At least this way of inquiring into the relationship between evangelicalism and Presbyterianism would not assume that evangelicalism is the norm for evaluating all forms of Protestantism, as if it is the purest or most biblical expression of Christianity. It might be obvious that certain Presbyterians are evangelical, but no one would reasonably expect evangelicals to be Presbyterian because evangelicals have not warmed up to either the five points of Calvinism or infant baptism for starters.

The reason for these different ways of looking at the relationship between evangelicalism and Presbyterianism was precisely the point of my talks. However it had happened, the common expectation in Presbyterian circles was for the heirs of John Knox and John Calvin to adopt the ways of evangelicalism so that Presbyterians would be indistinguishable from the likes of Billy Graham, Charles Colson, or James Dobson. But ironically, Presbyterians would never expect evangelical institutions such as *Christianity Today* or Promise Keepers to advocate Presbyterian teachings and practices. This situation seemed unfair—sort of like expecting immigrants to the United States to give up their culture for the English language, fast food, and political equality—and, I argued, it was odd for Presbyterians, proud of their theological heritage, to allow non-Presbyterians to dictate what was most important about the Christian religion.

Since that weekend conference, I have become convinced that to understand the relationship between the Christian faith and its practices, the question Are evangelicals Presbyterian? yields more insight than the query Are Presbyterians evangelical? Other questions would work just as well. For instance, Are evangelicals Lutheran? or Are evangelicals Episcopalian? The reason is that evangelicalism presumes a simple set of theological boundaries, mostly preserving the deity and supernatural redemptive work of Christ in history and the human soul, coupled with a set of religious practices that are virtually independent of the church as a worshiping communion. To spot an evangelical, one only need look for someone who carries a Bible (often in some sort of canvas or vinyl cover), leaves tracts, wears some expression of devotion such as a WWJD bracelet or T-shirt, witnesses to neighbors and strangers, refrains from cursing, and avoids such delights as tobacco and alcohol (though this is changing). In contrast, Presbyterians (along with other churchly forms of Protestants) possess a lengthy creedal statement of Christianity, and this understanding of the faith is nurtured through a distinctive form of public worship, relies on the ministry of clergy who preach and administer the sacraments, is reinforced through a system of church government, and expects Presbyterian families to engage in family worship and catechesis that buttress the ministry of the church. To be sure, this contrast may border on caricature, but it does point out the problems of asking whether Presbyterians are evangelical. If this question commits Presbyterians to practices that obscure the Reformed faith's churchly piety, then being an evangelical may actually be a curse rather than a blessing. Presbyterians intent on being evangelical may end up abandoning the very practices that have been crucial not simply for marking Reformed Christians but also for embodying the convictions of Reformed theology.

Of course, devout Presbyterians who delight in thinking of themselves as evangelical have generally not thought through the relationship between theology and practice. All they usually mean by being
evangelical is something as valuable as taking Christian commitment
and the Bible seriously. The habit of asking Presbyterians to be evangelical is not designed to ignore such matters as Sabbath observance,
public worship, or memorization of the catechism. Yet the evangelical
stress on conversion and believing in the Bible has obscured the range
of practices that various Christian communions believe the Bible requires and that fortify believers in their pilgrimage. It would be wrong
to say that evangelicalism emphasizes faith while other forms of Protestantism stress faith plus practice, since evangelicalism has its own set
of practices that flow quite naturally from its piety. But it would not be
unfair to say that the contrast between evangelicalism and, in this case,
Presbyterianism is one between practices geared toward the freedom
and creativity of the laity to express their devotion as they see fit and
practices oriented toward the corporate church through its ministry of
Word, sacrament, and discipline.

Although he is neither a Presbyterian nor an evangelical, the Duke
Divinity School ethicist Stanley Hauerwas, self-described as a high
church Mennonite, has written insightfully about the relationship between faith and practice and the importance of embodying one's religious convictions in visible and formal exercises. His basic point is
that Protestantism, whether in evangelical or liberal versions, has become an abstraction, something that is disconnected from the communal life of the church, defined as a worshiping community. In other
words, Hauerwas argues that doctrine, something dear to Reformed
Christians, cannot be isolated from the practices of the church. He
raises the stakes as well by asserting that the faith of Christians does
not achieve genuine significance until it is embodied in the ways and
patterns of participating in the life of the church. "What makes Christians Christian," Hauerwas writes, "is our worship of God." "Of
course," he adds, "the praise of God cannot be limited to 'liturgy,' but
it is nonetheless the case that Christians learn how to be praiseworthy
people through worship." An evangelical rendering of Hauerwas's
point might involve the idea that the way Christians show their regeneration is by saving other souls. But this interpretation misses Hauerwas's argument about the body of Christ as a worshiping community
and the unique responsibilities given to those who minister Word and
sacrament. Identifying worship as the central and essential task of the
church, Hauerwas observes, "counters some of the unclarity surrounding" ordination and embodies the presumption "that there is lit-

erally nothing more important for the Christian people to do than praise God."[1]

Reformed Christians may need to learn about the importance of the church and worship from a post-liberal Methodist ethicist because they have for so long thought of themselves as evangelical first and Presbyterian second. What is particularly clear is that Presbyterians who take their tradition seriously need to be reminded of the churchly and liturgical character of the practices that make good Presbyterians. Here it may be interesting to remember Question 85 of the Westminster Shorter Catechism: "What does God require of us to escape his wrath and curse?" Aside from showing Calvinism's gruffer side with the language of God's righteous retribution for sin, the answer is revealing for what it says about the relationship between faith and practice. The response states: "To escape the wrath and curse due to us for sin God requires of us faith in Jesus Christ, repentance unto life, and the diligent use of the outward and ordinary means whereby Christ communicates to us the benefits of redemption." Most evangelicals and conservative Presbyterians are on fairly familiar terms with the first two parts of that answer, namely, faith and repentance. Salvation requires trust in Christ for redemption and sorrow for sin, and without those two marks of regeneration, churches have difficulty spotting a genuine profession of faith. But diligently attending the means of grace is a notion foreign to many Presbyterians under the influence of evangelicalism. And so when the Shorter Catechism goes on to explain that the "outward and ordinary means" are Word, sacrament, and prayer, some proponents of the Reformed faith are caught off guard because they have so emphasized either conversion or doctrine that they have abstracted the Christian religion from the Christian practices that mark the body of Christ. Yet if the Westminster divines have anything to say about the Christian life, participating in the churchly practices of the Word preached, the sacraments administered, and corporate prayer is as necessary for a credible profession of faith as are trust in Christ and repentance from sin.

Interestingly enough, the Shorter Catechism's identification of Word, sacrament, and prayer as the ordinances necessary for salvation also highlights the importance of church and worship for genuine Christianity. Consequently, according to the Reformed tradition, participating in public worship and attending the means of grace are crucial to the making of Christians. In other words, practice is as vital to

1. Stanley Hauerwas, "The Liturgical Shape of the Christian Life: Teaching Christian Ethics as Worship," in *In Good Company: The Church as Polis* (Notre Dame: University of Notre Dame Press, 1995), 154.

the Christian life as is conversion or correct doctrine. The practice of corporate worship is essential to the life of the believer not because this activity functions as a sign or testimony to onlookers, indicating that the worshiper is truly a believer. To be sure, worship does help to set believers apart from those who do not worship Christ as Lord. But the main reason why worship is vital to the believer is that, as the Shorter Catechism also explains, the means of grace in Word and sacrament actually "communicate the benefits of redemption" (Ans. 88). Through the Word preached believers are "built up in holiness and comfort" (Ans. 89), and through the sacraments they have "Christ and the benefits of the new covenant . . . represented, sealed and applied" to them (Ans. 92). The practices of Christian worship, accordingly, are not trivial matters that can be packaged as if a commodity to attract a new set of customers or discarded in favor of the small-group Bible study. Instead, they are the elements that put flesh on the bones of faith and repentance. In the case of Presbyterianism, Reformed worship embodies Presbyterian convictions and piety. In the language of Hauerwas, Presbyterian worship is where Presbyterians learn what it means to be Reformed.

Nor are Presbyterian beliefs independent of the church. In Reformed teaching, as in other churchly traditions, the outward and ordinary means of Word, sacraments, and prayer are not practices that simply any believer may perform. In fact, one of the complications of the loss of a churchly Presbyterian piety is a low view of church office and authority. Exactly which is the chicken and which is the egg—does a low view of worship lead to a low view of ordination or vice versa?—is a difficult question to answer. Nevertheless, it is clear that a high view of the church and a high esteem for corporate worship rise and fall together because the service ministers perform is practically defined by the elements of public worship. But once a Christian thinks Sunday worship is a supplement to the more vigorous and personal weekly practices of the Christian laity, the ministry of church officers also becomes nonessential. As Nathan Hatch argued in his important book *The Democratization of American Christianity*, since 1800, American evangelicalism has thrived on motivating the laity to take control of their religious lives by throwing away the training wheels of the clergy. Not without surprise, since the early nineteenth century, American Protestantism has also experienced a dramatic neglect of corporate worship. It is no wonder that Presbyterians would join this movement because the camp of churchly Protestantism has been a lonely one. Still, the question that only a few Presbyterians have asked is whether the content of Reformed Christianity can be sustained on evangelical forms of piety, ones for which worship and the church are of secondary importance. If

Presbyterianism is a churchly expression of Christianity, as the West-minster Standards appear to indicate, the answer to that question is fairly obvious.

The Virtue of Nominal Christianity

The question of faith and practice and specifically the issue of whether evangelicalism and Presbyterianism require different kinds of devotional exercises point to an interesting feature of American reli-gion. In conversations about specific Roman Catholics or Jews, it is common to hear them described as either observant or nonobservant. In both cases, the line between observance and nonobservance is easy to spot because the person either does or does not practice the ceremo-nies and religous routines that constitute the community of faith. Prot-estantism, however, has no such language. Instead, discussions along these lines about Protestants usually employ the words *genuine, nomi-nal, authentic,* or *dead*. Part of the reason for this linguistic shift is that specifically religious practices, such as baptism, the Lord's Supper, Sunday worship, and ordination rites, are believed to be inconsequen-tial to being a true Protestant.

The fact that American Protestants do not use the nomenclature of observance demonstrates just how complete the triumph of evangeli-calism has been. Since the rise of pietism in the seventeenth century and the Anglo-American revivals of the following century, the goal among God-fearing Protestants has been to eliminate observant Prot-estantism. Of course, this is not how pietist or evangelical leaders iden-tified the enemy. The words they used were *dead* religion or *formalism,* and what they had in mind was a nominal Protestant faith whose ob-servance was one of simply going through the motions. Even so, the ob-jection to nominal Christianity launched a strain of suspicion against the very forms of devotion that characterize a churchly Christian piety, whether Reformed, Lutheran, Episcopalian, or Roman Catholic. With the religion of the heart triumphant, going to church was too easy a way of showing one's religious devotion. After all, people could nap through sermons, hypocritically partake of the Lord's Supper, or mouth the words of a hymn. And going to church involved only one day in the said Christian's weekly routine. To test the believer's mettle, more strenuous forms of piety needed to be devised, ones that demanded time and were apparent for all to see. Thus, antiformalism ironically launched both the forms of evangelical kitsch that sell briskly in Christian bookstores and the presumption that truly heartfelt religion will be eye-felt as well.

The irony that hostility to nominal Christianity generated its own forms of observance has not always been sufficiently appreciated. So prevalent are the associations of serious Christianity with extra-ecclesiastical forms of devotion that study Bibles, small groups, Christian cable television, and parachurch organizations are taken for granted as part of the way American Protestants do Christianity. And yet these practices may be performed just as perfunctorily as participating in any church service or ecclesiastical ceremony. In fact, the quest for heartfelt religion did not notice that its judgments rely on sense perceptions just as much as the dead formalism it opposes. Neither evangelicals nor Presbyterians can see into the heart, though the latter have been more candid about admitting this. Nevertheless, the rigors of devotion outside church continue to set the pace for American Protestantism, with pollsters and social scientists continuing to grade believers according to their performance away from worship services overseen by clergy.

What has also eluded notice is how the higher octane fuels of extra-ecclesiastical Protestantism have made it difficult to be content with the ordinary and relatively private duties of church membership because of fears of participating in nominal Christianity. The result is such that a Presbyterian who attends two services on Sunday and prays and reads the Bible before and after meals during the week will be deemed impious by his evangelical peers in the workplace—assuming he worships not at the Bible but at the Presbyterian church—if he neglects the after-work Bible study, the midweek lunchtime prayer meeting, or even the water cooler banter about things of "the Lord." His churchly piety, since it is not worn on his sleeve, will not be evident to any but those who know him on a more intimate basis. Conversely, one of his fellow Presbyterians, who sometimes goes into the office on Sundays to lower the stacks on his desk but makes time for fellowship with the evangelicals at work in the Bible study and prayer meeting, calling it the "real work of the church," will be included as one of the more devout persons in the company. The identification of observant Protestantism with nominal Christianity means it is possible to be a good Christian and a nonobservant Presbyterian. It may even be the case that thanks to the triumph of extra-ecclesiastical Protestantism, one's chances of being a good Christian increase as one's observances of the practices of a particular communion decrease.

Drawing a contrast between Presbyterianism and evangelicalism is not an entirely original exercise. Recently, Ted V. Foote Jr. and P. Alex Thornburg, both Presbyterian pastors in Oklahoma, wrote the book *Being Presbyterian in the Bible Belt*, a work that according to its subtitle is designed to be a "survival guide" for Presbyterians living in a land in which evangelicalism has become the norm. This book is interesting if only because the authors raise the possibility that Presbyterianism is different from evangelical Protestantism, so much so that members of Presbyterian churches might need guidance about how to avoid becoming assimilated into the evangelical mainstream. The authors offer advice on differences between Presbyterians and evangelicals on such topics as the conversion experience, inerrancy, Christ's second coming, hell, and sin. Unfortunately, for these mainline Presbyterian pastors (PCUSA), the idea of being Presbyterian is one heavily shaped by the history of mainstream Protestantism in the United States. As such, the mainstream's tradition of tolerance and theological breadth causes Foote and Thornburg to err on the side of not giving offense. In their rendering, Presbyterians are really ecumenical Protestants who think differently about the faith, in ways more complex and less definite than evangelicals, thus making Presbyterians less judgmental and more ecumenical.[2]

Still, these Presbyterian pastors are right to draw contrasts between the theological heritage of their church and evangelicalism. Foote and Thornburg could have made this contrast even more noticeable had they looked to the differences between evangelicalism and Presbyterianism regarding the church and her worship. The closest they come is in their discussion of conversion. There they point out that Presbyterians have understood conversion to be a lifelong process, not an instantaneous decision or a moment of crisis. And according to Reformed theology, the unfolding of sanctification in the believer's life—that is, dying to sin and living to righteousness—takes place in the context of the church and depends mightily on the means of grace that comprise the worship service.

Unfortunately, Foote and Thornburg have little to say about the church and worship. But it is fairly clear that one of the items that has made Presbyterians uncomfortable with evangelicals, and vice versa, is the way each group practices the faith. Most of the time, Presbyterians have come across as "God's frozen chosen" and have explained their frigidity with the bumper sticker rejoinder that Presbyterians do it decently and with order. But the reason for these different approaches to worship and the church's ministry goes much deeper than some sort of Presbyterian proclivity for appointing study committees and following Robert's *Rules of Order*. It concerns a different understanding of the Christian life and the believer's dependence on the church for growth in grace. Presbyterians practice the faith differently than do evangeli-

2. Ted V. Foote Jr. and P. Alex Thornburg, *Being Presbyterian in the Bible Belt: A Theological Survival Guide for Youth, Parents, and Other Confused Presbyterians* (Louisville: Geneva Press, 2000).

cals because they believe that the ministry of the church is truly effective and sufficient. This is not true only of Presbyterians. Books by the title *Lutherans in the Bible Belt* or *Episcopalians in the Bible Belt* could also be written. But Presbyterians do practice the faith differently than do evangelicals, and part of the reason is that Reformed theology grounds the salvation of the body of Christ in the God-ordained means that mark the church and comprise public worship.

Are Presbyterians Sectarian?

This way of looking at the relationship between Presbyterianism and evangelicalism raises a related question, namely, whether an emphasis on the singularity of Presbyterian identity through the lens of its practices winds up painting adherents of the Reformed faith into a corner all by themselves, without ties to other Christians. Indeed, part of the appeal for Presbyterians to think of themselves as evangelical is that emphasizing Presbyterian uniqueness is a lonely enterprise. Conversely, evangelicalism has been one way of affirming the articles of faith that bind Christians of a conservative stripe. Which explains why it is fairer to ask Presbyterians whether they are evangelical than to inquire of evangelicals whether they are Presbyterian. The point of being evangelical—or at least a chief one—is to find a common denominator for bringing Christians together for more effective witness and defense of the faith once delivered. So to ask evangelicals if they are Presbyterian is to raise an oxymoronic question. The point of being evangelical is to transcend (some might prefer "escape") the rough edges of particular Christian traditions that prevent believers from joining hands in fellowship and witness. In this case, being a committed evangelical is inherently an ecumenical proposition, while being a serious Presbyterian limits numbers at the Saturday morning men's prayer breakfast.

One way to defend Presbyterianism against sectarianism is to respond that all Christians are in some sense sectarian because no one church has managed to gather all believers into one communion. At the same time, it should be noted, even though evangelicalism is a broader movement in North America than various Presbyterian and Reformed ecumenical agencies, born-again Protestantism bears a reputation, as the authors of *Being Presbyterian in the Bible Belt* contend, for being sectarian, at least from the perspective of mainline Protestants. So there is singularity and then there is sectarianism, and the difference is in the eye of the ecumenical beholder.

Nevertheless, the charge of sectarianism that usually accompanies assertions of Presbyterian (or any communion's) uniqueness is worth thinking about if only because of the point it makes about the importance of churchly practices. The religious duties that Presbyterians usually have to shed when they join the ranks of evangelicals are those matters that mark a Reformed church's ministry and worship. To be sure, evangelicals are not generally any more desirous to adhere to the Westminster Standards' views on election or the efficacy of the atonement, and why these creedal differences have not given evangelically inclined Presbyterians greater pause is a constant source of confusion. Still, as far as evangelicals are from Presbyterians on doctrine and its importance, even greater (arguably) is the distance separating them concerning questions of church polity and liturgy. Do church officers actually hold the keys of the kingdom? Is church membership really necessary for salvation? Do Word and sacrament accomplish anything more significant than quiet times and potluck suppers? For Presbyterians who gather with evangelicals, these questions are generally off limits because evangelicalism is inherently a pietistic form of Christian devotion that stresses the unmediated and therefore individualistic character of the gospel. Presbyterianism, however, like other confessional traditions, possesses within it a sacramental and corporate understanding of Christianity in which belonging to the body of Christ and attending the means of grace are crucial in marking and sustaining the children of God.[3]

If this is a useful way of looking at the tension between evangelicals and Presbyterians, then it should be apparent that the process of becoming evangelical exacts a high price from Christians who look to the church and its ministry for nurture. It is responsible to say that evangelical Protestantism has been highly suspicious of the church in its official and liturgical ways. Sometimes this distrust has been legitimate, such as when churches abuse their authority and practices, and evangelicalism certainly inherited reservations about churchly ways from the Protestant Reformation. But evangelicals went well beyond the Reformers when they began to see the church as a barrier to genuine faith and so deemed matters of office and worship as things indifferent. For Presbyterians who understand their heritage properly, as for Lutheran and Episcopal heirs of the Reformation, to say that the church and worship are optional if not impediments to vital Christianity is to give up a large part of what it means to be a Christian. One analogy might be that of amputation in which certain limbs are removed to save the patient. But this is not the best analogy if the church and worship are not simply limbs but Christianity's vital organs. In this case, the price of becoming

3. On confessional Protestantism, see D. G. Hart, *The Lost Soul of American Protestantism* (Lanham, Md.: Rowman & Littlefield, 2002).

an evangelical may not only be high but fatal. And if the Christian religion itself, not just the Presbyterian expression of it, is also deeply dependent on the ministry of church officers in the service of worship, then it is not inappropriate to ask whether evangelicalism has been the healthiest development for genuine, that is, churchly Christianity.

So an emphasis on what makes churchly Presbyterianism different from evangelicalism need not be a sectarian effort if it points Presbyterians back to those practices, even though observed differently, that they share with the church catholic and apostolic. Indeed, recovery of a high view of the church and worship along with the distinctive patterns of Presbyterian ecclesiology and liturgy may actually be an exercise characterized not by narrowness but by breadth, for it should involve a recognition of those elements of the faith that Christians throughout the ages and around the world have observed for the good of their souls. In this case, churchly Presbyterianism would be no more sectarian than an Episcopalian concern to preserve the liturgy of the Book of Common Prayer or a Lutheran commitment to the importance of Christ's real presence in the Lord's Supper. To be sure, an appreciation of other Christian communions will go only so far thanks to the singularity of Presbyterian convictions. Even so, a greater esteem for the church and worship may alert Presbyterians to what unites them with the historic Christian faith and how their flirtation with evangelicalism has obscured practices vital not simply to Presbyterianism but to the catholic faith.

In the end, the effort to make adherents of Reformed Christianity more faithful to the churchly character of their religion is not necessarily parochial or sectarian. It may legitimately stem from a greater concern for all Christians to recognize the means that God has ordained and promised to bless in the salvation of his people. Presbyterians in the United States may require more exhortation than other Protestants because of their proclivity for revivals, experiential piety, and biblicism. Still, a call for Presbyterians to recover mother kirk is intended not simply for the benefit of Reformed Christians but for the church more generally. Consequently, although the health of Christianity ultimately depends on God, who is sovereign and does all things well, it also depends on the well-being of the church's ministry and her worship *because* God has ordained the church and worship as the means to sustain his people. For that reason, recognizing the importance of the church and worship to the gospel of Jesus Christ is not sectarian but biblical.

Subject Index

Scripture Index